Critical Trajectories: Culture, Society, Intellectuals

Critical Trajectories:
Culture, Society, Intellectuals

Tony Bennett

Blackwell
Publishing

BLACKWELL PUBLISHING

350 Main Street, Malden, MA 02148-5020, USA
9600 Garsington Road, Oxford OX4 2DQ, UK
550 Swanston Street, Carlton, Victoria 3053, Australia

First published 2007 by Blackwell Publishing Ltd

1   2007

Library of Congress Cataloging-in-Publication Data

Bennett, Tony, 1947–
    Critical trajectories : culture, society, intellectuals / Tony Bennett.
      p. cm.
    Includes bibliographical references and index.
    ISBN 978-1-4051-5698-1 (hardcover : alk. paper) — ISBN 978-1-4051-5699-8 (pbk. : alk. paper) 1. Culture. 2. Cultural policy. 3. Popular culture 4. Intellectuals. 5. Culture—Study and teaching. I. Title.

    HM621.B486 2007
    306.01—dc22

                                                          2007010759

A catalogue record for this title is available from the British Library.

Set in 10.5/13pt Minion
by SPi Publisher Services, Pondicherry, India
Printed and bound in Singapore
by C.O.S. Printers Pte Ltd

The publisher's policy is to use permanent paper from mills that operate a sustainable forestry policy, and which has been manufactured from pulp processed using acid-free and elementary chlorine-free practices. Furthermore, the publisher ensures that the text paper and cover board used have met acceptable environmental accreditation standards.

For further information on
Blackwell Publishing, visit our website:
www.blackwellpublishing.com

Contents

Contents

List of Illustrations

Acknowledgements

Although I shall not repeat them here, the debts I recorded to the many friends and colleagues who commented on the essays collected here when they were first published still stand. I do need to add, though, my appreciation for the support of the UK's Economic and Social Research Council (ESRC) as the final essay – "The Historical Universal: the Role of Cultural Value in the Historical Sociology of Pierre Bourdieu" – was completed as a part of the ESRC-funded project *Cultural Capital and Social Exclusion: A Critical Investigation* (Award R000239801). I owe a debt to the participants in the symposium that was held at the University of Oxford in 2004 as a part of this project for their helpful comments as well as for their encouragement that the line of argument developed in an early version of the essay was worth pursuing. Special thanks to Elizabeth Silva and Derek Robbins for their comments in this context. I am also grateful to both the anonymous reviewers commissioned by the *British Journal of Sociology* for their insightful and helpful comments on the first draft of this paper. These, together with Mike Savage's generous and helpful comments, helped make this a much better essay than it might otherwise have been.

This final essay was completed during the early phases of the work of the ESRC Centre for Research on Socio-cultural Change at the Open University and the University of Manchester. I should like to acknowledge my appreciation of the stimulating intellectual environment this Centre has produced and my debt to the free exchange of ideas that are so central an aspect of its culture and commitment.

I owe a special debt too to Jayne Fargnoli at Blackwell – first for her encouragement that this was a project worth doing, and second for her support and advice at various stages in compiling the book regarding the balance I should aim for between the different aspects of my work that it brings together. My thanks too to the anonymous reviewers Jayne commissioned to review my initial proposals regarding the structure and content of the collection: these proved invaluable in guiding me to the final selection and organizational structure I have opted for.

I should also like to thank Ken Provencher at Blackwell for guiding the book through the production process so effectively.

But my final and greatest debt is to Karen Ho at the Open University both for her help in materially assembling the text as well as for her more general efficient and effective support which made it possible for me to find the time needed to bring this book to fruition.

All the essays that appear in this book were originally published in the following:

Bennett, T. (1990) "Severing the aesthetic connection" in T. Bennett *Outside Literature*, London and New York: Routledge.

Bennett, T. (1982) "Texts, readers, reading formations," *Bulletin of the Mid-Western Modern Languages Association*, winter: 3–17.

Bennett, T. (1996) "Figuring audiences and readers" in J. Hay, L. Grossberg and E. Wartella (eds.), *The Audience and its Landscape*, Boulder, CO: Westview Press.

Bennett, T. (2002) "Culture and governmentality," in Jack Bratich, Jeremy Packer, and Cameron McCarthy (eds.), *Foucault, Cultural Studies and Governmentality*, New York: SUNY Press, pp. 47–66.

Bennett, T. (2000) "Acting on the social: art, culture and government," *American Behavioural Science*, 43(9): 1412–28.

Bennett, T. (2002) "Archaeological autopsy: objectifying time and cultural governance," *Cultural Values* vol. 6, nos. 1–2: 29–48.

Bennett, T. (2005) "Civic seeing: museums and the organisation of vision," in S. MacDonald (ed.) *Companion to Museum Studies*, Oxford: Blackwell.

Bennett, T. (1999) "Intellectuals, culture, policy: the technical, the practical and the critical," *Pavis Papers in Social and Cultural Research*, no. 2, Milton Keynes: Pavis Centre for Social and Cultural Research, The Open University.

Bennett, T. (2005) "The historical universal: the role of cultural value in the historical sociology of Pierre Bourdieu," *British Journal of Sociology*, 56 (1): 141–64.

Introduction: Critical Trajectories:
Culture, Society, Intellectuals

Two principles have informed my selection of the work that is gathered together in this collection.[1] First, I have aimed to illustrate the trajectories along which my work has developed in response to the changing intellectual, political, and institutional contexts in which it has been conducted over the period from the late 1970s to the present. Second, I have, with one exception, avoided republishing work that is already easily available in earlier books in favor of work that does not merely exemplify the critical pathways my work has taken but also adds to and more fully amplifies the theoretical logics underlying those pathways. The ordering of the collection is, as befits the nature of trajectories, to some extent chronological, although the logic of this ordering is more cumulative than sequential in the sense that there is a strong continuity running through the different phases of my work as I have returned to earlier preoccupations, approaching them from a different perspective to take account of changing intellectual and political contexts and the availability of different theoretical instruments.

These are questions I return to in more detail in introducing the essays collected in each part of the book. Before I come to these, however, some more general remarks are called for regarding my own intellectual formation and my relations to cultural studies. As is well known, cultural studies in Britain was initially shaped through a process of critical dialog with the forms of cultural analysis and traditions of commentary on the relations between culture and society that had been developed in association with the discipline of English.[2] Richard Hoggart, Raymond Williams, and Stuart Hall all had their initial university trainings in English, and all were deeply shaped by its legacies to the extent that these defined the traditions they worked both with and against in attempting to clear an intellectual space for the development of new and more politically-focused forms of cultural analysis. It was principally through their engagements with "Leavisism," in which the discussion of literary texts served as a vehicle for a broader social and cultural commentary,[3] that they sought to work through the legacies of nineteenth-century critics like John Ruskin and Matthew Arnold in order to cast off their

1

elitism and purely moral forms of anti-capitalism and, in their place, to substitute a concern with "ordinary culture": that is, with the forces shaping the "ways of life" of subordinate social strata.[4] This was, of course, a politically motivated concern orientated, particularly in the case of Williams and Hall, toward the transformation of those ways of life to generate the momentum for the production of a common culture via the socialist transformation of society.

As my first two books – *Formalism and Marxism* (Bennett, 1979) and *Outside Literature* (Bennett, 1990a) – were primarily concerned with questions of literary and aesthetic theory, it is often assumed that I too was trained in literary studies which, in Britain, usually meant studying English at university level. However, my interests in the relations between culture and society were developed via a quite different intellectual and disciplinary trajectory. My university training was focused on the social sciences with, initially, a degree in politics, philosophy and economics from the University of Oxford and, after that, postgraduate studies in sociology at the University of Sussex with a special focus on the sociology of art and literature. This led to doctoral studies on the work of Georg Lukács, particularly his concepts of realism and class consciousness, through which I became acquainted with post-Kantian aesthetics and the varied subsequent political inflections of this tradition associated with the aesthetics theories of western Marxism – that is, the tradition which, in Perry Anderson's account, ran from the 1920s through to the 1970s comprising, as its leading figures, Antonio Gramsci, Georg Lukács, Karl Korsch, Walter Benjamin, Max Horkheimer, Galvano Della Volpe, Herbert Marcuse, Henri Lefebvre, Theodor Adorno, Jean-Paul Sartre, Lucien Goldmann, Louis Althusser, and Lucio Colletti (Anderson, 1976: 25–6). In Anderson's assessment, this tradition of Marxist thought was most distinguished from earlier work in the Marxist tradition by its preoccupation with questions of aesthetic and cultural analysis, just as he regards the fruits of this work as the richest legacy of this tradition. Yet, while not disagreeing with this assessment, many aspects of the ways in which the relations between Marxist thought and aesthetics were posed in this tradition struck me as seriously misdirected. This was especially true of those attempts, evident in the work of Lukács, Goldmann, Della Volpe, Marcuse, and Althusser, to develop a philosophical aesthetics – that is, an account of the aesthetic as an invariant mode of mental relation to reality distinct from both science and ideology – based on Marxist premises. While it was perfectly clear that Marx's own thought had been profoundly influenced by Enlightenment conceptions of the aesthetic, especially those of Kant and Hegel, and that these had shaped his critique of alienation in ways that became clearer, in the 1960s, with the publication of his early writings,[5] the endeavor to develop a Marxist aesthetic seemed to me mistaken for three reasons.

First, and this is a striking aspect of this literature, the key to the truth of a Marxist account of the aesthetic always turned out to reside in a pre-Marxist philosophical position – that of Hegel for Lukács, that of Kant for Colletti, and that of Spinoza for Althusser. I thought this a peculiar outcome given that, at the same time, each of these thinkers argued that Marxism superseded, displaced or transvalued the problematics of earlier "bourgeois" philosophies. If this were indeed so, how could the kernel of a Marxist aesthetics always prove to consist in a philosophical position that preceded it? Second, the construction of the aesthetic as an invariant mode of mental relation to reality was, in my view, hard to reconcile with the conception of Marxism as a science of history which aimed to offer a thoroughgoing historicization of all social and cultural phenomena. How could such a program be carried out if, at root, all individual literary and artistic practices were already determined, in their most significant aspects, as particular manifest-ations of an aesthetic mode of mental relation to reality whose constitution was universal and therefore trans-historical? This could only result in a weak materi-alism – a *materialism manqué*, so to speak – that would only be able to account for the incidental, ephemeral, aspects of such practices and not their essence since this was given in advance of any analysis of the particular historical circumstances of their production, circulation and reception by their constitution as, precisely, an invariant mode of aesthetic perception. Third, and finally, all of this, within the purview of western Marxism, was true only of genuinely great or authentic art and literature, leaving no analytical space in which "the rest" – the texts of popular culture, or ways of life – could be engaged with other than as "merely ideological."[6] This, in a formulation I used in *Formalism and Marxism*, reflected a commitment to establishing a "holy trinity of the superstructure" in which science, ideology and the aesthetic were distinguished from each other abstractly, after the fashion of Kant's transcendental account of the relations between the power of judgment and the operations of pure and practical reason.[7]

These, then, are the aspects of Marxist literary and aesthetic theory that I thought ought to be contested since they were so sharply at odds with the principles of historical reasoning that I took to be a defining feature of Marxist thought but one which, when it came to the analysis of "the aesthetic," most Marxists seemed content to set aside. However, I was not at this time (the mid 1970s) acquainted in any detail with the ways in which Williams had sought to clear a space for new kinds of cultural analysis via his critical assessments of those traditions of cultural criticism that had informed the development of the discipline of English.[8] Nor was I directly familiar with those traditions themselves; I only became acquainted with indigenous English critical traditions much later. My intellectual trajectory in these respects thus reflected both a disciplinary training and a generational experience that was quite different from Williams's. For, as he later recorded (Williams, 1971), his acquaintance with the aesthetic theories developed in the context of western Marxism came only after he had tried to settle his accounts with the English critical tradition. While this influenced the formu-lations of his later work, particularly in *Marxism and Literature* (Williams, 1977), Williams's concerns in his earlier and, from the point of view of the development of cultural studies, his most influential texts – *Culture and Society* (1958) and *The Long Revolution* (1961) – were strikingly different from those that had shaped the concerns of western Marxism. The aesthetic theories developed in the context of the latter aspired to be full-developed accounts of the specificity of the aesthetic as a mode of mental relation to reality that characterized all the arts. There had been no intellectual enterprises of a similar kind in British Marxist thought.[9] This is partly because Kant's account of the aesthetic never enjoyed the same degree of influence in Britain as it had in continental Europe, particularly in Germany, with the consequence that the aesthetic was never quite so clearly separated off from other modes of thought as a power or faculty in its own right. Of course, the broader formations of *Bildung*, in which culture serves as an instrument of character formation, and the associated tradition of *Kulturkritik* in which culture serves as the standard of a higher morality from which existing forms of political authority and action can be judged insufficient, did influence the nineteenth-century traditions of cultural criticism that helped to shape the development of English as a moral discipline. But these aspects of German aesthetic thought were inflected in specific directions via the influence of both Romanticism and different schools of religious thought to yield conceptions of the aesthetic as an essentially religious-cum-moral response to art (in the case of Ruskin, for example) that could be adapted to serve as an instrument of character development within the newly developing machineries of popular schooling (as in the case of Arnold).

These traditions formed the deep historical backdrop to the twentieth-century development of the discipline of English out of which British cultural studies developed. This is not to suggest that all of those who contributed to the early development of cultural studies shared this disciplinary background, or that the early development of British cultural studies can be accounted for solely in terms of its relations to English. There were historians who followed in the footsteps of Edward Thompson,[10] and a key aspect of the work of the Birmingham Centre for Contemporary Cultural Studies – its analysis of youth subcultures (Hall and Jefferson, 1976) – was strongly influenced by American sociology. While these were strong tributary currents in shaping cultural studies as an interdisciplinary *rendezvous* for varied traditions of analysis concerned with the ways in which culture is tied up with the exercise of power, it was Williams's critique of the Coleridge-Ruskin-Arnold lineage of cultural criticism that was most effective in providing a theoretical space in which such concerns could be brought together and fashioned into a coherent program that had a strong sense of effecting a break with the prevailing critical tradition.

This was not, however, a complete break. The political and analytical orientation of Williams's early work was clearly defined by its concern to work both with and against the intellectual traditions that had shaped the development of English: with them in the sense of endorsing and accepting their often stridently anti-capitalist critiques and their construction of culture as a vantage point from which the moral and aesthetic insufficiency of existing economic, social, and political arrangements might be judged; against them in the sense of seeking to redeploy this critical machinery by connecting it to socialist traditions of thought and political action, and so overcoming its elitism by harnessing it to the creation of a common culture. This was, however, less a definitive breach with nineteenth-century English aesthe-tico-moral traditions of cultural criticism than the construction of an intellectual context in which the forms of moral authority these had invested in the persona of the cultural critic could be redeployed in the context of a left-wing critical project in which cultural analysis was again able to claim a central political significance. It was in this way that the distinctive moral voice that had been cultivated in the nineteenth-century critical traditions, and that had later been shaped into the twentieth-century critical project of Leavisism, was shifted into a new position in being bent to the left where it furnished a rationale for the centrality that was accorded questions of culture within the priorities of the New Left. The price to be paid in all of this, Ian Hunter (1988a and 1988b) and Francis Mulhern (2000) have argued, was a tendency to repeat the deep structure of post-Kantian *Kulturkritik* through an over-valuation of the role of culture and a corresponding underestimation of the significance of organized politics in anticipation of the day when the latter might finally be subordinated to the higher authority of culture.

There are, in this regard, significant similarities between the position Williams staked out in relation to the antecedent traditions of English criticism and those which, in continental Europe, western Marxism had staked out in relation to pre-Marxist aesthetics to the degree that, in both cases, the conceptual architecture of the earlier traditions continued – like Hamlet's ghost – to have a continuing influence on the traditions of thought that claimed to break with them. These were not, however, the aspects of Williams's work that first engaged my attention. I was much more interested in his own more explicit engagement with the tradition of western Marxism that was expressed in his concern, evident in his work in the early 1970s, to develop a specifically Marxist account of literature as part of a broader project of "cultural materialism." While the influence of this aspect of Williams's work is evident in *Formalism and Marxism*, it also gave rise to my first personal connections with both Raymond Williams and Edward Thompson through a weekend conference on the relations between Marxism and literature that I arranged while working at the University of Bristol in the early 1970s.[11] I became interested and involved in the debates surrounding the development of cultural studies only some time later, after I had moved to the Open University in 1975 and, more particularly, from 1978 when I took on the responsibility of developing the Open University's "Popular Culture" course.[12] It was in this context that I first became acquainted with the work of the Birmingham School and its leading figures,[13] a relationship that was to become closer when, in the early 1980s, Stuart Hall left Birmingham to join the Open University as Professor of Sociology. It was also in the context of developing the Open University "Popular Culture" course that I became interested in the earlier phases of Williams's work and its role in constructing the intellectual space in which British cultural studies had been formed but from which it was also then evidently moving on in terms of both the increasing influence of feminist perspectives and, particularly in the work of Hall, a shift of attention to questions of race and ethnicity.

This was above all, though, the moment of the "turn to Gramsci." While aspects of Bourdieu's work were immediately influential in suggesting new approaches to the relations of culture and class,[14] his overall theoretical framework, with its intersecting concepts of capitals, field and habitus, had little impact on British cultural studies (its impact on sociology was to prove much greater).[15] Similarly, aspects of Althusser's work were influential, particularly his re-reading of the concept of ideology.[16] But Althusser's work was always carefully filtered of its theoretical anti-humanism in Birmingham cultural studies which – in dividing the field between culturalists and structuralists – was critical of what it character-ized as the more thoroughgoing structuralist engagements with Althusser repre-sented by the short-lived, but productive, journal *Theoretical Practice* and the work of Barry Hindess and Paul Hirst. The work of Foucault was similarly treated with caution by Birmingham cultural studies in contrast to the journals *Ideology & Consciousness* and *Economy and Society* which became the major fora for the development of Foucauldian work in Britain.

The "turn to Gramsci" was an event of a quite different order, eclipsing theoretical engagements on other fronts to provide the intellectual basis for a program that was to have sustained long-term consequences for the future trajec-tories of British cultural studies (see Turner, 2003, for a more detailed account). Evident in the work of Williams as well as that of Hall (see Williams, 1977; Hall, 1981, 1986a, b and c), and the fruit of personal relationships as well as of theoretical ones,[17] this interest in Gramsci's work was prompted by a number of considerations. His concept of hegemony provided a framework within which class struggle could be theorized in a non-reductive fashion which accorded due weight to the role of cultural and ideological forces, as well as to the role of non-class actors subject to the limitation that only a class with a fundamental role in the relations of production could play the leading role in organizing a ruling power bloc or coordinating the struggle against such a bloc. This resonated well with the highly divided and still predominantly class-based politics of the late 1970s and early 1980s. It also, in the leadership roles it envisaged for organic intellectuals, provided a theoretical space in which the moral voice of the cultural critic that had been refashioned in the earlier history of cultural studies might find a role. And its conception of the national popular as being shaped by the struggles of competing forces to articulate national popular traditions to their philosophies and values provided a means of conceptualizing popular culture as a mobile formation, consisting of varied elements that were capable of being articulated together in different configurations and of being connected to social struggles in complex and varying ways. This provided an immeasurable advance on the forms of class essentialism that had characterized earlier conceptions of popular culture, includ-ing those arising from Williams's influential conception of culture as ways of life. It was this aspect of Gramsci's thought that had the greatest impact on my own work at this time. It provided the main architectural principle for the Open University "Popular Culture" course as well as for a number of parallel and subsequent publications addressing different aspects of both the theory of popular culture and the history and formation of different aspects of British popular culture, most notably my work on the organization of pleasure at the popular British seaside town of Blackpool (Bennett, 1982d, 1986a) and, with Janet Woollacott, a study of the various phases in James Bond's career as a popular hero (Bennett and Woolla-cott, 1987).

The first two of the essays that are brought together in Part I represent different aspects of these two early phases of my work – my critique of the aesthetic theories of western Marxism, and my involvement in British cultural studies at the moment of its "turn to Gramsci" – while also traversing them. My concern in "Severing the Aesthetic Connection" is both to dispute the cogency of those conceptions of the literary which construe it as part of a more generalized mode of aesthetic cognition and to locate, in Foucault's work, an alternative construction of the literary and of the aesthetic as particular technologies of subjectivity. It does so by arguing that the production of the autonomy of art and literature is a necessary precondition for their instrumentalization within programs of aesthetic-ethical self-formation. The argument is developed via commentaries on the work of Peter Bürger, Terry Eagleton and, as a counterpoint to these, that of Ian Hunter whose work provided an intellectual vantage point outside the traditions of British cultural studies from which the latter could be usefully relativized and historicized.

The central preoccupation of the second essay, "Texts, Readers, Reading Forma-tions," is with the status that is to be accorded to texts from the point of view of the concerns of sociological and historical analysis. Its arguments are directed against, first, metaphysical constructions of texts as ideal essences that are unaffected by the variant conditions of their reception, and, second, those constructions of texts which privilege one set of text–reader relations – usually those marking the originating conditions of a text's production and reception – over others. The concept of reading formation elaborated in the essay proposes a way of under-standing how text–reader relations are organized in particular circumstances that avoid the passive implications of "reception studies." Conceived as a set of discur-sive and institutional conditions that produce texts for readers as well as readers for texts, reading formations productively activate both texts and readers – and the ground between them – in specific ways. The argument is developed via a discus-sion, and qualification, of Carlo Ginzburg's (1980a) account, in *The Cheese and the Worms*, of untutored readings of the Bible and of Michel Pêcheux's (1982) account of the relations between ideology and language.

The concern that is evident in this essay with the question of popular readings reflects my preoccupation, at that time, with Gramscian approaches to the study of popular culture. This was evident too in my subsequent application of the concept of reading formation to the variant ways in which the "texts of Bond" (the James Bond novels, films, and publicity materials) have been discursively and institu-tionally organized to be read in different ways for different readers/viewers at different moments in the history of "the Bond phenomena," paying particular attention to the differences between popular and culturally knowing or parodic readings of these texts (Bennett, 1984c). There are, of course, some similarities between the concerns addressed in these essays and those that were worked through in British cultural studies through the encoding/decoding approach to audiences and, later, the "active audience" tradition. However, my approach to these questions was ultimately quite different and was, to some extent, an attempt to overcome what I saw as an important limitation of these traditions: namely, their inadequate understanding of the nature of texts and of textual historicities. The final essay in Part I, "Figuring Audiences and Readers," written a decade or so later, addresses these issues by counterposing the implications of the concept of reading formation to the figure of "the active reader" that played such a prominent role in the cultural studies approaches to the analysis of audience practices that were developed in the late 1980s and early 1990s. Its criticisms of the political voluntarism of the endeavor to find resistive readings everywhere reflected an increasing skepticism of the value of the polarized political topographies – governed by relations of resistance versus domination – that still held sway over much of cultural studies, particularly in Britain.

This skepticism partly reflected the experience, after I moved to Australia in 1983, of living and working in a society whose intellectual, political and cultural coordinates were quite different from those of Britain in a number of ways. As there is not space to go fully into these matters here, I shall limit myself to three points. The first concerns the considerably diminished intellectual presence of the distinctive moral voice of culture that had been developed in association with the development of English. While Leavisism did affect the teaching of English at a number of Australian universities, its influence on the terms of public intellectual debate was less strong than in Britain. This was partly because the voice of the cultural critic mattered less than that of the prophetic historian in view of the particular salience of questions concerning the national past in a country that was in the process of renegotiating its relationship to its colonial history. Of course, the same was true in Britain, but from the "other side" so to speak, where debates concerning "the end of empire" formed a significant point of reference for cultural studies. This was especially true of the account offered in *Policing the Crisis* (Hall et al., 1978) of the role played by racist responses to post-war immigration into Britain in reorganizing the texture of class politics and the significance, in this respect, of the historical prophecy of the Conservative politician Enoch Powell in his dire warnings of the rivers of blood that would carry the British people away in a tide of racial strife if the flow of immigration were not halted. The unique symbolic position of Indigenous Australians, however, gave debates concerning the relations between nation, culture, and history a particular force in Australia, and a particular complexity of a kind that I had not encountered before. Symbolically fêted as the First Australians in the nationalist discourses of the 1970s and 1980s, and using this to their advantage whenever possible, Indigenous Australians also staked their claims to a longer history than that of the nation and, moreover, to a history, that of the Dreamtime, whose complex temporality, while by no means that of a static eternity, confounded the progressive linear narratives of national histories.

Here, then, was a set of issues that had helped to shape the distinctive trajectories of Australian cultural studies alongside those it shared with cultural studies in Britain. They are also ones which had profoundly unsettling implications for the theoretical underpinnings of the "Gramscian moment" in cultural studies. For the program of organizing a counter-hegemonic struggle against the power bloc by organizing a "national popular" that would articulate the interests and values of subordinate social strata to those represented by a "fundamental class" was unable to make any connection whatever with the histories that had produced the unique and specific forms of material and symbolic dispossession that Australia's Aboriginal peoples had experienced. At the same time, the more dispersed distribution of power in federal political systems like Australia made Gramscian conceptions of a power bloc centered on the state seem far less probable than in highly centralized political systems like Britain's.

This coincided with my increasing interest in the work of Foucault, particularly his essay on governmentality (Foucault, 1991) and his critique of western political theory for its historical lag in continuing to apply forms of political reasoning associated with the principles of sovereignty developed in monarchical political systems. The perspectives of population and biopower, Foucault argued, had prompted the development of new forms of power concerned with the conditions of life of populations which exceeded the ambit of traditional state-centered forms of political power and authority. I was immediately interested, when I first read this essay, in its implications for the ways in which cultural studies had mostly concerned itself with the relations between culture and power. For, beyond the concern with the relations between ideology and state power that characterized forms of cultural analysis informed by the principle of sovereignty, it opened up a set of different questions concerning the ways of acting on and shaping populations by cultural means that had been produced by the development of specifically cultural forms of knowledge and expertise over the "modern" period. It also provided a counter to that tendency in cultural studies which, by this time, had become more or less a mantra in which culture, as a site of resistance, was invoked as the *vis-à-vis* of government.

The virtue of Foucault's work, per contra, was that it suggested ways in which culture and government might be placed on both the same and on different sides of the equation by seeing culture as simultaneously an instrument of governance and its object. It is the former as an inherited repertoire of cultural forms and practices that have been sequestered from the social, providing resources that are organized and deployed by agents acting within the frameworks of particular cultural knowledges in the context of particular institutional apparatuses for acting on the social. It is the latter insofar as it is culture in its more extended sense of ways of life that constitutes the surfaces through which such apparatuses seek to connect with and act upon the social.

These, then, are some of the changes in intellectual orientation that informed what became a significantly new organizing focus for my work in the late 1980s through to the 2000s: the relations between culture and governance as an umbrella theoretical setting for the analysis of and practical engagement with cultural policy as, then, a relatively new area of work in cultural studies. The essays in Part III all, in their different ways, examine the kinds of theoretical reformulation of the concerns of cultural studies that are called for in order to accommodate a focus on the relations between culture and the practices of government in the broadened sense implied by the Foucauldian optic of governmentality. These are questions that I had considered, first, in an essay, "Putting Policy into Cultural Studies" (Bennett, 1991b), and later and at greater length in *Culture: A Reformer's Science* (1998b) where I argue that culture, understood in terms of the relations between its various contemporary meanings, has to be understood as a field of government in which some forms of culture are enlisted as a means of reforming others in the context of varied programs of social management.

In the two essays collected here, I build on these earlier discussions, first, to review the implications of the concept of governmentality for the terms in which the relations between culture and the social should be approached. These are distinguished from those constructions of such relations, informed by linguistic versions of the cultural turn, which, as in Stuart Hall's work, tend to merge culture and the social by seeing culturally organized relations of meaning as being centrally implicated in the construction of the latter. In contrast to this the varied technical mediations through which, in governmentality theory, discourse operates to format the social for action in varied ways provides a more plausible, because more concrete and differentiated, account of the ways in which culture organizes and acts on the social and of the varied forms of agency (compliant and non-compliant) it encounters. "Acting on the Social: Art, Culture, and Government" continues the same vein of argument by suggesting that the historical specificity of modern forms of cultural governance can only be understood if the analytical focus on the relations of mutual permeability between culture and the social that is proposed by the "cultural turn" is called into question. Rather than being merged together, it is suggested that culture and the social are more usefully regarded as distinct if analysis is to engage adequately with the ways in which culture has been shaped into a historically distinctive means for acting on the social within the strategies of liberal government. The argument is carried by means of two case studies. The first examines how art was enlisted as a means of acting on the social – conceived as a realm of problematic class behaviors – in the reforming programs of mid-nineteenth-century English liberalism. The second considers the varied roles accorded art as a means of acting on communities in the programs of advanced liberalism. Consideration is also given to the implications of the perspectives on the relations of art, government, and the social that are developed in the case studies for the status of the work of art.

If the essays in Part II address questions of culture and governance as a set of general historical and theoretical questions, those collected in Part III deal with similar issues but in a more concrete way by focusing on the role of museums and art galleries as cultural technologies that have played key roles in the organization of modern relations of culture and governance. My interest in museums was initially prompted by a fascination with the role that they played in reassembling the national past in the Australian museum boom of the 1980s, and led from there to an interest in the history and theory of museums focused particularly on the civic and cultural logics characterizing the development of public museums in nineteenth-century Europe and North America. The first manifestation of this broader set of concerns was the essay "The Exhibitionary Complex" (Bennett, 1988a) leading, alongside other work, to *The Birth of the Museum* in which, by tracing the relations between the development of the public museum and the parallel birth of the prison, I tried to sketch a Foucauldian genealogy for the public museum.[18] The two essays collected in Part III belong to a later phase of work, but one whose concerns are recognizably continuous with those introduced in these studies. The first essay, "Archaeological Autopsy: Objectifying Time and Cultural Governance," looks at the use of the historical sciences in the context of late nineteenth-century museums of natural history and ethnology as a means of producing self-developing subjects in the context of the new perspectives of developmental time that were opened up by Darwinian accounts of evolution. Covering such museums in Britain, the USA, and Australia, the chapter examines the ways in which the artifactual field was re-ordered as a consequence of developments in the historical sciences and outlines how the management of this field was related to conceptions of the museum's new role as a technology for managing the subject's insertion into new relations of time in the context of nineteenth-century conceptions of liberal government. In these regards, the essay embodies a more fully elaborated Foucauldian approach to the relations between museums and governmentality theory than is evident in *The Birth of the Museum*, while also drawing on elements of actor-network theory and science studies in the account it offers of the processes of reassembling culture and nature that evolutionary museums effected. As such it serves as a condensed version of the argument developed at greater length in *Pasts Beyond Memory: Evolution, Museums, Colonialism* (Bennett, 2004b).[19] In "Civic Seeing: Museums and the Organization of Vision," my interests focus on the conception of museums as "civic engines" for acting on the social with a diversity of ends in view. However, it brings a particular perspective to bear on these concerns by considering the different ways in which different kinds of museums, operating within the contexts of different regimes of vision, have sought to regulate the visual practices of their visitors in order to direct their looking to the attainment of specific civic ends.

The aspects of my work that are represented in Parts II and III were initially developed in research institutes whose work was primarily focused on questions concerning the relations of culture and government, and of cultural policy in particular. The first comprised the work of the Institute for Cultural Policy Studies at Griffith University which I directed from 1987 to 1990, and the second the Australian Key Centre for Cultural and Media Policy which I directed from 1995 to 1998, when I returned to Britain. The work that was produced by these research centers had a controversial reception within cultural studies, most of which, in my view, merely confirmed the theoretical, political, and ethical shortcomings of the intellectual traditions that the focus on the relations between culture and government had been pitched against.[20] There were, inevitably, those who saw the very idea of a concern with cultural policy as equivalent to being co-opted by the state. And, in spite of much careful argument to the contrary, there were many more who thought that studying the operation of agents within governmental apparatuses necessarily means taking their side – which, of course, sometimes it might just as, sometimes, it might not. And the old topographies informing the view that a concern with policy entailed a focus on the operations of power from "the top down" at the expense of a concern with the movement of opposition and resistance from "the bottom up" were endlessly rehearsed by those who had no inkling of what it might mean to follow Foucault and try to cut off the king's head in cultural theory as well as political theory or of his contention that, although intellectuals now find themselves inevitably placed within government, this does not stop them being restive in relation to it.

There were, in these debates, very few who saw that, in their opposition to concerning themselves with the mundane realities of cultural policies and in seeking a position outside the entanglement of culture with the processes and mechanisms of government – in Habermas's discourse ethics, for example, or in the purity of resistance theory – they were reproducing those traditions of English cultural criticism in which culture had been fashioned as a higher plane of moral authority than the political. I had, in this regard, always found Bourdieu's comments on the illusions of intellectuals – that is, their strong disposition to entertain misplaced, and often simply fantastic, conceptions of their relationship to the conditions of their activity as intellectuals – a sober corrective to the moralizing posturing that goes with the notion of *critique* and of invaluable assistance in developing an ethical demeanor, cast more in a Weberian spirit, appropriate to the conduct of intellectual practice in the present.[21] This entailed, then, apart from theoretical and historical work on the relations of culture and government, a preparedness to work for and with varied agencies of cultural administration by producing work that might have an impact on actually existing cultural policies. There is, of course, no reason why such work should take away the entitlement or, indeed, the responsibility to also be critical of such policies where, as is only too often the case, the rhetorics that drive them serve to obfuscate the issues they are supposed to address.

Yet the allure of inherited conceptions of criticism and its function have proved well-nigh irresistible for the ways in which the roles of intellectuals have been elaborated within, or in close relation to, cultural studies. Since I have always found these problematic and disabling for the conduct of seriously critical intellectual practices, I have taken issue with them on a number of occasions. Indeed, this has been a continuing thread of my work from my early engagements with literary theory – where I took issue with the conceptions of criticism, and the related functions of the critic, that were proposed by Terry Eagleton, Fredric Jameson and Edward Said[22] – through my responses to the issues raised in the "cultural policy debates" of the 1990s to, since my return to Britain in 1998, my more active re-engagement with debates in sociology. The essays collected in Part IV illustrate these concerns. A significant point of engagement for the first of these is Edward Said's later work on intellectuals, and his conception of their central obligation as being that of "speaking the truth to power." However, these conceptions are placed in a broader context by being related to the Habermasian tradition of the public sphere and its construction of an opposition between the critical functions of "intellectuals proper" and the purely technical functions of those intellectuals who work in the bureaucratic machineries of government. Taking its point of departure from contemporary debates about whether and, if so, how intellectuals should concern themselves with and relate to the bureaucratic concerns of cultural policy, the chapter disputes the cogency of both Habermas's construction of the relations between different kinds of intellectual and his account of the historical formation and subsequent deterioration of the public sphere. In doing so, it argues for a role for intellectuals in the mundane process of culture's governance that does not construe an involvement in such technical questions as – by definition – critical reason's compromised Other.

The final essay focuses on the work of Pierre Bourdieu who, as I have indicated, often wrote trenchant criticisms of the tendency for intellectuals to overestimate their own power. Yet, in his final years, Bourdieu became an almost Sartrean figure as, in his opposition to neo-liberalism and to the state, he also claimed a major public and universal significance for intellectuals. The argument of this essay is that – in spite of appearances to the contrary – Bourdieu had always subscribed to Enlightenment and universal conceptions of cultural value. The argument is developed by a reading of the evolutionary and historicist conceptions informing Bourdieu's account of the historical development of the artistic and literary fields in *The Rules of Art* (Bourdieu, 1996b). The resulting conception of the "historical universal" value that is deposited and accumulated in great art gives rise to a related conception of the intellectual's function, to be realized through the practice of historical anamnesis, as being that of speaking for and extending the influence of the historical universal against the encroachments of state and economy.

It is worth, in concluding, saying a few words about the context for my engagement with Bourdieu in this last essay. The last major research project I was involved in before leaving Australia was a statistical survey of cultural practices in Australia. Convened by John Frow, this project was designed to explore how far Bourdieu's assessment of the part played by culture in processes of social distinction was also true of Australia in the 1990s (Bennett, Emmison and Frow, 1999). I have, since 2003, been involved in a similar project, but focused this time on Britain, and developed with a research team operating across the Open University and the University of Manchester.[23] I have also, over the same period, been coordinating a research program that brings a Foucauldian optic to bear on the relations between culture and liberal government over the period from the late eighteenth century to the present.[24] I mention this because both of these projects have returned me to questions concerning the relationships between aesthetics and society that preoccupied me in the early stages of my intellectual career. I also mention it because it underlines the respects in which, while I see my work as amounting to a prolonged interrogation of the relations between culture and power, I have, depending on the purpose to hand, sometimes done so by engaging with the work of Foucault and sometimes by engaging with the work of Bourdieu.

Introduction

This is not to suppose that their positions are easily reconcilable. To the contrary, Bourdieu's class-centrism clearly has no place in Foucault's work, any more than does the way in which he partitions economic, political, and cultural power into separate fields. And, by reverse, it is difficult to see how Foucault's work could result in the kinds of statistical investigations Bourdieu has pioneered, except to see these as themselves aspects of modern technologies of governance – which, indeed, they are. There are, then, significant and irresolvable tensions between these two bodies of work. While it has never been my purpose to seek to fuse them, I have, found them useful for different purposes. It is, I think, Foucault who provides a better overarching framework for investigating and intervening in the relations of culture and power so far as these concern the operations of specific cultural knowledges within particular cultural apparatuses and their implications for the ways in which the social is laid out to be acted on. These are questions which rarely occur to Bourdieu: the theoretical space he constructed is not one in which such questions can be posed since what matters for Bourdieu is less the content of particular forms of expertise, or how they operate in fashioning the social, than how they are placed relative to one another in the context of the competitive strivings which govern the architecture of the various fields (the economic, the cultural, the political, the journalistic, the scientific, and so on) into which he partitions power. By reverse, however, Foucault's work offers no purchase on the distributional aspects of the relations between culture and power of the kind that statistical inquiries modeled on Bourdieu's investigations into the relations between cultural and economic capital are capable of doing by demonstrating the systematic and endemic differences and inequalities that characterize our relations to culture when measured in terms of class, gender, or ethnicity. The virtue of both bodies of theory, then, is that of providing good locations, and vocations, for intellectual practice by allowing one to be both engaged with, and restive within, modern relations of culture and government.

And this, perhaps, is as good a note as any on which to conclude. For if there is an aspect of cultural studies that I have always been wary of, it is that tendency, less influential now than it used to be, to look for a position outside such relations that might provide both a situation and validation for intellectual practice. There is, though, no such position for there can be no outside in relation to the multiple ways in which practices of culture and practices of government are mutually implicated with one another. This ought not, however, to be a cause for regret for its consequence is to multiply the interfaces between such practices at which intellectual work can be critically and productively engaged.

Notes

1   I draw in what follows on aspects of a related collection of essays published in Chinese translation under the title *Culture and Society: Collected Essays* by Guangxi Normal University Press in 2007.

2   The classic texts here are Williams (1958, 1961). These are, however, important not only for their own arguments but in functioning as nodal texts for a much larger literature which, when seeking to place cultural studies in relation to earlier critical and intellectual traditions, takes it bearings from Williams's discussions.

3   See Mulhern (1979) for a thorough discussion of Leavis's work in the context of the broader critical tradition of which it formed a part.

4   While this is evident in Hoggart's classic text *The Uses of Literacy* (Hoggart, 1957), this remains strongly under the influence of Leavis in its negative assessments of many of the popular cultural practices it discusses. Hall's early writing on popular culture – his essays in *New Left Review*, for example, and the book he co-authored with Paddy Whannel (Hall and Whannel, 1964) – is more concerned with popular culture as a site for political mobilisation by connecting popular pleasures to the political agendas of the new left.

5   Marx's *Economic and Philosophical Manuscripts* and other early writings first became widely available in English translation in Bottomore (1963).

6   I discuss the operation of this logic in some detail in Bennett (1981).

7   Although I still think these criticisms are valid, the Foucauldian perspective of liberal government opens up a more productive way engaging with the history of aesthetic thought in terms of its positive effects in relation to new practices of governing through freedom. This orientation means paying more attention to the transformations to which Kant subjected both the Wolffian tradition of Prussian aesthetics and the civic humanist tradition developed in England and Scotland. For accounts of these transformations (not, though, from a Foucauldian perspective) see Caygill (1989), and Guyer (2005).

8   I had, however, read excerpts from both Hoggart and Williams during my secondary schooling in a pedagogic context I have discussed more fully in Bennett (1996b).

9   The work of Christopher Caudwell came closest to developing a Marxist approach to literary and cultural phenomena. His work is discussed by both Williams (1958) and Thompson (1977), but with much more enthusiasm by the latter.

10 This included, at Birmingham, the work of the history group coordinated by Richard Johnson (see Johnson et al., 1982) and continuing as an active focus of work at the Birmingham Centre in the period of Johnson's directorship, and, under the leadership of Raphael Samuel, the work of the journal *History Workshop*.

11 Like both Williams and Thompson, I began my career in an extra-mural department – the sections of British universities which, at that time, were responsible for developing courses for mature-age students. The connections between cultural studies and the history of adult education in Britain are interestingly discussed in Steele (1997).

12 This was a collaborative, team effort in which I worked most closely with Graham Martin, Ken Thompson and Janet Woollacott. Open University courses are large, multi-media courses which, apart from being available to the University's students, are also publicly available and so are often widely used in other universities and colleges. This was true of 'Popular Culture' which, according to O'Shea and Schwarz (1987), had a significant influence on the development of cultural studies teaching in Britain.

13 I had earlier had stronger associations with the Society for Education in Film and Television (SEFT) and, in the early 1980s, was more closely involved in working with James Donald in developing and contributing to, first, *Formations* and, later, *New Formations*.

14 See, for example, Willis (1978).

15 See Neveu (2005) for a discussion of the relations between Bourdieu and British cultural studies.

16 Hall's essay on the structuralist and culturalist paradigms in cultural studies – taking from both, but with a leaning in favor of the latter – proved decisively influential, providing the terms of reference through which British cultural studies was to "story itself" throughout the 1980s: see Hall (1980a).

17 There were institutional links between the CCCS at Birmingham and the Instituto Universitario Orientale at Naples, and strong person links between Hall and Lydia Curti and Fernando Ferrara at the IUO.

18 For retrospective assessments of the concept of the exhibitionary complex, see Bennett (2006c) and Hall (2006).

19 Although not published until 2004, the research for this book was supported by a grant from the Australian Research Council and was mostly completed by the time I left Australia in 1998. However, completion of the manuscript for the book was delayed for a number of years owing to the demands of my administrative and teaching duties at the Open University.

20 See, for examples of some of the issues raised in these debates, Jones (1994), McGuigan (1996) and, more interestingly, O'Regan (1992).

21 See, for example, Bourdieu (2000).

22 My discussions of these can all be found in Bennett (1990a).

23 The project – *Cultural Capital and Social Exclusion: A Critical Investigation* – was funded by the Economic and Social Research Council. Mike Savage, Elizabeth Silva, and Alan Warde were the co-holders of the award and Modesto Gayo-Cal and David Wright the Research Fellows on the project.

24 I refer to the research theme "Culture, Governance and Citizenship: The Formation and Transformations of Liberal Government" that forms the research program of the ESRC Centre for Research on Socio-cultural Change (CRESC). I have developed this theme in close collaboration with Patrick Joyce from the University of Manchester.

Part I   The Literary, the Aesthetic, and the Popular

Chapter One   Severing the Aesthetic Connection

In introducing a selection of Marx's and Engels's writings on literature and art, Stefan Morawski cautions that "we should distinguish the writings which explicitly and coherently elaborate a topic from the fragments which contain a thesis about a topic but which leave it undeveloped in part and thus rather unclear, and from the hasty or opaque comments which, as such, don't offer a reliable basis for a thesis" (Baxendall and Morawski, 1974: 7). Morawski goes on to note that, for the greater part, the themes clustered under the first of these categories concern the functional aspects of specific attributes of artistic structures. By contrast, he numbers the following among the themes associated with the second and third categories: the distinguishing traits of aesthetic objects and aesthetic experience; the recurrent attributes and enduring values of art; the distinction between science and art; and the hierarchy of artistic values.

The founding texts of Marxism thus seem to authorise, quite clearly and directly, the concerns of a historical and sociological approach to the analysis of artistic forms and functions. The degree to which they also authorise the concerns of a Marxist aesthetic, understood as a theory of a distinct mode of cognition or experience embodied in works of art, is less certain. Marx and Engels undoubtedly had views on such matters and interpolated them into their writings from time to time. Yet it is not clear how much reliance can be placed on these as indicative of the arguments they might have advanced had they given such questions their sustained attention. Moreover, even if this conundrum could be resolved, it would hardly be decisive. The considerable pains Marx devoted to establishing the existence of a separate Asiatic mode of production have had few binding consequences for the subsequent development of Marxist thought which, on balance, has judged this an unhelpful suggestion.

Unfortunately, these fragmentary writings are not always approached so circumspectly. They have rightly attracted a good deal of attention from scholars concerned to deepen and extend our understanding of the various tributary sources of Marx's and Engels's intellectual development. Margaret Rose's *Marx's Lost Aesthetic* is a recent case in point, offering a detailed and persuasive reconstruction of 'what Marx's aesthetic theory might have been' by considering his stated views on art and literature in the context of contemporary aesthetic theories and artistic movements (Rose, 1984)[1]. Difficulties arise, however, when such reconstructed accounts are used to justify the view that Marxist thought should ongoingly engage with the concerns of philosophical aesthetics. For the issues are distinct. The first is a historical matter concerning the biographical fullness of thought of a specific (although exceptionally richly) historically determined individual while the second concerns the current theoretical and political requirements of an intellectual tradition whose very commitment requires some degree of adaptability to changing circumstances.

I put the matter this way because I would hesitate to push too hard the contrary view that a concern with the traditional preoccupations of philosophical aesthetics cannot be reconciled with the analytical logic of Marxist thought. Indeed, empirically, the tradition of Marxist aesthetics is largely definable in terms of its attempts to effect such a reconciliation. Nor can there be much doubt that Marxism's political vision has been profoundly – and often disastrously – affected by the influence of Romantic aesthetics on Marx's conception of communist society as a vehicle for the full realisation of humanity. That said, my own view is that the concerns of philosophical aesthetics *do* pull in an opposite direction from what is, for me, the most important and most lasting innovation of Marxist thought: its socialising and historicising logic – even though this, its 'rational kernel' so to speak, has often to be won from the particularity of Marx's own formulations. If we compare the procedures governing the formation of objects of thought which Marx deployed in his social and economic analyses with those regulating the formation of objects of thought within philosophical aesthetics, then these do seem incompatible. Marx's argument, in the *Grundrisse*, that the concrete is the concrete because it is the concentration of many determinations whose interaction can only be grasped by the violent abstraction of thought, thus embodies a methodological orientation that is precisely the reverse of that of philosophical aesthetics (Marx, 1973: 101). It suggests, for example, that questions relating to the effects of works of art require that the labour of theoretical abstraction be orientated to examining the modes of interaction of the complex concatenation of factors regulating the reception of such works. Within philosophical aesthetics, by contrast, the process of abstraction pulls in the opposite direction. Here, it embodies a procedure for disengaging works of art from the mundane particularities regulating their reception in different contexts in order to arrive at a conception of their effects as being always subject to the influence of an invariant aesthetic relation, itself rooted in an unchanging faculty of the subject deduced from a transcendental analysis of the constitutive properties of art in general.

Aspects of this tension were recognised by Georg Plekhanov in his insistence that, while Marxist categories could account for the socio-genesis of works of art, they could neither explain nor illuminate the nature of aesthetic experience as such. This is not to endorse Plekhanov's view which left the sphere of aesthetic experience and judgement in a position of untouched transcendence. None the less, the point is worth making if only to recall that the alignment of Marxist approaches to art and literature with the concerns of philosophical aesthetics occurred at a relatively late point in the development of the Marxist tradition. The first work to propose such an alignment was Mikhail Lifshitz's *The Philosophy of Art of Karl Marx* (Lifshitz, 1974), first published in 1933 coincidentally with the first collection (co-edited by Lifshitz) of Marx's and Engel's writings on art. Lifshitz's work was inspired by the publication, a year earlier, of Marx's *Economic and Philosophical Manuscripts*, just as it, in turn, prompted Lukács to draw on the same source in elaborating his historicised man-centred aesthetics in which art is viewed as affording a specific mode of self-consciousness of the processes of man's historical self-making.[2]

Even then, not everyone subscribed to the commitment, derived from this period, to establish a Marxist aesthetic which could rival – and, of course, surpass – the aesthetic theories of the nineteenth century in its capacity to offer alternative explanations of such enduring problems as the defining attributes of art, the hierarchy of artistic values and so on. Brecht didn't. But most of the theorists comprising Perry Anderson's tradition of western Marxism did, and wholeheartedly in the sense that such questions came to supply the organising centre of their inquiries into the spheres of art and literature. Work of this sort still goes on, of course. The cutting edge of most recent Marxist literary theory, however, has tended in the opposite direction, seeking to sever the aesthetic connection rather than to constrain inquiry within its confines and, in doing so, to bring a more thoroughgoing socialising and historicising logic to bear on questions which had previously been resolved abstractly or philosophically. While I argue that the structure of aesthetic discourse is incompatible with the socialising and historicising impetus of Marxist thought, I want first to resist a conclusion which is sometimes drawn from this: that the category of literature should be abandoned. To the contrary, I argue that it is vital, both theoretically and politically, that such a category should be secured – but only on the condition that its specificity is conceived non-aesthetically.

As a prelude to this argument, however, it will be useful to identify a number of linked problems which derive from the theoretical alignments the tradition of Marxist aesthetics has sought to effect. I shall focus on two such problems. The first concerns the tendency toward an idealist reductionism which, in spite of their socialising and historicising rhetoric, has characterised Marxist approaches to the question of aesthetic value. The second concerns the related tendency for the concepts and procedures developed to enable Marxism to address the concerns of aesthetics to be carried over into adjacent areas of inquiry – those concerning the social determination of works of art, for example – such that the issues pertinent to such areas of inquiry are subjected to a "logic of aesthetic overdetermination". The consequence, in both cases, is that the scope of social and historical categories of analysis tends to be restricted while also, through the way their application is conceived, being subject to an idealist inflection.

An Idealist Reductionism

> We could say then that art, like all autonomous, qualitatively distinct spheres, exists as such to the extent that it transcends the particularity of its social conditioning. This transcendence, which in essence resides in the very bowels of art, is the exact opposite of all sociological reductions. Consequently, if Marx's theory of aesthetics had no other objective than to explain art from the perspective of its social conditioning – expressed, in turn, by its ideological content – it would never amount to more than a sociology of art. (Vazquez, 1978: 97)

This argument might have been excerpted from any of the classic texts comprising the tradition of Marxist aesthetics. Here, it is Sanchez Vazquez speaking, but it could just as easily have been Lukács, Lifshitz, Goldmann, Lefebvre, Fischer or Althusser, or, more recently, Eagleton or Jameson.[3] That Marxism is not a mere sociology of art is a constantly recurring trope within the tradition. Marxism respects art's transcendence of its social conditioning. Yet, at the same time, it is not content merely to register this fact or to posit, in the spirit of neo-Kantianism, a simple duality between a socio-genetic approach to art and the question of its value. Marxism both respects art's transcendence and seeks to explain it in terms of – and this is the central paradox of the tradition, a discursive contradiction which it can never entirely disguise – precisely its social and historical conditioning.

Viewed in this light, the argument forms part of a double disclaimer through which Marxist aesthetics, in telling us what it is not, has sought to negotiate a specific position for itself within the field of available discourses about art and literature. If the formulation of a Marxist *aesthetic* warns us that its concerns are not to be confused with those of a "mere sociology", the fact that it is a *Marxist* aesthetic that is on offer also tells us that its concerns will not be subjective or formalist either. If Marxist aesthetics thus differs from the sociology of art in the attention it accords questions of aesthetic value and experience, it also differs from traditional aesthetics in rebutting the contention that the specific nature of the aesthetic experience consists in relations of mutual support between the abstracted form of the art-work and the constitution of a transcendental subject. In the more sophisticated versions of the argument, these two moments of differentiation are integrated by positing an ideological affinity between the subjective formalism of bourgeois aesthetics and the "pseudo-objectivism" of sociology. Lukács, seemingly with Plekhanov in mind, thus accuses 'vulgar sociology' of adopting an abstract and entirely external approach to art which relinquishes the question of aesthetic experience to the hold of equally abstract subjectivist formulations:

> And the social insights of "sociological" literary criticism are on an even lower level and thus even more abstract and schematic than those of general sociology; this approach treats aspects of literature it sets out to illuminate as abstractly and formalistically and as much in aesthetic isolation as the non-sociological approaches to literature. The affinity of vulgar sociology to aesthetic formalism, often remarked

upon, is not a speciality of those who distort Marxism. On the contrary, it is from bourgeois literary criticism that this tendency toward aesthetic formalism passes into the labour movement. One can discover this direct, inorganic mixing of abstract, schematic sociological generalisations with the aesthete's subjective approach to literary works in full bloom in such "classics" of sociology as Taine, Guyau or Nietzsche. (Lukács, 1970: 198)

Having defined the field of discourses about art as being governed by an antinomy whose terms are ideologically complicitous, Marxist aesthetics defines its own function as that of overcoming the effects of this opposition. It will return to sociology a concern with aesthetic questions while simultaneously grounding such questions in the analysis of social and historical relations. In the classical statements of the position, this is accomplished by conceiving both aesthetic objects and the subjects of aesthetic judgement as being marked by the processes of their historical formation. While this avoids formalist conceptions of aesthetic transcendence and idealist conceptions of the givenness of the subject, it does so in such a way that subject and object are still regarded as the mutual supports of one another. For, in so far as the aesthetic relation between them is concerned, neither the subject nor the object is regarded as being unduly influenced by the immediate social and historical determinations which condition the forms of their inter-relation in specific contexts. Rather, the historicisation of subject and object takes the form of their being written into a long and continuous history of the humanisation of the senses in which – incompletely at first but, once the alienating effects of the division of labour have been overcome, fully – the value inherent in the art-work which embodies this history is recognised by the subject which that history helps to produce. In this way, no matter what stage has been reached within these mutually supportive histories, the aesthetic relation between subject and object is represented as a relation of fundamentally the same type: one in which the subject recognises itself as the product of the processes of man's historical self-making, processes which, in turn, the art-work embodies while also heralding their completion. Any examination of the differential structure of the varying social relations within which works of art are valorised, and of the different functions which their valorisation plays within those relations, is thus pre-empted to the degree that such relations are held to be ultimately elevatable to a general subject–object relation susceptible to a philosophical definition.

This idealist reductionism – a reductionism upwards, so to speak – is a conse-quence of the statute of limitation placed on socialising and historicising categories which results from their deployment *within the discursive field of aesthetics*. Yet the appearance of idealism which this orientation brings in its tow is avoided by the recurrent use of an argument which seems uncompromising, indeed excessive, in the role it accords history. This consists in the view that if art transcends its social conditioning, it is able to do so only by virtue of that social conditioning – by virtue of the fact that, as genuine art, its relations to history are deeply determined. Marked indelibly by the conditions of its production, the genuine work of art is able to rise above those conditions precisely because its value consists in and derives from its relations to them. It is only where the force of historical determination is weak – where a text is affected by history only shallowly or by its more superficial aspects, as popular fiction is often viewed within the tradition – that it proves also to be a limitation.[4]

There are many versions of this argument. Perhaps the most fully elaborated, however, is Lukács's theory of the vocation for universality which derives from the social typicality of the experience reflected in the art-work and the degree to which this experience represents the progressive tendencies of the historical epoch to which the work in question belongs. Through the application of these two criteria, Lukács is able both to construct a canon and effect discriminations within it. All those works of literature which give a shape and coherence to the experience of significant social classes have a place within world-historical literature. However, the place of literary texts within this most totalising of literary canons varies in accordance with the historical functions of the classes whose world-views they fashion. Where the class which provides a literary text, however indirectly, with its ultimately determining social base is of a limited significance within a particular mode of production and, accordingly, has only a tangential bearing on the central political and cultural tendencies of the epoch, then that text's capacity for universality is assessed as a limited one. The same is true of classes which have passed their prime and which, like the bourgeoisie after 1848, act as a halter on the forces of historical development rather than representing their progressive tendencies. If such classes support the texts which constitute the troughs of realism – still   important components of world-historical literature, but not its highest achievements – the peaks are constituted by those texts which embody the world-views of those classes which represent the developmental tendencies of their epoch, with an exception clause (the Balzac clause) which allows declining social classes to enrich realist literature through their ability to supply a critical perspective on the development of capitalist social relations.

The internal consistency and elegance of this theory has often been remarked upon. It rests on a view of history as a continuous process – marked, of course, by the vicissitudes of the dialectic, but still pursuing its ever-onward course – in which literary texts can be assigned a definite relation to one another in terms of their relations to the objective tendencies of historical development. Yet this ordering of relations between texts requires that the process of history can be counted on to produce a subject capable of recognising – fitfully at first, but eventually fully – the respects in which both the troughs and peaks of realist literature offer a mediated reflection of the contradictory processes of that subject's self-making. As a consequence, Lukács's assignation of relative value and meaning to literary texts is dependent on an idealist conception in which their future value and meaning is allowed to overdetermine their past and present ones.[5] In this way, the vocation for universality which derives from a text's relations to its conditions of production is, in the final analysis, subject to a future determination. For the way Lukács construes the relations between a text and the social and ideological conditions of its period is always informed by a prior conception of that text's relations to earlier and subsequent texts as specified by the degree to which its conditions of production enable it both to continue earlier realist tendencies and to anticipate later ones. The objective meaning and value of literary texts is thus determined by the place which their conditions of production produce for them within a meta-text of History which Marxism claims to know but whose final judgements – which can only be delivered once the process of History has been completed – it can only anticipate. Hence Lukács's constant insistence that the meaning of a period and its texts will become clearer to us the more distant we are from it – not just because, with time, perspectives settle, but because, with the unfolding of each stage of historical development, we move a little closer to the post-historical unified subject, Man, to whom the meaning of History and, therefore, that of each text within it will finally become luminously transparent.

Yet this future-structured conception of a text's meaning and value does not negate the fact that its vocation for universality is thought of as deriving from its relations to the conditions of its production. For it is still the history which flows into the text from behind it that, come the day of History's final hermeneutic reckoning with itself, is held to determine its relative value. As a consequence, the yet-to-be fixed past of the text is accorded a priority over the real history of its differential valuation and reception within different valuing communities. Indeed, this latter question is rendered devoid of any possible significance as an area of analysis. Discrepant systems of valuation of the same text simply don't count for much within this scheme. Their ontological weight is weak compared with that of the historical forces which prepare the judgements of empirical subjects for their eventual *rendez-vous* with those of Man. Foucault throws some light on this matter in contrasting the functioning of utopian representations within the classical and the modern *epistemes*. Whereas, in the classical period, utopias functioned as fantasies of origins, the development of historical systems of thought in the nineteenth century effects a transformation in the temporal orientation of utopic thought. Concerned "with the final decline of time rather than with its morning", Foucault argues, the modern utopia projects a future situation in which "the slow erosion or violent eruption of History will cause man's anthropological truth to spring forth in its stony immobility; calendar time will be able to continue; but it will be, as it were, void, for historicity will have been superimposed exactly upon the human essence" (Foucault, 1970: 262). Foucault's purpose in this discussion is to draw attention to the structural similarities which underlie Ricardian and Marxist economics in spite of their differing end-of-history scenarios – a confrontation with finitude and scarcity in the one case and a leap beyond it in the other. These similarities are precisely mirrored in the complicity between bourgeois and Marxist aesthetics. For in both the aesthetic sense is projected as a utopian condition that will mark the end of time and which, in so doing, will finally legislate the proper modes for the deployment of the faculty of judgement. To concern oneself overmuch with particular histories of valuation would, in this light, be merely vain labour given their impending engulfment within a general history of the formation of a unified subject of judgement.

25

The Logic of Aesthetic Overdetermination

In *Criticism and Truth*, Barthes argues that the call to respect the specificity of literature "seems to be the last will and testament of old criticism, so religiously is it held to" (Barthes, 1987: 53). Its advantage as a slogan, he suggests, consists in its pretension to establish literary studies as an autonomous science "which would at last consider the literary object 'in itself', without ever again owing anything to historical or anthropological sciences" (Barthes, 1987: 57). Yet this ambition, he argues, can only place literary studies on a road to nowhere:

> "*On the subject of the gods*", recommended Demetrius Phalereus, "*say that they are gods.*" The final imperative of critical verisimilitude is of the same kind: *on the subject of literature, say that it is literature.* This tautology is not gratuitous: at first, they pretend to believe that it is possible to talk of literature and to make it the *object* of discourse; but this discourse leads nowhere, since it has nothing to say of this object other than that it is itself. (Barthes, 1987: 54–5)

Marxist literary theory has also found a way of saying this in its insistence that literature must be regarded as relatively autonomous: that is, as being characterised by specific formal and organisational properties which, in differentiating literature from other semiotic forms, are also the product of determinants unique to it. It is true, of course, that neither these determinants nor their literary effects are envisaged – as they are in Barthes's "old criticism" – as operating in isolation from other social and historical relations. To the contrary, when adequately formulated, the problem of relative autonomy in Marxist literary theory concerns precisely how to theorise the modes of interaction which characterise the relations between those determinations which are construed as specific to literature and the more general economic, political and ideological determinations which Marxist thought contends are relevant to the analysis of any practice.[6] Yet, whatever their precise pattern in different circumstances, it is foreordained that such modes of interaction will give rise to the same result in supporting those attributes of texts' formal structures which qualify them as instances of literature.

It is in such formulations of literature's relative autonomy that the logic of aesthetic overdetermination most clearly manifests itself. For literature's relative autonomy – its specificity – can be secured only if all texts counted as literary are deemed to be so in essentially the same way in spite of the manifold differences between them in other respects: whether they are texts produced for performance or for reading; the historical circumstances of their initial production and reception; their placement within particular genre systems, etc. Moreover, to specify and account for literature's relative autonomy, analysis must orientate itself to differing historical relations of literary production precisely with a view to abstracting from these some recurring set of determining relations capable of accounting for the recurrence of an underlying commonality in formal structure which confers on such texts their literariness in spite of their differences in other respects. In thus setting out from the assumption that texts nominated as literary *must* have some underlying set of attributes in common, Marxist analysis is led away from the domain of social and historical particularity which it has always claimed as its own.

In these respects, Marxist concern with the question of literature's relative autonomy constitutes the locus of an attempted (but impossible) reconciliation of, on the one hand, an approach to the analysis of the composition and functioning of forms of writing in the contexts of the historical circumstances of their production and social deployment with, on the other, an immanent analysis of literature understood as a distinctive, trans-historical semiotic system. This tension was evident in one of the earliest, and still most influential, formulations of the problem: that developed by Medvedev and Bakhtin in their critique of Russian Formalism. Taking the Formalists to task for positing a division between the extrinsic (systems of patronage, literary markets, etc.) and intrinsic (formal) "facts" of literature, and for denying the former any influence on the latter, Medvedev and Bakhtin seek to undercut this duality by insisting on the inherent sociality of any influence which literature exerts on itself. In so doing, they are able to deny any essential distinction between the extrinsic and the intrinsic, the social and the literary, studies of literature:

> From within it [the literary work] is determined by literature itself, and from without by other spheres of social life. But, in being determined from within, the literary work is thereby determined externally also, for the literature which determines it is itself determined from without. And being determined from without, it thereby is determined from within, for internal factors determine it precisely as a literary work in its specificity and in connection with the whole literary situation, and not outside that situation. (Medvedev and Bakhtin, 1978: 29)

What, then, is the nature of this interior determination which allows literature to contribute to its own social determination? For Medvedev and Bakhtin, the answer consists in literature's differentiation from other semiotic systems as determined by the specific forms and devices through which it reflects and refracts reality:

> Literature is one of the independent parts of the surrounding ideological reality, occupying a special place in it in the form of definite, organised philological works which have their own specific structures. The literary structure, like every ideological structure, refracts the generating socio-economic reality, and does so in its own way. But, at the same time, in its "content," literature reflects and refracts the reflections and refractions of other ideological spheres (ethics, epistemology, political doctrines, religion, etc.). That is, in its "content" literature reflects the whole ideological horizon of which it is itself a part. (Medvedev and Bakhtin, 1978: 16–17)

When it comes to identifying the exact nature of the specific mode of reflecting and refracting reality which the literary work effects, Medvedev and Bakhtin are somewhat vague. The most they offer is a restatement of the metaphor of the artist as seer in which this capacity is (partially) transferred from the personality of the writer to the impersonality of the literary structure:

> Literature is capable of penetrating into the social laboratory where these ideolo-gemes are shaped and formed. The artist has a keen sense for ideological problems in the process of birth and generation. (Medvedev and Bakhtin, 1978: 17)

This penchant for theorising literature's specificity by means of metaphors of sight recurs in Althusserian Marxism, as does Medvedev's and Bakhtin's charac-terisation of literature as a secondary system of signification whose distinctiveness consists in its relations to other semiotic or ideological systems. For Althusser and Macherey, literature's specificity thus consists in its capacity to help us "see", "feel" or "perceive" the ideologies to which it alludes and which provide the ground upon which it works – and works precisely to transform by rendering the occlusions and contradictions of those ideologies perceptible.

Two preliminary difficulties with this conception may briefly be mentioned. First, as must be the case, the relative autonomy of literature, and thereby its capacity to determine itself, is secured only by attributing to it an invariant function and effect. The argument, as Frow puts it, rests on the assumption "that literature can be described as a distinct ontological realm with a specific difference from the realm of ideology and an invariant function, the demystification of illusion through its parodic formal reproduction" (Frow, 1986: 25–6). If this is so, the nature of the literary function and effect must elude the reach of social and historical analysis. As the "literiness" of literature is held to consist in its invariant relation to ideology, the most such analysis can do is to identify the contingent factors which condition the specific modes in which such an invariant function/effect is realised in particular circumstances. The result is, indeed, an endless demonstration that literature is literature; or rather, and to propose a correction to Barthes's argument, an endless demonstration that literature isn't something else – in this case, ideology – and so must be itself.

The second difficulty relates to the assumption that literature is a second-order system of signification. Medvedev and Bakhtin thus argue not only that literature refracts social reality in its own way but also that it "reflects and refracts the reflections and refractions of other ideological spheres". Since this mechanism is not said to work in reverse – since, that is, literary refractions of reality are not said to be, in turn, subject to a further refraction in other ideological forms – the effect is to install literature as the queen of the superstructures, "reflecting the whole of the ideological horizon of which it is itself a part". Similarly, Eagleton, in a sub-variant of the Althusserian argument,[7] contends that literature signifies history indirectly via its signification of ideological significations of history. History enters the literary text not as history but as ideological significations of history, these latter significations being transformed in the work so as to produce the distincti-vely literary effect: "the literary text's relation to ideology so constitutes that ideology as to reveal something of its relations to history" (Eagleton, 1976: 69).

Ideology here is conceived as a first-order system of signification with literature functioning as a second-order system of signification operating upon it within what seems, again, a non-reversible relation between them.[8]

It is clear that the terms of such arguments, and consequently the implied hierarchy of forms of which they form a part, can easily be deconstructed. There is no reason, for example, why the argument should not be simply up-ended by arguing that, in certain regions (criticism, for instance), history also does not enter into ideology directly as history but only as already signified by literature. In brief, when account is taken of the complex networks of reciprocal signification which characterise the relations between different semiotic systems, the distinction between first- and second-order systems of signification breaks down. All ordered systems of signs involve – and work by and through – their relations to other such systems, all of which, so to speak, are equally close to or distant from god so far as their relations to "history" are concerned. If, in the Marxist conception, literature and ideology are placed in a hierarchical relation to one another, this is only made possible by the fact that the structure of that hierarchy is secured by the role accorded science. For it is science (= Marxism) which, in knowing history, can also know ideology's relations to history. In sum, if literature is able to be represented as "queen of the superstructures", it is because that place is secured for it by science's functioning as the "king of the superstructures".[9]

It can be seen from this how both problems coalesce and have their provenance in a broader set of difficulties: the pressure to theorise literature's specificity in terms of its difference from ideology. Or rather, since this is only half of the story, the root difficulty with Marxist theorisations of literature's relative autonomy is that this has to be conceived in relation to the places already occupied by science and ideology within the economy of the superstructure. Typically, then, literature is defined by means of a double differentiation: its specificity consists in the conjunction of those properties which allow it to be differentiated from ideology on the one hand and from science on the other. Nor is this true solely of Althusserian Marxism. While differing in content, the procedures deployed by Lukács and Goldmann to identify literature's specificity are structurally identical – literature has in some way to be defined in relation to what are taken to be the already given and fixed poles of reference of science and ideology. As a consequence, Marxist conceptions of literature's relative autonomy typically result in a proliferation of not-statements: literature is not ideology and it is not science, but it is not entirely not ideology either, since it is in some way connected to it by virtue of its function. Nor is it entirely not science for, depending on the formulation, it is either said to constitute a staging post on the royal road which leads the subject from the illusions of ideology to the truths of science (Althusser) or to offer a form of knowledge which, albeit organised differently, is as objective as that offered by science (Lukács).[10]

It is in regard to this definitional issue that the logic of aesthetic overdetermination has borne most consequentially on the concerns of Marxist literary theory, introducing a quite radical ahistoricity into its most basic procedures. For there are no reasons, apart from those derived from epistemology, to assume that literary texts should stand constantly in the same relation to other texts nominated as ideological or scientific. The concern to so argue clearly derives from, as it can now be seen, a historically and theoretically contingent pressure to install literature in an acceptable niche within Marxist variants of the triadic conceptions of the mental economy of the subject inherited from classical epistemology. Indeed, the history of Marxist aesthetics consists largely of competing attempts to map such triadic conceptions of the economy of the subject onto a triadic conception of the organisation of the superstructure: why else, indeed, should it be thought that the superstructure's economy should necessarily be triadic? In consequence, the possibility of examining historically differing sets of relations between different intellectual practices is radically curtailed: science, ideology and literature – these are always there (at least once art and science have been differentiated from magic),[11] and they always exist in the same relation to one another just as each always induces in the subject an invariant mode of mental relation to reality. Viewed from this perspective, differences within the Marxist tradition – between its Althusserian and Lukácsian components, for example – are of quite minor significance. Indeed, virtually the only point at issue between them concerns which pre-Marxist epistemology and aesthetic (Kantian, Hegelian, Spinozan, etc.) should govern the terms in which the relations between ideology, science and literature are to be conceived.

That aside, the problems inherent in this definitional procedure are apparent. They are, in effect, variants of those generated within the sociology of genres by the attempt to characterise genres in terms of a definite positivity. For, that positivity always turns out to be relationally conceived as a set of differences from the properties of other genres whose defining attributes, while assumed as given for the purposes of defining the genre in question, are similarly theorisable only as sets of differences from other genres. This, in turn, means that such genres cannot function in the manner required of them if they are to serve as stable points of reference in relation to which the specific differences of other genres might be defined. The whole ground of inter-generic relations is too slippery, fluid and mobile to allow the process which this procedure of genre definition requires to be initiated: namely, that a particular genre, definable solely in terms of its self-identity, might be abstracted from these relations and so serve as a fixed point around which a series of negatively defined generic differentiations might rotate. To the degree that Marxist characterisations of literature's positivity are dependent on the series of not-statements which govern the process of literature's definition – literature is not science and it is not ideology – then so, similarly, that positivity turns out to consist of a set of negatively defined relational attributes subjected to a misleading ontologisation.

Consideration of a more closely related analogy – the Russian Formalists' attempt to theorise the specificity of poetic language in terms of its differentiation from practical language – may help make the point. The result of this endeavour, Medvedev and Bakhtin argue, was an entirely negative definition of poetic language (its capacity to defamiliarise the automatism of practical language) whose cogency depended on an unwarranted ontologization of an arbitrarily selected set of differences between poetic and practical language. In being called on to serve the purpose of providing a standardised form of communication in relation to which the *differentia specifica* of poetic language might then be theorised, practical language was able to fulfil this function only because it was itself subject to an arbitrary definition. In focusing purely on narrowly technical forms of utterance in which the communicative function is dominant, Medvedev and Bakhtin argue, the Formalists suppressed those aspects of practical language which included a de-automatising propensity. Once such attributes are included as a part of practical language use and, accordingly, of its definition, then they are clearly unable to serve as criteria whereby practical and poetic language might be differentiated as ontologically distinct realms.

Similarly, then, if literature is to be defined negatively in relation to both science and ideology, these latter must be capable of being defined on their own terms and in a definite relation to one another. There are now more than sufficient grounds for doubting this to be the case. Quite apart from the difficulties associated with the concept of ideology in its own right – its assumption of the attributes of the subject it is supposed to account for, for example, as well as its conventional association with a dualistic ontology of the social, divided between 'the real' and its representations[12] – the very organisation of the epistemological space in which ideology is theorised as the opposite of science has been tellingly called into question in recent debates.[13] Frow, reflecting on these criticisms and urging the need for the category of ideology to be redefined to take account of them, suggests this might be achieved if ideology, rather than being ontologised as a particular kind of discourse, is thought of "as a *state* of discourse or of semiotic systems in relation to the class struggle" (Frow, 1986: 61). This ideological state of discourse, he further suggests, consists in "the tactical appropriation of particular [discursive] positions by a dominant social class"(Frow, 1986: 62).

While this avoids many difficulties, others remain. Two might usefully be singled out here: first, the arbitrary restriction of the category to the sphere of class relations; second, the equally arbitrary reservation of the term for those tactical appropriations of discourse associated with the dominant class. The effect of these two considerations taken in combination is to equate ideology with dominant ideology, thereby attributing to it the function of reproducing relations of class power via the organisation of consent, and to envision, as its opposite, not truth but resistance. Frow is careful not to ontologise the terms of this distinction. Resistance, like ideology, is, for Frow, a specific use of discourse rather than discourse of a particular kind. Thus understood, he argues, resistance is "the possibility of fracturing the ideological from within or of turning it against itself...or of reappropriating it for counterhegemonic purposes" (Frow, 1986: 63–4). None the less, the dichotomous organisation (domination/resistance) he proposes for the field of discourse seems unlikely to account for the full complexity of the different states in which discourse is appropriated and mobilised in the context of different fields of political and power relations.

If these difficulties are to be avoided, and the conditions Frow specifies be met, my own view is that the term ideology must be accorded a much looser and more general function. Capable of specifying neither a particular kind of discourse nor a state of discourse produced by specific forms of its political appropriation, it serves a useful purpose in suggesting that discourse can never be neutral with regard to power relations. To refer to discourse as ideological is thus not to attribute specific properties to it but serves rather as a way of indexing that it is to be examined with a view to disclosing its functioning as a component of the rhetorical strategies through which particular forms of power – and not solely those associated with class relations – are organised or opposed. This is by no means saying nothing; the risk of trying to pin the concept down more tightly, however, is that this seems invariably to result in theoretically arbitrary restrictions of the term which obscure its value at this more general level.

What is certain, however, is that if we cannot fix ideology as a particular kind of discourse defined in terms of an identifiable set of properties which exhibit a definite and unchanging relation to science, the very attempt to define literature in terms of its differences from these two categories collapses. It is important to be clear about the nature of this objection. For it applies not merely to this or that Marxist theory of literature's specificity or autonomy. How, in any particular version of the argument, the box of "literature" happens to be filled is contingent to the objection which concerns, rather, the very procedure of theorising literature's specificity in terms of an epistemologically derived triadic conception of the economy of the superstructures. The objection also applies to those instances where the procedure of defining literature in relation to ideology is uncoupled from the assumptions of epistemology and deployed in historically limited terms. *Formalism and Marxism* offers an instance of this approach in its suggestion that the capacity of literary texts to estrange or defamiliarise ideology should be regarded not as an invariant effect of literature, conceived as a trans-historical category, but rather as true only of historically specific forms of writing associated with the formation of the bourgeois literary system. It is clear, however, that this attempt to operate with a historically limited category of literature whose specific formal attributes might then be grounded within historically specific relations of literary production offers less a way round the classical Marxist procedure for defining literature's literariness than its last ditch. For the structure of the argument remains the same: literature's specificity consists in its relations to ideology which the analysis must take as a given in order to secure a point of reference in relation to which literature's literariness can be defined.[14]

There are, of course, other difficulties with Marxist theories of literature. Not the least of these concerns a strong tendency toward conventionalism when it comes to determining which writings should fall under the category of literature. With isolated exceptions, this question is usually resolved by duplicating the hierarchy of forms posited by bourgeois criticism. So far as its empirical determination is concerned, literature always – or nearly always[15] – turns out to comprise the self-same works which it is conventionally thought to include (the Great Tradition) while also excluding the broader field of fictional writing from which it is conventionally distinguished: popular or mass fiction.

The difficulties with this procedure are now sufficiently well known not to require further rehearsal. The consequences which follow from it, however, have been less remarked upon. At root, these stem from the fact that the procedure sits ill at ease with that through which the category of literature is defined *as a category*. So far as this is concerned, as we have seen, literature's definition is governed by the statements that it is not science and not ideology. However, when it comes to the empirical task of *filling that category*, a different system of not-statements is brought into play: literature is not popular fiction or mass fiction. There is an obvious procedural inconsistency here. In defining the category of literature, it is a matter of fitting it into the space mapped out for it within the already-determined triadic structure of epistemological reasoning. However, the terms in which that category is then empirically fleshed out derive from the quite different system of distinctions posited by a culturally relative hierarchy of forms. The result, not surprisingly, is a series of contradictions and torsions at the points where these different systems of not-statements meet and, since they cannot entirely be reconciled, mutually abrade one another.

The most obvious casualty of this abrasive collision consists in Marxist theorisations of popular fiction. For since, in the second system of not-statements, popular fiction is distinguished from literature, there is then no way in which this system can be reconciled with the first, in which literature is distinguished from science and ideology, except to argue that, as popular fiction isn't literature and as it clearly isn't science either, it must fall under the category of ideology. The endless reiteration of this argument, in other words, is entirely the effect of a definitional necessity. If the literature/popular fiction distinction is to be inserted into the already mapped-out set of epistemological distinctions between science, literature and ideology, then there is literally nowhere else that popular fiction could be placed except under the category of ideology which would not call into question the terms in which the category of literature has already been theorised.

As a consequence of these contradictory definitional procedures, Marxists have been constrained to approach popular fiction as merely a disguise system for the reproduction and relay of ideology. The effects of this can best be seen by contrasting the procedures deployed in Marxist approaches to literature with those characterising Marxist analyses of popular fictions. In the former, to take the Althusserian version of the argument, the study of literature is an occasion for demonstrating its non-coincidence with ideology. Attention thus focuses on the functioning of those formal devices specific to literature which initiate a process of ideological distanciation through which the contradictions of particular ideologies are rendered perceptible. The Marxist analysis of literature thus offers us a knowledge of the way literary texts work to nudge into our field of vision those aspects of their relations to history, as known by Marxism, which ideologies occlude or repress. When it comes to the study of popular fiction, however, this double relation is denied or, if admitted, rendered inconsequential: since, for definitional reasons, popular fiction cannot be differentiated from other ideologies, its relation to these is one of simple duplication.

An early essay by Roger Bromley, written from within an Althusserian framework, offers a convenient illustration of this argument.[16] Popular fiction, Bromley suggests, "should be regarded as a specific ideological practice within an ideological apparatus (publishing, communications, media, etc.), and as such participates in the permanent insertion of individuals and their actions in practices governed by ideological apparatuses" (Bromley, 1978: 42). The specificity of popular fiction, however, consists entirely in its secondariness: popular fiction "is not a primary site of ideology (cf. the educational system) but is one of the secondary areas where ideological components are represented and reinforced...." (Bromley, 1978: 40) This secondariness, however, is one without specific consequence since its only effect is to do again what ideology, in its own definition, does to and for itself: represent itself as a natural horizon. Popular fiction thus functions complicitly with ideology, assisting it to pass unnoticed, "uniform, unambiguous and non-contradictory" (Bromley, 1978: 39).

The task of Marxist analysis, accordingly, is to read through popular fictions in order to identify the ideologies they transmit and for whose transmission they serve as otherwise empty vehicles. Extrapolating from a discussion of late nineteenth-century romance fiction, Bromley thus suggests that popular fictions are typically characterised by a system of absences and presences:

Absent	*Present*
The current relations of production.	Personal relations.
The bourgeoisie (the real ruling class) as personified in economic categories.	Aristocracy (fraction offered at the level of style and code as *real* ruling class).
The working classes, defined in relation to capitalism as economic personification of *labour*. That is to say: Capital and Labour in its fundamental relations of antagonism under capitalism.	The petit-bourgeoisie personified in the *woman* particularly (and in authorial ideology).
Exchange relations in the economy.	Marriage: non-antagonism. House as property, self-owning and self-growing.
Division of labour.	No divisions other than natural.
Society.	Nature Self-consciousness. (Bromley, 1978: 204)

It is clear, here, that the master-text governing the left-hand column is none other than *Capital* and that the effect of the analysis is to demonstrate that popular fiction does not represent social relations in the same way that Marxism does: in other words, that it is *not* Marxism (science) but *is* ideology. What is most important to note, however, is the absence of a third column charting the fictional modes in which the ideological themes comprising the second column are represented. For this absence is a definitional requirement if it is to be demonstrated that popular fiction is, indeed, ideology, and, thereby, the terms of its own differentiation from literature can be reconciled with the contradictory terms in which literature is differentiated from ideology.

Literature Without Aesthetics

To summarize: the purpose of the foregoing has been to query not merely this or that Marxist theory of literature but the logic governing the procedures through which, however it may be formulated, a conception of literature's specificity is arrived at. The central problem, I have suggested, thus concerns less how the space of literature is filled within any particular theory than the way in which this space itself is conceived. The inherent instability of the science/ideology couplet undermines the ground necessary to secure a conception of literature either as a form of writing that is invariantly distinct from ideology or as a historically specific form of writing whose differentiation from ideology is the effect of a specific configuration of the field of ideology in general.

Does this mean, then, that there can be no such thing as a theory of literature? Terry Eagleton takes this view. After reviewing the difficulties associated with attempts to differentiate literature from other semiotic systems so that it might serve as a bounded object of knowledge for a specific science, he concludes that the logic of "recognising that literature is an illusion is to recognise that literary theory is an illusion too" (Eagleton, 1983: 204). Given the impossibility of securing the boundaries of the literary, Eagleton argues, the point is not to counter conventional theories of literature with a Marxist theory. Rather, it is to rethink the study of literature as part of a larger intellectual project concerned with the study of discursive or signifying practices, a project which would include analysis of those texts conventionally called 'literature', albeit that the ways in which these would be investigated in being viewed in this wider context would be significantly transformed.

While in general agreement with this conclusion, it is none the less important to insist that, within this broader project, there should be reserved a place for a theory of literature – but for a non-literary theory of literature which will theorise its object as a set of social rather than formal realities and processes. For that there may not be a *literary* theory of literature does not rule out the possibility of there being *other* kinds of theory of literature. The significance of the distinction I have in mind here can perhaps best be clarified by looking more closely at Eagleton's reasons for issuing literary theory/theories of literature with their obituary notices.

The root objection to literary theory, he argues, is that "the one hope it has of distinguishing itself – clinging to an object named literature – is misplaced" (Eagleton, 1983: 204). Since there is no such thing as literature, there can be no literary theory nor any theory of literature except as discourses which deal entirely with their own self-generated problems.

Stephen Heath, pointing to the respects in which this still leaves Eagleton with the practical difficulty as to how, then, to negotiate his own relation to the literature which he has declared non-existent, but which still so obviously supplies the condition for his activity, argues he pays a high price for this iconoclastic gesture. Unable to offer a *political* retheorisation of literature – that is, one in which literature is not argued away as non-existent but is rethought as a non-essentialist ensemble of textual articulations of language and experience – Heath suggests that Eagleton's options are reduced to those of reviving old forms of criticism (rhetoric) or contriving new and ever more radical readings, thereby, in either case, leaving literature in much the same place that it was before issued with its obituary: "an academic object for the oldest criticism or the newest readings" (Heath, 1987: 310). A further difficulty with Eagleton's argument consists in its empiricism. Christopher Norris, commenting on the application of a related argument to the more general concerns of aesthetics, usefully identifies its shortcomings. To dismiss the concerns of aesthetics as being "wholly self-induced by the discipline which sets out to explain or resolve them", he argues, runs the risk of missing the point that "the same is true to some extent of any branch of knowledge that defines its subject area by singling out questions of especial theoretical interest" (Norris, 1985: 123).

It should be noted, in the light of these considerations, that my critique of the logic of aesthetic overdetermination has not rested on the empiricist argument that there is no such thing as literature or art. Rather, it has rested on a demonstration of the theoretical inconsistencies which result from the attempt to translate the transcendental distinctions of philosophical aesthetics into the typically triadic structure of Marxist conceptions of the economy of the superstructure. The objection is thus less that literature, as a special kind of writing, does not exist – although this is surely true – than that the system of concepts upon which this construction of literature depends is itself flawed. The problem, in other words, lies in how the space of the literary is theorised. Yet if this is so, it then remains at least a possibility that this space may be rethought and a cogent conception of literature elaborated which is disabled neither by the theoretical objections I have rehearsed nor by the argument that literature, as a special kind of writing, does not exist. The critical question here concerns the nature of the distinctions the category is used to effect. That the category cannot designate an ontologically distinct realm of writing is clear. However, this need not hinder its capacity to designate distinctions of another kind. Let me indicate some possibilities:

1 That the term literature be used to refer to a particular socially organised space of representation whose specificity consists in the institutionally and discursively regulated forms of use and deployment to which selected texts are put, the

empirical question as to the actual identity of those texts being regarded as a contingency which does not affect the definition. Clearly, a theory of literature proceeding from this definition would have no need to secure, either theoretically or empirically, literature's existence as a special kind of writing. Its concerns would rather centre on the constitution of a region of social practice whose specificity consists in the modes of use and deployment of the texts it constitutes as its occasions rather than in a set of formal properties. The effect of this move is to rethink the ontological status of literature such that it is taken to refer to an observable set of social processes rather than to an (as it has proved so far) unfathomable essence.

2   That literature, so defined, be regarded as a historically specific set of institutional and discursive arrangements regulating the use and deployment of the texts it constitutes as its occasions. In effect, this is to limit the concept of literature to the modern period, distinguishing it from earlier institutional and discursive organisations of the field of writing. This is not, however, the same thing as a distinction between modern and pre-modern forms of writing. The processes whereby forms of writing deriving from earlier periods are retro-spectively literarised by abstracting them from the sharply different institutional and discursive forms regulating their initial use and organising their relations to adjacent fields of social practice would form a part of literature under this definition.

3   That literature, so defined, be regarded as a set of social realities and processes which interact with other spheres of social practices *on the same level*. This is to deny those depth models of the social structure which support the hermeneutic project of deciphering literary texts in terms of the underlying realities they express. The grounds for this denial consist in the contention that all social practices are simultaneously institutional and discursive in their constitution.

It can be seen how, if these steps are taken, the way is opened for a theory of literature that will construe its object as a historically specific, socially organised and maintained field of textual uses and effects. And if it is important to insist, in this sense, on the specificity of literature, this is because, thus understood, it is by no means a mere illusion. Although we can already see beyond its rims, this socially organised field of textual uses and effects has had very real conse-quences, historically, and continues to function as an influential set of social practices which have inescapably to be taken into account in present-day political/critical calculations. To conclude, because literature cannot be secured as a formal reality, that its analysis should be dissipated into an undifferentiated study of signifying practices is to miss what ought properly to have been the focus of analysis in the first place: the functioning of a definitely organised field of uses and effects in which strategies of boundary construction and maintenance are central to the functioning of a *socially differentiated region of textual uses and effects* (rather than kind of writing).

Notes

1 For other studies of a similar kind, see Prawer (1978) and Demetz (1967).
2 Lukács, who had worked with Ryazanov at the Marx-Engels-Lenin Institute in 1930–1 in preparing Marx's 1844 manuscripts for publication, developed a close friendship with Lifshitz after his emigration to the Soviet Union in 1933 and explicitly acknowledged his indebtedness to Lifshitz for rekindling his interest in aesthetic questions.
3 Jameson, for example, posits a distinction between the social and historical concerns of musical semantics and those of 'aesthetic value proper' in his introduction to Attali (1985: ix). For Eagleton, see the final chapter of Eagleton (1976).
4 Here, as elsewhere, Marxist thought is content merely to invert dominant aesthetic discourses. The view that genuine literature transcends its social determination, and hence exceeds sociological analysis, whereas popular fiction is riven by its determination, and hence amenable to such analysis, is a commonplace which finds its mirror reflection in this aspect of Marxist aesthetics.
5 I have developed this argument more fully elsewhere. See Bennett (1984a).
6 More often than not, however, the issue is not posed in these terms. In being conflated with the problem of value, the question of literature's relative autonomy is often translated into a concern with its seeming ability to transcend its determinations. Posed in this way, the analysis of literature's autonomy concerns itself less with the relations between different forms of determination than with stressing the limitations of any account of literature which focuses on its determining conditions, however these might be conceived.
7 While Eagleton is sharply critical of Althusser's and Macherey's use of figurative language to express the relations between literature and ideology, his argument is none the less a variant of the Althusserian schema in installing literature, as Frow puts it, in an 'epistemological no man's land' between science and ideology. See Frow (1986: 27).
8 There is, however, another aspect to Eagleton's position here: the contention that it is ultimately ideology itself which governs the process of its signification by literature ("The process of the text is the process whereby ideology produces the forms which produce it..." (Eagleton, 1976: 84)). Still, however, literature enjoys the special status of being the privileged instrument through which ideology thus effects its self-production.
9 While these gendered metaphors are intended only loosely, an investigation of the degree to which the relations between science and aesthetics are typically represented in gendered terms in epistemological and aesthetic discourse would, I suspect, prove amply rewarding. Useful bearings for such an analysis can be found in Lloyd (1984).
10 An excellent example of the contradictory entanglements produced by this proliferation of not-statements is offered by Frow in his discussion of Macherey. See Frow (1986: 26).
11 In the aesthetics of writers such as Lukács, Lifshitz and Vazquez, their (largely speculative) anthropological accounts of the processes of art's differentiation from magic constitute the only point at which historical – or, more accurately, pre-historical – considerations enter into their specification of the aesthetic mode.
12 For the most sustained criticisms of the first of these criticisms, see Hirst (1976).
13 See, for example, Foucault (1980).

14 In truth, *Formalism and Marxism* places its bets both ways here. While arguing that the Althusserian view of literature's capacity to produce an internal distanciation of ideology is true only of historically specific forms of writing, it then undermines the ground necessary to support this argument in contending that the science/ideology distinction must be understood as political rather than epistemological. This disqualifies ideology from performing the role of a differentiating point of reference for literature's definition even in a historically limited sense.

15 Macherey (1978), for example, is concerned with the more general category of fiction rather than with the conventionally more restricted concept of literature.

16 For a further elaboration of the points which follow, see Bennett (1981).

Chapter Two   Texts, Readers, Reading Formations

> The frontiers of a book are never clear-cut: beyond the title, the first line and the last full-stop, beyond its internal configuration, its autonomous form, it is caught up in a system of references to other books, other texts, other sentences: it is a node within a network . . . The book is simply not the object that one holds in one's hands; and it cannot remain within the relative parallelipiped that contains it: its unity is variable and relative. As soon as one questions that unity it loses its self-evidence; it indicates itself, constructs itself, only on the basis of a complex field of discourse.
>
> (M. Foucault, *The Archaeology of Knowledge*)

I want, by exploring the issues which Foucault points to here, to open up a set of questions concerning reading, especially popular reading, and the determinations within which it is produced. Although my primary concern is with the reading of written texts, especially fictions, I intend the term "reading" in the more general sense of referring to the means and mechanisms whereby all texts – literary, filmic and televisual, fictional or otherwise – may be 'productively activated' during what is traditionally, and inadequately, thought of as the process of their consumption or reception. For reasons that I hope will become clear, I venture the concept of the "productive activation" of texts as a means of displacing the concept of interpretation and the construction of the relations between texts and readers which it implies rather than as a substitute for that concept, another way of saying the same thing.

I should also explain that I do not intend the term "popular", in a narrowly exclusive sense, as having a singular class articulation. Rather, in speaking of "popular readings", I have in mind what might, from another perspective, be classified as 'untutored readings'; readings produced outside the academy, at a considerable remove from and relatively untouched – and, one might add, untroubled – by the discourses of textual criticism which circulate within it. However, I prefer 'popular readings' to 'untutored readings' because of its more positive connotations; it implies readings which may be assessed as valid and productive on their own terms. "Untutored readings", by contrast, implies an absence or a lack. It is a negative definition entailing a negative judgement – readings which "don't count" and whose only destiny, unless they're earmarked for preservation as curiosities, is to be "corrected".

So much for preliminaries. Before going further, let me give an example of what would count as a popular reading under my definition and, in doing so, outline what I mean by a "reading formation". The case I have in mind is that of Menocchio, the sixteenth-century miller whose reading habits constitute the subject of Carlo Ginzburg's *The Cheese and the Worms* (Ginzburg, 1980a). Menocchio was twice hauled before the Inquisition, once in 1584 and again in 1599, to account for his belief that God and the angels were created from the worms which emerged from a vast, primordial cheese before the elements had separated.[1] In unravelling the sources of this extraordinary cosmogeny, Ginzburg, at one level, in his practical handling of the difficulties, says all that needs to be said on the subject of 'texts, readers and reading formations'. At another level, however, Ginzburg occludes the issue, covers up what he has uncovered in – residually, when he's not looking so to speak – using theoretical formulations which preserve intact the conventional view of texts as "things" which have 'meanings' which readers may variously 'interpret'.

The problem which exercises Ginzburg concerns the roots of Menocchio's inspired cosmogeny, his "fantastic opinions" (Ginzburg, 1980a: 32). From whence did these come? Clearly at odds with those of the Catholic Church, they also differed significantly from those of Lutheranism and Anabaptism whilst sharing elements with both. Where, then, did they come from? Menocchio, when pressed on this, answered: "My opinions came out of my head" (Ginzburg, 1980a: 27). Ginzburg seeks to disclose what put these opinions in Menocchio's head by examining the books he read and the way he read them, and by tracing-in the cultural sources which produced his, on the face of it, singularly aberrant readings. The key text at issue here, of course, was the Bible, which Menocchio had read in the vernacular, and especially Genesis for, again when his back was to the wall, Menocchio would claim a textual warrant for his materialist account of creation by invoking the authority of the Biblical account itself.

In a later essay, Ginzburg theorizes the relationship between clues and scientific method within the human and social sciences by means of an analogy with the situation of the hunter who learns "to construct the appearance and movements of an unseen quarry through its tracks" (Ginzburg, 1980b: 12). Later in the same essay, he likens the situation of the historian of ideas to Gaboriau's detective hero, Monsieur Lecocq, "who felt he was crossing 'an unknown territory, covered with snow', marked with the tracks of the criminal, like 'a vast white page on which the people we are searching for have left not only footprints and traces of movements but also the prints of their innermost thoughts, the hopes and fears by which they are stirred'" (Ginzburg, 1980b: 23). In *The Cheese and the Worms*, Ginzburg too is a hunter, with Menocchio – "his thoughts and his sentiments – fears, hopes, ironies, rages, despairs" (Ginzburg, 1980a: xi) – as his quarry. The clues he works from are those provided by the transcripts of Menocchio's trials. Hunting down the books Menocchio read – lives of the saints and of the Virgin Mary, medieval chronicles, the *Travels* of Mandeville, Boccaccio's *Decameron*, and perhaps the *Koran* in Italian translation – he seeks the key to the way Menocchio read them by tracing the correspondences, the fits and the near-fits, the inversions and mutated echoes of these texts in the text of Menocchio's testimony before the Inquisitors.

Ginzburg ultimately tracks his quarry down to the sphere of the intertextual. He finds his key to Menocchio's reading of the Bible in the relations between two written cultures – the official Biblical culture of the Church and the fringes of the new intellectual humanism that reached him – and, beyond that, in the interaction, in Menocchio's head, between these two written cultures and the orally transmitted under-culture of the Italian peasantry. Placed in this context, Menocchio's fantastic cosmogeny is rendered intelligible: a materialist subversion of the Biblical myth of creation effected by reading the relations between Genesis and the intellectual humanism and materialism of Renaissance culture through the filter of the belly materialism, the cheese and worms materialism, of the oral culture of the peasantry. This, then, is what I mean by a "reading formation": a set of intersecting discourses which productively activate a given body of texts and the relations between them in a specific way. Menocchio's reading, his "productive activation" of the Bible and of the texts of Renaissance humanism, working them against one another so as to establish a "teeth-gritting harmony" between them, is the product of his installation within a network of intersecting but contradictory cultures, each with its own rules and procedures, within which the yeast, the active, fermenting ingredient was supplied by his native peasant culture.

Moreover, this reading formation had its historical and material foundations in reading relations, or social relations of reading, of a particular kind which Ginzburg summarizes as follows:

> In Menocchio's talk we see emerging, as if out of a crevice in the earth, a deep-rooted cultural stratum so unusual as to appear almost incomprehensible. This case, unlike others examined thus far, involves not only a reaction filtered through the written page, but also an irreducible residue of oral culture. The Reformation and the diffusion of printing had been necessary to permit this *different* culture to come to light. Because of the first, a simple miller had dared to think of *speaking out*, of voicing his own opinions about the Church and the world. Thanks to the second, *words* were at his disposal to express the obscure, inarticulate vision of the world that fermented within him. (Ginzburg, 1980a: 58–9)

Indeed, Ginzburg ventures a more precise social location for the reading formation to which Menocchio's fantastic cosmogeny bears witness. Considering the heresies of another miller, Pellegrino Baroni, heresies which suggested an abrasion between Biblical culture, Renaissance humanism and the oral culture of the peasantry similar to that which organized Menocchio's reading, Ginzburg notes that the social situation of millers rendered them uniquely exposed to the contradictory cultural cross-currents of the period. In close and everyday contact with the peasants who brought their grain to the mill, yet also distanced from the peasantry by virtue of the mistrust which traditionally characterized the peasant's attitude to the miller, millers were also economically tied to the feudal nobility, who retained possession over the milling privilege, and, accordingly, they were often involved in quasi-familiar forms of social interaction with the local nobility – and hence, indirectly, with the secular intellectual culture of the period – in ways that would have been inconceivable for the vast mass of the peasantry.

However, Menocchio is not Ginzburg's only quarry in *The Cheese and the Worms*. He also hunts down, although in a different way, two adversaries. The first is the view that readings, and especially popular readings, can be inferred from the analysis of popular texts. In his Preface, he takes issue with Robert Mandrou's analysis of the literature of *colportage*, especially the view that its constituent texts can be defined as the "instruments of a victorious process of acculturation, 'the reflection…of a world view' of the popular classes of the *Ancien Regime*" (Ginzburg, 1980a: xv). This implies, Ginzburg argues, that popular reading is a process characterized by a "complete cultural passivity" (Ginzburg, 1980a: xv) and rests on a "hypodermic syringe" model of the relations between texts and readers and, in this case, of the relations between dominant and subordinate cultures. Leading on from this, Ginzburg's second adversary is the view, variously attributable, that the traffic between the official or high culture of a society and its popular culture is all one-way, exclusively from the former to the latter. Against this, Ginzburg appeals to the authority of Bakhtin's *Rabelais and His World* in its demonstration of the degree to which the intellectual culture of Renaissance humanism was fuelled by the popular, materialist belly of carnival. Indeed, *Rabelais and His World* is the master text of *The Cheese and the Worms*, the text which productively activates Ginzburg's own reading of the way Menocchio read the texts he read. As Bakhtin listens for the echoes of carnival in Rabelais's *Gargantua and Pantagruel*, so Ginzburg, in listening to the evidence of Menocchio's testimony, interrogates the relations between his materialist cosmogeny and the humanist writings of the period to hear, in the former, not the diluted, handed-down versions of the latter, but an independent voice, vigorously materialist, humanistically tolerant, a voice "from below", speaking through Menocchio, actively influencing the intellectual culture of the period and, in some respects, considerably in advance of that culture. A secularly inclined, humanistic utopianism; a tendentially scientific account of the spontaneous generation of life from inanimate matter; a universal tolerance of the diversity of faiths; a tendential reduction of religion to morality – Ginzburg finds aspects of all of these in Menocchio's testimony, not as watered-down versions of intellectual humanism but as more vigorously, and more materialistically inflected extensions of it. Menocchio's "heresies", in short, in their philosophical if not their literal sense, were destined to become orthodoxies; orthodoxies, moreover, which would claim their warrant in the very texts which Menocchio seemed to have so violently traduced.

It is surprising, therefore, that Ginzburg sometimes – but not always – speaks of Menocchio's relation to his texts as one of misrepresentation. Here's how he opens up the general issue of popular reading:

> The almanacs, the songsters, the books of piety, the lives of saints, the entire pamphlet literature that constituted the bulk of the book trade, today appear static, inert, and unchanging to us. But how were they read by the public of the day? To what extent did the prevalently oral culture of those readers interject itself in the use of the text, modifying it, reworking it, perhaps to the point of changing its very essence? Menocchio's accounts of his readings provide us with a striking example of a relationship to the text that is totally different from that of today's educated reader. They permit us to measure, at last, the discrepancy that … existed between the texts of 'popular' literature and the light in which they appeared to peasants and artisans … As far as the quantitative history of ideas is concerned, only knowledge of the historical and social variability of the person of the reader will really lay the foundations for a history of ideas that is also qualitatively different. (Ginzburg, 1980a: xxii)

It may be no more than a quibble, but it's the notion of "essence" that I balk at here. Who said that texts had "essences"? And how can an essence be "changed"? And why should the relationship between popular texts and their readers be conceived as a "discrepancy"? What does it mean to say this? Or again:

> Any attempt to consider these books as "sources" in the mechanical sense of the term collapses before the aggressive originality of Menocchio's reading. More than the text, then, what is important is the key to his reading, a screen that he unconsciously placed between himself and the printed page: a filter that emphasized certain words while obscuring others, that stretched the meaning of a word, taking it out of its context, that acted on Menocchio's memory and distorted the very words of the text. (Ginzburg, 1980a: 33)

The problem Ginzburg is dealing with here is clearly the problem of *difference;* of the *difference* between the "aggressive originality" of Menocchio's readings and more established readings. And he clearly wants to theorize this difference non-hierarchically; to place Menocchio's readings *alongside* those of the Church, *alongside* those of contemporary humanists and equal with them, to restore the grid of intelligibility to Menocchio's apparently demented discourse so as to bring him 'very close to us: a man like ourselves, one of us' (Ginzburg, 1980a: xi). Yet, from time to time, this relation of *difference* is theorized as one of *misrepresentation* or *distortion* – as a difference not between Menocchio's readings and other readings but between Menocchio's readings and the "texts themselves". Although everything else Ginzburg has to say works against it, it is through such formulations that there occasionally obtrudes the view that texts are *things* which *have* meanings which may be *traduced*.

It is this view I want to dispute, and indeed which must be disputed if Ginzburg's project of a history of ideas that will be qualitatively different as a result of taking account of "the historical and social variability of the person of the reader" is to be realized. Meaning is a transitive phenomena. It is not a *thing* which texts can *have*, but is something that can only be produced, and always differently, within the reading formations that regulate the encounters between texts and readers. To be sure, some readings regularly carry more cultural weight than others and some, like Menocchio's, may never settle to provide the framework for an enduring pattern of "response". But meanings are meanings, and marginalized, subordinate, quirky, fantastic and quixotic ones are just as real, just as ontologically secure, just as much wrapped up in the living social destinies of texts as dominant ones.

Although the problem is a general one, applicable to the analysis of all texts, it has a particular pertinence, or so it seems to me, to the study of popular fictions. In the case of canonized texts, there is a considerable degree of coincidence between the discourses of academic criticism and the reading formations which productively activate such texts inasmuch as, for most readers, some form of acquaintance with those discourses constitutes a necessary apprenticeship for reading, the means by which they are socialized into the literary community. In the case of popular fictions, no such coincidence exists. Academic criticisms, of all varieties, have dissected popular texts, analyzed their internal relations, made suppositions about their effects on thier readers – all without interrogating the necessary disparity which exists between the discourses of criticism and the reading formations, circulating outside the academy, through which popular reading is organized.

I

These, then, are the questions I want to explore: the determinations which bear on the formation of popular reading. Before coming to these, however, I would like to give my concerns a more general theoretical location by relating the problem of text/reader relations to some contemporary problems in linguistics. For it is linguistics that has provided the master code for the various ways in which, within literary theory, the question of the relations between texts and readers has been addressed.

Broadly speaking, there have been two lines of approach to the subject. First, there are those approaches which concern themselves with the textual production of a position for reading; with the production, within the organization of the text, of what has been variously described as the implied reader, the model reader or the preferred reader.[2] Such approaches operate at the syntactical level of textual analysis: their concern is with the ways in which a place or places for reading are constructed within the system of relation between those signs which constitute a text's mode of address. Whilst a necessary level of analysis, this approach is also necessarily insufficient when confronted with the real variability of reader response. Stephen Heath puts the objection succinctly:

> It is possible with regard to a film or group of films to analyse a discursive organ-ization, a system of address, a placing – a construction – of the spectator...This is not to say, however, that any and every spectator – and, for instance, man or woman, of this class or that – will be completely and equally in the given construction, completely and equally there in the film; and nor then is it to say that the discursive

organization and its production can exhaust – be taken as equivalent to – the effectivity, the potential effects, of a film. (Heath, 1978: 105–6)

Something eventuates in the interaction between text and reader which cannot be deduced from the construction or placing of the reader effected by the text's organization of the process of its own reading. However, the second approach, which aims to confront the empirical reader and his/her historical variability, is also couched within the terms of a linguistic paradigm, construing the relationship of readings to a text on an analogy with the Saussurean distinction between *parole* and *langue*. Here, the semiotics of reading stands in relation to the semiotics of the text much as the study of *parole* stands in relation to the study of *langue;* it's a question of *first* analyzing the structure of the text and *then* disclosing the ways in which that structure is variantly realized as a consequence of the different determinations which are brought to bear on it, through the reading subject, in the act of reading. To the text, as to Saussure's *langue*, there belong all those systematic properties of structure. The text supplies the objective datum within the analysis – the object to be read – which, in its objectivity, is also the realm of necessity, the realm in which those laws and structures which *necessarily* constrain the act of reading (although they may not *entirely* determine it) hold away. The study of reading and of the reader, by contrast, as with Saussure's *parole*, is the study of the subjective and contingent, of the random and chance determinations which animate the text via the person of the reader.

In short, the study of reading occupies the same relation to the study of the text as, in linguistics, pragmatics occupies in relation to syntax. It is the area in which the reign of the subject, excluded from the analysis of textual structures just as much as from the study of *langue*, is triumphantly re-installed. The terms of theorization used construct a terrain in which subject (the reader) encounters object (the text), a paradigm in which what is at issue is the use of the text, its interpretation or decoding by the subject. No matter what the particular terminology used, and no matter how sociological the analysis of the determinations moulding and configuring the activity of the reader, this approach construes the text as an object, a structure, a system of necessary relations, call it what you will, that is pre-given to the reader. Readings may vary but, when all is said and done, they are all readings of the same thing, of the text as a set of necessary and objective relations conceived as existing in some pure and limiting condition of 'in-itselfness' independently of the historically active reading relations which regulate its productive activation in the different moments of its history. (This condition of 'in-itselfness', it needs to be added, is not of the text's making but is a space specifically produced for it by the terms of theorization employed.) Such an approach cannot help but be normative, cannot help but to rank and assign readings their place according to the degree of their conformity to that reading which the analysis of the 'text itself' confirms as the most correct, the most meaningful, the most valid or appropriate or whatever.

Let me give an example, Umberto Eco concludes his discussion of Eugene Sue's *Les Mystères de Paris* as follows:

The whole of the foregoing examination represents a method of study employed by one particular reader relying on the "cultivated" codes that were supposedly shared by the author and his contemporary critics. We know perfectly well that other readers in Sue's day did not use this key to decipher the book. They did not grasp its reformist implications, and from the total message only certain more obvious meanings filtered through to them (the dramatic situations of the working classes, the depravity of some of those in power, the necessity for change of no matter what kind, and so on). Hence the influence, which seems proved, of *Les Mystères* on the popular uprising of 1848 ... For this reason we must keep in mind a principle characteristic of any examination of mass communication media ...: the message which has been evolved by an educated elite ... is expressed at the outset in terms of a fixed code, but it is caught by diverse groups of receivers and deciphered on the basis of other codes. The sense of the message often undergoes a kind of filtration or distortion in the process, which completely alters its 'pragmatic' function. (Eco, 1981: 140–1)

That seems eminently fair and reasonable, a model of openness. But it is caught within precisely the system of polarities I have been describing: *first* the analysis of the text and its "fixed code", *then* the analysis of its differing pragmatic functions. The difficulty here is that what is presented as the 'fixed code' turns out, on Eco's own admission, to be a *relational code* located not in the text of *Les Mystères de Paris* itself but in its relations to the "cultivated" codes supposedly shared by the author and his contemporary critics. Why start there, especially in analyzing a popular novel which, again on Eco's own admission, had its most significant impact within reading relations of a different kind? Further, those other readings, those "under-readings" produced outside the cultivated codes that circulated between writer and critics, are conceived as a lack, a failure: the product of a "filtration" which produces a "distortion" of the "fixed code" of the text, a reading that is marked by an incomprehension, a failure to grasp that text's reformist implications as a result of abstracting only "the most obvious meanings" from the "total message". The domain of pragmatics, it turns out, is entered one-sidedly: there are those uses of the text which are uses of the 'text itself' – not really uses, in fact, but functions dictated by its "fixed code" – and then there are those uses, uses properly speaking, which, however, are not uses of the 'text itself' but uses of the selectively filtered, distorted, inadequately understood text.

The question arises: what if Eco had started from the other direction, using popular rather than "cultivated" codes as the "key" with which to "decipher the book"? Would not the "fixed codes" of *Les Mystères de Paris* then look different as a result of their having been analytically inscribed within a different network of signifying relations? The point of asking this is not to recommend such a simple strategy of reversal. Rather, it is to question the procedure whereby the relations between different readings are conceived as differences between valid and invalid, more or less appropriate responses, and in which the criteria of validity or appropriateness are supplied by the critic's own construction of the "text itself".

II

In order to suggest an alternative to the question of reading, and to indicate why an alternative is needed, let me return to Saussure. In his *Language, Semantics and Ideology,* Michel Pêcheux characterizes Saussure's notion of *parole* as "the 'weakest link' of the scientific apparatus set up in the form of the concept of *langue*"; Saussure's *parole* is, he argues, "the very type of anti-concept, i.e., a pure ideological excipient 'complementing' in its evidentness the concept of *langue,* i.e., a stop-gap, a plug to close the 'gap' opened up by the scientific definition of *langue* as systematicity in operation" (Pêcheux, 1982: 174). The couples langue/parole, system/speaking subject and the series of antinomies they entail – object/subject necessity/contingency – describe, Pêcheux argues, an ideological circle in which each term begets the opposite it implies and which, in turn, it requires as a condition of its own existence, intelligibility and functioning. *Parole* requires *langue* as the system against which it manifests itself as a creative departure. *Langue,* in turn, requires *parole* as the creativity which prevents the total closure of the system of rules which comprise it. By means of this circular exchange, *langue* preserves its own status as a closed system yet prevents the total closure of that system in opening itself up, via *parole,* to the impact of a residue of determinations, not given within *langue* itself, which operate on it via the speaking subject and his/her situation. In this way, Saussure's theory accounts for what it can't account for simply by pointing to what it can't account for: the full range and variability of language in use.

In like manner, the relations between textual and reading semiotics have been developed along the path of a mutually numbing symbiosis. The reader, within this construction, requires the "text itself" as that against which his or her reading can be registered as a creative departure, a use or interpretation that is in no way pre-ordained. The subject triumphs: contingency overrules necessity, the subject conquers the object, Man has his day. On the other side of this exchange, the "text itself" requires such a reader as the means of affirming its own objectivity and necessity; misunderstood, maybe, but still intact, indissoluble into the acts of reading through which, in Robert Escarpit's terms, it is "creatively betrayed" (Escarpit, 1961). The text and its readings, meanings and their different interpretations, the "fixed code" and its variant "de-coding": the terms are retained in their separateness, although never without threatening to dissolve into one another.

It is precisely such a dissolution that I wish to recommend: not, however, the dissolution of the "text itself" into the million and one readings of individual subjects but its dissolution into the reading relations and, within those, the reading formations which concretely and historically structure the interaction between texts and readers. As a result of such a dissolution, the interaction between, on the one hand, the 'text itself' as a pure entity uncontaminated by any exterior determinations and, on the other, the "subject" – whether conceived as "raw" and unacculturated or as situationally formed – but as an interaction between the *culturally activated* text and the *culturally activated* reader, an interaction that is structured by the material, social, ideological and institutional relationships in which *both* text and readers are inescapably inscribed. To develop my argument here, I want to take another leaf out of Pêcheux's book. In an earlier critique of Saussure's concept of *langue*, Volosinov had argued that the constitution of *langue* as a system of objective and universal rules ignored the struggle over meaning that took place within language as a result of the opposition between "differently orientated social interests within one and the same sign community" (Volosinov, 1973: 23). Pêcheux argues that the unity of *langue*, although real (he rejects the notion that there are separate, class-based languages within the given sign community), is only *tendential*. Not merely at the level of its practice, of its use, but at that of its structure, this tendential unity is riven by the contradictions and antagonisms between different *discursive formations* which initiate, in relation to *langue*, different *discursive processes* resulting in "contrasting 'vocabulary syntaxes' and 'arguments' which lead, *sometimes with the same words,* in different directions depending on the nature of the ideological interests at stake" (Pêcheux, 1982: 9).

Langue, then, constitutes the basis, a definite set of phonological, morphological and syntactic structures, in relation to which there form antagnostic discursive processes. Pêcheux goes to some pains to stress that what he has in mind here is not another variant of *parole*. A discursive process, he writes, "is not a 'concrete' individual way of inhabiting the 'abstraction' of the *langue*" (Pêcheux, 1982: 58). A discursive process is rather the putting into use, the manifestation, on the basis of *langue*, of a discursive formation rooted in a specific ideological class relationship. Individual speech acts, or the events of *parole*, if the term is to be retained, are not the product of individual and subjective uses of *langue* but are rather located in the intersection between the class-based discursive processes which traverse *langue* and which, in so doing, make its unity only tendential rather than actual.

What I am interested in here are the implications of this position for the analysis of meaning. Pêcheux summarizes these as follows:

> The first consists of the proposition that the meaning of a word, expression proposition, etc., does not exist "in itself" (i.e., in its transparent relation to the literal character of the signifier), but is determined by the ideological positions brought into play in the socio-historical process in which words, expressions and propositions are produced (i.e., reproduced). This thesis could be summed up in the statement: *words, expressions, propositions,* etc., *change their meaning according to the positions held by those who use them,* which signifies that they find their meaning by reference to those positions, i.e., by reference to the *ideological formations*...in which those positions are inscribed. (Pêcheux, 1982: 111)

Again, Pêcheux goes to some lengths to make it clear that what he has in mind here is not another version of polysemanticity, or of what Volosinov called the "multi-accentuality of the sign". The concept of polysemanticity implies that a word may have several possible meanings before it has *a* meaning or that it has *a* meaning which may be variously interpreted. Pêcheux contests this assumption. He endorses Lacan's argument concerning the primacy of the signifier over the sign and over meaning and hence the view that meaning is produced within the relations of substitutability between signifiers – an effect of the ceaselessly mobile relations between signifiers rather than a property of the signifier as such. It follows from this, Pêcheux argues that "meaning does not exist anywhere except in the metaphorical relationships (realized in substitution effects, paraphrases, synonym formations) which happen to be more or less provisionally located historically in a given discursive formation: words, expressions and propositions get their meaning from the discursive formation to which they belong" (Pêcheux, 1982: 189).

Put another way, because the same signifier may function differently within different discursive formations, it is impossible to locate a linguistic space within which it may be said to have *a* meaning in relation to which other uses can then be conceived as distortions. The only way of doing so is by privileging the linguistic values at work within one discursive formation over those in evidence elsewhere but, as we have seen, this is precisely the means whereby the linguistic values of dominant social groups become reified in being viewed as properties of *langue* itself rather than of a specific mode of its social accentuation.

In short, Pêcheux concludes: "A meaning effect does not pre-exist the discursive formation in which it is constituted" (Pêcheux, 1982: 187). And so I want to argue that a "reading effect" does not pre-exist the 'reading formation" in which it is constituted. The analogy is not, of course, a strict one. It is clear that a text would count as an instance of what Pêcheux characterizes as a discursive formation. So too would what I have called a "reading formation", although I think it useful to retain this as a separate term singling out a region of discourse specifically concerned with the production of readings, with the operation of a hermeneutic. However, whilst it is true that a text always effects a certain embedding of meaning within a discursive formation – it consists not just of signifiers, but of a definite order of relations between signifiers – that meaning can always be dis-embedded and re-embedded in alternative discursive formations via the different ways in which that text is productively activated within different reading formations. Reading formations, it needs to be added, which are put to work within reading relations of different kinds as, in the course of its history, a text is constantly *re-written* into a variety of different material, social, institutional and ideological contexts. It is for this reason that I prefer the concept of "productive activation" to that of "interpretation". To speak of interpretation is to permit variability to enter the process of reading only through the person of the reader. In speaking of the "productive activation" of texts, I mean to imply a process in which texts, readers and the relations between them are *all* subject to variable determinations.

III

What are the practical consequences of this? To be honest, I'm not altogether sure. My concern has been less to provide answers than to raise akward questions. For the most part, these have concerned the status a text is to be conceived as having within a given critical or theoretical enterprise – a troubling question since, once the seductive facticity of the 'text itself' is questioned, there seems to be nothing to stop the text's total dissolution into a potentially infinite series of different readings, in which case there then seems to be nothing left for criticism to get hold of, nothing there for it to address. The only way out of this dilemma is for criticism to realize that what it has got hold of is different from the object it has traditionally supposed was given to it, and to modify its practice accordingly. This is the step Fredric Jameson recommends in his Preface to *The Political Unconscious*. Constructing criticism as an enterprise which "takes place within a Homeric battlefield, on which a host of interpretive options are either openly or implicitly in conflict," he disclaims any concern with "the criteria by which a given interpretation may be faulted or accredited" and addresses himself instead to the question of the relations between readings (Jameson, 1981: 13). *The Political Unconscious*, he writes, "presupposes, as its organizational fiction, that we never really confront a text, immediately, in all its freshness as a thing-in-itself", a supposition which "dictates the use of a method . . . according to which our object of study is less the text itself than the interpretations through which we attempt to confront and to appropriate it" (Jameson, 1981: 9–10). The method of the "meta-commentary" which Jameson here proposes is one in which a criticism seeks a validity – but a validity for its own time, for the circumstances in which it is written – by virtue of its ability to net other interpretations and locate them within its own rather than by appealing to the authority of the "text itself". It recognizes its own nature as a specific productive activation of the text, the product of a reading formation (Marxism) put to work within reading relations of a particular kind, just as it recognizes the need – the political need, a condition of effective intervention within the battleground of readings – to clear a space for itself by producing its own relation to contending readings. Where attempts are made to warrant specific readings and to discredit others by an appeal to the authority of the "text itself", this needs to be recognized for what it is – another way of entering the battleground of readings, another political strategy for reading in which the critic's own construction of the "text itself" is mobilized in an attempt to bully other interpretations off the field.

If, as distinct from criticism, one's concern is with the analysis of the social destinies of texts – with the real and varied history of their productive activation – the attribution of any authority to the "text itself" has the effect of bullying other readings not just off the field of battle but out of existence entirely. It is the means whereby, dismissed as "untutored readings", as distortions of misunderstandings, they are located as part of a history of incomprehension rather than as readings which, like Menocchio's, deserve to be understood on their own terms. The study of reading, as it has so far been developed, has been characterized by a marked one-sidedness. It has placed the reader into the melting pot of variability whilst retaining the text as a fixed pole of reference within the analysis. It is necessary, and high time, to place the text into the melting pot of variability too; to recognize that the history of reading is not one in which different readers encounter "the same text" but one in which the text readers encounter is already "over-worked", "over-coded", productively activated in a particular way as a result of its inscription within the social, material, ideological and institutional relationships which distinguish specific reading relations. It has no meanings which can be traduced.

As I've already indicated, I think these considerations apply with particular force to the study of popular texts. These are usually studied, and not infrequently condemned, for their effects on "other people" without any real attempt being made to take account of the specific determinations which mould and structure popular reading; that is, to recall my earlier definition, readings which are produced outside the academy and at a considerable remove from the critical discourses which circulate within it. Jameson writes that texts come before us as "the always-already-read", apprehended through the sedimented reading habits and categories developed within inherited interpretative traditions (Jameson, 1981: 9). That's true in so far as one is concerned with the canonized tradition where the most consequential activations of the relations between texts and readers consist of those forms of critical commentary which circulate within those cultural apparatuses (critical journals, educational institutions, publishing houses) which have a primary investment in the institution of Literature. But what about the popular reading of popular texts? What are the orders of inter-textuality within which such reading is located? What are the discursive forms and institutional apparatuses through which popular reading is superintended? We don't know, at least not in a detailed way. One might point to the operation of the star-system and to the social production of popular heroes as instances of the superintendence of popular reading, hermeneutic systems which pin down the meaning of popular texts in particular ways, fixing the ideological co-ordinates within which they are to be read. One might also point to the similar functioning of interviews with actors, actresses, writers and directors in publications which impinge directly on the social organization of popular reading – film reviews, fan magazines, and the like. But we scarcely have an adequate knowledge of the way in which these hermeneutic activators of popular texts work, and we know even less about the cultural resources which may be mobilized against such provided "reading triggers". It's not exaggerating to say that, in the absence of an adequate knowledge and theorization of these matters, any attempt to make a political intervention within the sphere of popular reading runs the risk of being radically inappropriate.

To put the point simply, the problem is that the text the critic has on the desk before her or him may not be the same as the text that is culturally active in the relations of popular reading. It is, accordingly, with the determinations which organize the social relations of popular reading that analysis must start if we are to understand the nature of the cultural business that is conducted around, through and by means of popular texts in the real history of their productive activation. Rather than taking the text as a given it is necessary to introduce a radical hesitancy into the analysis, a hesitancy such that the text will be *the last thing* one speaks of – and speaks of only in the particular historical reading relations in which it has been analytically located – if the study of the "living life" of written texts is to advance beyond the empty-headed gesture of stating that there are texts with "fixed properties" which may, of course, be variantly "interpreted". Whilst this displays a fine open-mindedness – anything is possible – it also singularly fails to broach the real issue: accounting for such *real* variations in the social destinies of texts as *have actually* taken place.

Notes

1   Menocchio provides a succinct summary of his cosmography as follows:

> I have said that, in my opinion, all was chaos, that is, earth, air, water, and fire were mixed together; and out of that bulk a mass formed – just as cheese is made out of milk – and worms appeared in it, and these were the angels. The most holy majesty decreed that these should be God and the angels, and among that number of angels, there was also God, he too having being created out of that mass at the same time, and he was lord, with four captains, Lucifer, Michael, Gabriel, and Raphael. That Lucifer sought to make himself lord equal to the king, who was the majesty of God, and for this arrogance God ordered him driven out of heaven with all his host and his company; and this God later created Adam and Eve and people in great number to take the places of the angels who had been expelled. (Cited in Ginzburg, 1980a: 5–6)

2   See, for example, Iser (1978), Slatoff (1970), Morley (1980a), and Hall (1980b).

Chapter Three Figuring Audiences and Readers

In a recent critical exchange on audience theory, James Lull entered the plea that, when speaking about television, we should get rid of the terms "texts" and "readers" (Lull, 1988: 239). It's not difficult to see why. The literary bias of both terms is obvious as is the inappropriateness of their unqualified application to audio-visual media. Television is not reducible to its texts while the complexity of our relations to and forms of involvement in this cultural technology clearly go beyond the notion of reading, no matter how generously we might interpret it.

Yet, if this is so, it is not clear why – as Lull implies – the term "audience" should present itself as automatically preferable. There are, after all, other terms that might be used – viewer, for example – just as there have been, historically, other alternatives whose theoretical and political force we should not lose sight of. The early history of sound broadcasting thus affords ample evidence of significantly contrastive views of the relations (actual or ideal) between radio and, as they were initially envisaged, its listeners: that is, as the subjects of an action. Lesley Johnson's work on Australian radio, for example, thus highlights the respects in which listeners were initially conceived as delighting in the act of listening as such, deriving their pleasure from marveling at radio's technical ability to render distant sounds present, rather than from program content (Johnson, 1988). Johnson, like Williams (1974), also stresses the enormous work of social and cultural definition through which listeners subsequently came to be conceptualized as, precisely, audiences – that is, as consumers of centrally produced and broadcast programs – rather than as, say, technical users or as differentiated publics, each regulating radio for its own purposes.

The modern concept of the audience (at least before it became "active") as the receivers of messages from a centralized source of transmission, then, was not present at the birth of the modern media but has emerged in tandem with their development and, in part, as a product of their own practices. What *was* present from the outset, however, was the mold in which such a conception of the audience might be cast. As Janice Radway has noted, the term "audience" derives, etymologically, from the contexts of face-to-face communication. It is important to add, however, that those contexts were typically hierarchically organized. To be granted an audience – as in the relations of a subject to a sovereign – was to be granted the right to listen to the enunciations of power; to hear and to take account of a message delivered by and from an authoritative source. If, as Radway suggests, virtually all early mass communication theories "retained the notion of the audience as a unified aggregate of similarly endowed individuals who passively read or hear the words and therefore the message of another" (Radway, 1988: 360), it is equally important to note that such message flows were also conceived as descending the hierarchy of discursive power.[1]

My point, then, is that if it is true that the term "readers" brings with it a particular set of associations, so, too, does the term "audience." Indeed, if the brief analysis hinted at above holds, traditional conceptions of the audience might be regarded as a part of the juridico-discursive conception of power bequeathed to us by the ways of envisaging power associated with absolutist regimes in which power seems to derive from some central and originating source: the sovereign or the state (see Foucault, 1976). However, this is not to suggest that we might either wish or be able to dispense with the term. For the same sort of points could be made in relation to any of the other terms that might be proposed as substitutes. The fact is that the inquiries that are presently conducted under the heading of audience studies – or under such alternative formulations as effects studies, reception theory, or reader-response studies – represent, or figure, their objects of study in different ways: as audiences, readers, publics, receptants, interpreters, viewers, spectators, or listeners. Whichever of these conceptions is chosen, moreover, will – if it is accorded any theoretical weight – affect how a particular inquiry is conducted: what it looks for, how it frames its object theoretically, what methods are used, how the results are represented, where and how those results are circulated, and to what effect.

Pierre Bourdieu's enigmatic contention that public opinion does not exist but its effects are real (Bourdieu, 1979) may help make the point I am after here. In maintaining that public opinion does not exist, Bourdieu's purpose is to dispute the supposition, quite common among advocates of opinion polling, and especially such pioneers of polling techniques as George Gallup and Saul Rae (Gallup and Rae, 1968), that there exists such a thing as a public whose opinions on any given topic are ready-made, simply lying there waiting to be discovered via the application of an appropriate polling method. The making of any statement regarding public opinion on any particular issue, Bourdieu argues, depends on a specific means of accessing a public and arriving at an assessment of its opinions. Yet the means deployed for these purposes serve more to constitute and shape a public rather than simply to discover one just as they often organize into being the very opinion they seem merely to report.

Thus, whether people are interviewed at home, over the telephone, via methods of random intercept or by post; whether they are interviewed singly or in groups, who they are interviewed by, and what manner of relations of power might exist between interviewer and interviewee; whether they are able to arrive at a means of expressing an opinion via discussion with each other and then voting; whether voting is by means of a public or private ballot; how the options within a questionnaire are structured and how they are phrased: these are among the considerations which can influence the kind of opinion likely to be attributed to a particular population. Whatever the means by which it is arrived at, moreover, such an opinion is subject to a further process of shaping via the discursive forms – from official poll reports through to editorializing comment – which regulate its circulation in the public domain.

Public opinion, then, is always shaped and organized by the very instruments which purport to measure it. No such instrument is neutral, simply revealing a set of opinions which pre-exists its application. Public opinion cannot be spoken of without, in the very process, giving it a determinate form – as a set of statistics, say, or as a set of exemplary views and preferences – which is the effect of the means of its measurement. All of which is to say that public opinion always takes the form of a representation – or, more accurately, a circuit of representations – which has been arrived at in determinate and specific ways. This is not to say that its existence is in the least chimerical or without consequence. While public opinion might not exist in the form that the early pollsters imagined – in the raw, so to speak – it certainly has a very real, if also fractured and contradictory, existence in the many complex and varying representational forms in which it is circulated. Nor is this field of representations in which the public and its opinions are diversely figured without consequence for political processes. Its consequences, however, are not those envisaged by Gallup who, viewing opinion polls as a means of making the will of the people luminously transparent to their political representatives, extolled their virtues as instruments of democracy. Rather, Bourdieu suggests, polling has developed into an instrument for making popular opinion responsive to political direction rather than vice versa. It affords a means whereby opinions, in being organized to conform to the shape in which they are represented, can be mobilized in support of particular political causes or projects.

Broadly similar arguments apply to the researches that are presently conducted under the various headings of audience studies, reception theory, effects or reader-response studies. For all such researches require some means of accessing their objects (whether audiences or readers), means which never simply allow "what is going on" in the situations they investigate to be fathomed in ways that are not affected by the means of access selected: participant observation versus postal survey, for example. Indeed, such "means of access" often organize their objects into being in that, and more often than not, audiences are artifacts of the instruments selected for their investigation. There is also little room for doubting the practical consequences of the ways in which the audience is represented, or figured, when the results of such inquiries are written up and circulated. The social and political fields in which such representations can be counted as having consequential effects are many – the relations between commercial broadcasters and advertisers, the activities of regulatory agencies, the investment strategies of publishers, pedagogical practices in the classroom, forms of assessment and examination. They may also occasionally have a bearing on the symbolic currency and strategies of major political movements as Lawrence Grossberg has argued was the case with the relationship between the "active-audience" conceptions of the 1920s and 1930s and American Progressivism (Grossberg, 1989).

Yet, however, familiar these perspectives may be, debate in these areas often proceeds as if the point at issue was that of somehow really fathoming out the audience, of finally getting to what audiences actually do with media, how they really interpret media messages, the *real truth* of their media lives. This is especially so where debate crosses the boundary lines between different paradigms. Thus, for James Lull, the value of much of the work that goes on under the heading of "cultural studies" audience research is discounted because, in his view, it is driven more by a priori theoretical considerations than by "descriptions and grounded interpretations of what audiences really think and do" (Lull, 1988: 240). Yet John Fiske, writing in the same colloquium, argues that the academic objectifications of audiences produced by the quantitative methods of the "communications studies" paradigm distort the relations of reciprocal fluidity which, in his view, really characterize text–reader relations. These, Fiske contends, are more accurately revealed by ethnographic approaches which he sees as allowing audiences/readers more control over the terms in which they describe their own activities (Fiske, 1988).

To suggest that debates conducted in this manner have not proved particularly productive – and, indeed, that they are unlikely ever to do so – is not to suggest that we have no means of deciding between competing approaches to the audience. We certainly do, but never in the abstract. The grounds on which, in practice and in particular regions of debate, such decisions are made are always pragmatic – and so provisional and circumspect – rather than abstractly theoretical in the sense of requiring a general validation of a specific method or paradigm. In short, and quite sensibly, they are dependent on the tasks to hand and the instruments that are judged most likely to assist in them. Academic debates concerning the relations between different paradigms of audience research are likely to be more productive if conducted in a similar spirit. This would involve an abandonment of the empiricist dream of some day being finally able to assess which approach had finally got the audience "figured out" correctly and focusing, instead, on the respects in which different ways of figuring audiences or readers – statistically or ethnographically, for example – are connected to, and calculated to produce effects within, quite different regions of practical activity.

I want, therefore, to develop this argument by considering the different fields of practical activity with which work falling under the heading of the "active-audience" approach has been associated. To object, as does Lull, that the empirical protocols for this way of figuring the audience are weak is correct. It would also be correct, in my view, to argue that such constructions of the active audience no more offer an adequate critique of more conventional empirical approaches to audience studies than they provide a usable alternative to many of the practical purposes such approaches serve. Yet these objections are, in a sense, inconsequential. For they miss what, in at least some of its variants, this way of representing audiences really aims for: the production of a figure of the audience or reader which, through its pedagogic deployment, can serve as a performative prop for a particular set of exercises through which actual readers – by aligning their reading practices with those associated with the exemplary figure of the active reader – are to be, so to speak, activated. This is said not to defend such approaches but rather to identify more clearly the grounds on which they might more usefully be criticized. For if, as I am suggesting, the figure of the "active audience" forms part of a specific technologization of the text–reader relation which aims at the transformation of reading, viewing or listening practices, the issue is not its descriptive adequacy but its role as part of an apparatus of textual criticism and pedagogy.

To substantiate this argument, however, will require that the notion of the active audience be, to a degree, deconstructed. For, the semantic currency of this term is now an extraordinarily wide and varied one. It is also, consequently, an imprecise one. If the audience has recently become "active," its activeness has been differently conceived and constructed in different regions of inquiry. However, the failure to accord these differences the attention they merit means that the image of the "active audience" now uneasily combines often contradictory conceptions arising from quite different disciplinary fields. Some disentangling will be necessary, then, to identify the different kinds of theoretical and political investments that have been made in this figure.

Audiences as Objects and Subjects

Before pursuing these contentions further, however, let me first summarize my argument so far and explore some of its collateral implications with a view to providing a broader context for the above remarks. My main purpose has been to suggest the incoherence of those empiricist conceptions of audience research according to which an objective knowledge of audiences is eventually to be arrived at via the progressive refinement of research techniques. Ien Ang has recently argued a similar position in disputing the assumption that the audience can be regarded as "a proper object of study whose characteristics can be ever more accurately observed, described, categorised, systematised and explained until the whole picture is 'filled in' " (Ang, 1989: 103). Her grounds for doing so, moreover, are broadly similar: that research in the area can only give rise to "historically and culturally specific knowledges that are the result of equally specific discursive encounters between researcher and informants" (Ang, 1989: 105).

Ang is at pains to make it clear that this argument applies with just as much force – neither more nor less – to "cultural studies" ethnographic approaches as it does to empirical survey techniques. Such approaches do not provide a privileged means of access to the real "media lives" of audiences, nor can the statements of viewers' preferences and activities they give rise to be viewed "as transparent reflections of those viewers' 'lived realities' that can speak for themselves" (Ang,

1989: 106). If understanding audience activity is thus "caught up in the discursive representation...of realities having to do with audiences" (Ang, 1989: 105), then the politics of audience research have to do with the manner in which those representations are arrived at, the form they take, where they are circulated, and the political projects they can be connected to.

This line of thought might be taken a little further by distinguishing between means of accessing and representing audiences according to whether the political programs they enable and support address audiences as objects or subjects. To clarify what I have in mind: the audience is constituted as an object within governmental or regulatory projects which, typically drawing on statistical representations of audience activities or preferences, aim to influence the nature of the services available to audiences or the conditions within which their activities are situated. In such cases, while audiences constitute the targets of such programs – and, indeed, are often brought into being by them – the programs themselves are conceived, put into effect and implemented by other agencies (by regulatory bodies like the Australian Broadcasting Tribunal, for example) which therefore also constitute the key reception points at which those representations of audiences effectively circulate. By contrast, where ethnographic studies give rise to representations of audience activities in the form of first-hand descriptions and reported statements whose effective reception points are within the pedagogic apparatus and the various quasi public spheres that apparatus is connected to, the political programs they support often aim to modify audience behavior directly – via the empowering effect which can arise from making marginalized readings publicly available, for example.

I do not, in distinguishing between these programs in this way, mean to imply a preference for the latter on the grounds of some abstract emancipatory potential. Valerie Walkerdine, writing of her experience in researching family uses of video, has noted that, as observer, she became "a 'Surveillant Other' not only watching but producing a knowledge that feeds into the discursive practices regulating families" (Walkerdine, 1986: 190). While, obviously, from both an ethical and a political point of view, the dangers inherent in this situation need to be kept in mind, it is equally important to avoid the kind of reflex politics in which surveillance and regulation are deemed to be axiomatically oppressive. To the contrary, it is clear that a vast range of progressive political agendas – egalitarian, socialist and feminist – cannot be even thought, let alone brought into being, without mechanisms of surveillance capable of making visible the fields of activity they address in a form that renders them amenable to political calculation and action.

It is thus true, to draw on an example from a related field of study, that the public museum has, from its inception, functioned as a space of surveillance in which conduct has been subjected to regulation by exposing it to a normalizing and controlling gaze: of security staff or fellow visitors, for example. It is also true (although little noted) that, like the prison and the asylum, the museum has functioned as a laboratory of observation which has served as the incubus for the development of techniques of observation and behavioral description – intercept studies on exit, the surveying of group behavior patterns, calculations of attention time-span – which have assisted the development of regulatory practices in a wide variety of domains: the design of shopping malls, for example. Yet it is also true that the development of modern political demands for more equitable patterns of access to, and participation in, museums has been made possible only by utilizing this space of observation so as to make visible the socio-demographic profile of its visitors.

Moreover, it is clear that there is now a self-fueling momentum built into the relationship between museum practices and visitor observation in the sense that new fields of museum policy are constantly being generated into being as the grid of observation to which visitors are subjected becomes more refined. While the notion of the "active visitor" is not yet current within the field of museum studies, it just as well might be. Although no more reducible to their textual components than are film or television, it is now widely recognized that many aspects of museums are text-like in their organization: the narrativization of the visitor's route from one gallery to the next, for example. Equally, this recognition is accompanied by an increasing awareness that museums and museum exhibits can be experienced and interpreted in significantly different ways by visitors with different socio-economic and cultural profiles in accordance with the discursive resources they can draw on to organize their readings of those exhibits or, more generally, to negotiate their relations to the museum environment. And this awareness, finally, is increasingly reflected in attempts to build polysemic possibilities into museum displays so as to enhance the prospects for multiple readings (see, for example, MacDonald and Silverstone, 1990).

Yet the museum visitor is not – or is only rarely – an effective agent within such fields of policy formation. The visitor – and, where programs are designed to make museums accessible to broader publics, the non-visitor too – is always the point of reference for the programs put into action by effective agents (curators, museum directors, boards of trustees, government funding bodies) within the museum sphere. However, owing to the nature of their relations to the institution – infrequent and transitory visits or, for non-goers, none at all – visitors themselves are rarely involved in these policy issues or the politics which accompany them except in the forms in which they are figured via the application of a range of observational techniques. The visitor, moreover, is typically unaware of the ways in which visitor needs, interests, and so on, are represented in policy debates and processes; nor, with few exceptions, are visitors actively enlisted in support of the programs constructed on their behalf. Constantly present figuratively, the museum visitor is yet constantly absent as agent and is seldom addressed as such. Certainly, I know of no studies of museum visitors – whether of their attitudes, behavior, or social and cultural characteristics – which have constituted those visitors as their addressees as well as their objects of study.

By contrast – and to come to the point I want to make by way of this digression – the very point at issue in many versions of the "active-audience" approach is precisely how they constitute and, in constituting, address audiences or readers as subjects. For, notwithstanding their pretensions to a general theoretical status, such constructions of audiences form part of a rhetorical politics which is concerned less with describing audience behavior than with altering it, less with accounting for reading practices than with changing them. They are, that is to say, parts of larger critical enterprises whose effectivity depends on how they map out and organize a role for the reader and on the mechanisms they deploy to induct real readers into that role and its performative requirements.

Yet, this is true only of some versions of the argument. It will therefore now be useful to return to my earlier commitment and, in the light of the above considerations, distinguish between a number of positions that are commonly grouped under the "active-audience" approach. While the use of a common designation has served usefully to differentiate these positions from other and earlier traditions (structuralism, for example) in which the audience was figured as passive, its course mapped out for it as an effect of its textual positioning, its indiscriminate application can prove a barrier to analysis and debate if allowed to occlude equally important differences between them. I shall, therefore, offer a breakdown of the "active- audience" approach into three positions. I shall call these the "determined active reader", the "indecipherably active reader" and the "over-active reader" approaches and I shall argue that they are distinct from one another with regard to both the means they employ in arriving at the figure of the reader they construct and the spheres of practical activity in which those figures of the reader, and of reading, are capable of surfacing and producing effects.

This will then allow me to argue that it is mistaken to limit criticisms of the "indecipherably active reader" and "over-active reader" approaches to their inadequacies as research paradigms. It is not that criticisms couched in such terms are wrong. Rather, it is that they fail to see that, however much they might masquerade as research paradigms, such approaches are more accurately viewed as interventions within the politics of reading. The figures of the reader they construct, that is to say, function as a means of rhetorically enlisting readers for certain reading practices while also providing them with a performative prop – a model – which they can use in arriving at readings of a similar kind. This therefore raises questions concerning their implications for the ways in which texts – televisual, filmic or literary – are to be pedagogically deployed, issues which need to be assessed in other ways and on other grounds.

Activating Audiences

By the "determined active reader," I have in mind those approaches which, while arguing that a text cannot dictate its readings and thus insisting on the activity of the reader within or vis-à-vis the text, do not construe that activity as being in any way voluntaristic or autochthonous. Rather, if the reader is active vis-à-vis the text, this is by virtue of the other forces or considerations – social position, intertextual relations, discursive mediations, etc. – which are accorded a role in the determination of reading practices. I would cite as examples here David Morley's study of the *Nationwide* audience (Morley, 1980b) as well as my own and Janet Woollacott's study of the varying reading formations which have affected the social reception of "the texts of James Bond" (Bennett and Woollacott, 1987).[2] For, while both attribute a degree of autonomy to the reader vis-à-vis the text, that autonomy is regarded as the result of the *other determinations* which bear upon the social organization of reading practices.

Both, moreover, shared a common impetus derived from their opposition to the "hypodermic syringe" model of ideological inoculation implied by the dominant ideology thesis. This is evident in their concern to theorize the social relations and determinations of reading in a manner that would allow for the possibility of resistive or oppositional readings of media texts. That said, however, neither implies that the active reader is, must be or should be a resistive or oppositional reader. For Morley, the readings of trade unionists, managers or tertiary students are all equally active in the sense that all are molded by similar configurations of extra-textual relations: the patterns of access to the discourse positions which govern their "decoding" activities. Similarly, in suggesting that the "texts of Bond" might be read in a plurality of ways, the analysis of *Bond and Beyond* allows the "active reader" to be figured as deeply misogynist or conservatively nationalist just as much as benignly resistive.

The "determined active reader", then, is one whose activity might best be thought of as being organized by a complex weave of determinations within which the operative influence of the text is always "overdetermined" by the concerted influence of a variety of extra-textual forces.

The means whereby this figure of the reader may be constructed are various, ranging, for example, from the techniques of focus group discussion to, where it is past reading practices that are at issue, appropriate historiographical methods of inquiry (see Parry, 1985). Similarly, the political currency of this version of the active audience is a varied one: whether or not you'd like a "determined active reader" as your best friend depends on the nature of the determinations which organize her or his reading practices. Given this, the figure of the reader that is constructed in this way cannot serve as a model for empirical readers. Nor is it the purpose of such approaches to directly politicize reading in this way. To the contrary, their political address is to the determinations which mold and structure the reader's activity. For it is only by virtue of transformations in these that the political quality of the audience's textual investments can be altered. Indeed, the political pay-off of this version of the active-audience approach has consisted in the contribution it has made to the demise of those forms of purely textual politics – the search for radical or progressive texts – in insisting on the need for questions concerning the political effects of cultural practices to be posed in relation to the broader fields of relations (discursive, institutional, inter-textual) which organize the cultural terrain of specific text–reader encounters.

If the provenance of the "determined active reader" has been largely sociological, that of the "indecipherably active reader" has been chiefly literary. The product of the uncoupling of the text–reader polarity engendered by deconstruction's insistence on the reciprocal iterability of text and reader (now no more than an intertextual nodal point), the "indecipherably active reader" is one whose activity, while subject to an endless theoretical affirmation, is simultaneously unfathomable since neither the place of the reader that reads nor that of the text that is read is susceptible, even in principle, to a definite determination. Literary in origin, this construction of the reader also constitutes a means whereby the regime of truth which characterizes modern literary studies – a regime which rests on the production of a text whose meaning is for ever undecided and undecidable – is extended from the literary text to the domain of its readings.[3] As such its effect, in undermining any attempt to make audiences or readers the objects of a positive knowledge, is to produce an enlarged field in which the protocols of the literary reading might be applied. As a consequence, the type of analysis to which (assuming they could be isolated) particular reading practices might be subject is one which can never be finalized. The reading that is to be read – since, by definition, it exceeds the scope of any particular set of methods – always remains, in some way, indecipherable, out of reach.

Notwithstanding its literary provenance, this figure of the reader has acquired a much broader circulation within the field of audience studies. This has been mainly due to the influence of postmodernist debates, especially as mediated via Ernesto Laclau's and Chantal Mouffe's deconstructive conception of the discursive (and hence undecidable) organization of social relations (see Laclau and Mouffe, 1985). Janice Radway's conception of the dispersal and nomadicity of audiences provides a case in point, and an instructive one in the disjunction between her subscription to such a conception of the audience and her attempts to devise a research method appropriate to it. Noting that most audience studies proceed from the assumption that texts can be categorized as entities of a particular sort, Radway thus argues:

> Audiences, then, are set in relation to a single set of isolated texts which qualify already as categorically distinct objects. No matter how extensive the effort to dissolve the boundaries of the textual object or the audience, most recent studies of reception, including my own, continue to begin with the "factual" existence of a particular kind of text which is understood to be received by some set of individuals. Such studies perpetuate, then, the notion of a circuit neatly bounded and therefore identifiable, locatable, and open to observation. (Radway, 1988: 363)

Insisting, against such conceptions, that neither texts nor audiences can be treated as simply givens – or as existing in given relations to one another – Radway proposes that the study of audiences should give way to a more diffusely defined object of analysis:

> Instead of segmenting a social formation automatically by construing it precisely as a set of audiences for specific media and/or genres, I have been wondering whether it might not be more fruitful to start with the habits and practices of everyday life as

they are actively, discontinuously, even contradictorily pieced together by historical subjects themselves as they move nomadically via disparate associations and relations through day-to-day existence. In effect, I have begun to wonder whether our theories do not impress upon us a new object of analysis, one more difficult to analyse because it can't be so easily pinned down – that is, the endlessly shifting, ever-evolving kaleidoscope of daily life and the way in which the media are integrated and implicated within it. (Radway, 1988: 366)

The challenge, as Radway enunciates it, is thus whether it is possible to design a research strategy that will "provide for a collective mapping of the social terrain equal to the ambitious, majestic scope of our recent theories of subjectivity and intertextuality" (Radway, 1988: 367–8). The difficulty is that, in seeming to respond positively to this challenge, Radway reinstates assumptions which run counter to the very grain of the challenge they are meant to meet. For Radway suggests – although clearly in an exploratory and hesitant fashion – that an appropriate response to such a challenge might take the form of a team-based ethnographic analysis of "the range of practices engaged in by individuals within a single heterogeneous community as they elaborate their own form of popular culture through the realms of leisure and then articulate those practices to others engaged in during their working lives" (Radway, 1988: 368). This does, in truth, sound a little like rediscovering "the real media lives" of small-town America after the fashion of the Lynds (1929) or Vidich and Benseman (1960). The more general difficulty, though, is that this solution is bought at the price of suppressing the conditions which generated the problem in the first place. Lawrence Grossberg – on whom I have drawn in much of the foregoing discussion – thus argues that, in spite of her ostensible commitment to the fluidity and transience of audience/ media, reader/text relations, the methods Radway appeals to for the analysis of such relations re-inscribe them within objectifying frameworks in which their separateness and self-identity are reaffirmed (see Grossberg, 1988).

Grossberg's point in developing this critique is to insist on the need for ways of speaking about audiences or readers which lack the objectifying potential – and especially the division between researchers and audiences, "us" and "them" – inherent in Radway's continuing reliance on ethnography as an acceptable research tool. Mine, per contra, is to suggest that Radway's mistake consists in the supposition that *any* set of research techniques might prove adequate to the task of reconstructing the "real media lives" of "non-audiences" that would be equal to "the ambitious, majestic scope of our recent theories of subjectivity and intertextuality." For the effect of such theories, where they are of literary derivation, is always such as to put the analysis of *any and all* social relations beyond the reach of a determinate research technique and to constitute them, instead, as a resource for a project of reading which – since the possibility of arriving at a correct reading is denied – is simultaneously the project of a re-reading that can never be completed.

To ask whether definite and specific research methods might be deployed in a field in which audiences and texts, and the relations between them, have been deconstructed in this manner is, in short, to make a category mistake. For the very point of such a deconstruction is, precisely, to place such questions beyond the sphere of positive methods so that the domain of reading and audience practices might be reconstituted for other purposes. In being rescued from the domain of methodology, the "indecipherably active reader" is thereby made available as a resource for extending the sway of literary readings beyond the confines of the literary text. The reader, figured in this fashion, is not a possible object of analysis. Rather, it supplies a means for cultivating and exercising a particular reading competence, one which develops the ability to hold to many different meanings at the same time but without being able to (or feeling the need to) decide between them; one which, in literarizing life, extends the spheres in which it is possible to speak without saying anything definite, without any sense of a referential horizon or responsibility. In short, the "indecipherably active reader" forms part of a distinctive technology of reading which – originating within the literary branches of the academy, but now enjoying a broader circulation within specific regions of other humanities and social science disciplines – has to be assessed in terms of the specific intellectual skills and capacities it gives rise to. While this is not a task I shall undertake here, it is surely clear that intellectuals formed by means of such a technology will display a limited ability to contribute in a definite manner to specific endeavors.

The difficulty with the "over-active reader", by contrast, is that of recruiting empirical readers, too easily, and too automatically, for reading practices conducted in the name of resistance. Like the "determined active reader," this figure of the reader was fashioned in critique of the "hypodermic syringe" model of ideological inoculation associated with the dominant ideology thesis in both its capitalist and patriarchal versions. It differs, however, in two key respects. First, the active reader here is always represented as occupying a position of social subordination and as the subject of a reading which is usually valorized in being portrayed as manifesting a resistive, oppositional or transgressive potential. Second, the methods through which this figure of the reader is produced are hypothetical-deductive rather than empirical. Rather than relying on ethnographic, statistic or historiographic techniques of inquiry, that is, the more usual procedure here is to deduce what the reading practices of particular subordinate groups might be by positing correspondences between the formal attributes of specific textual regimes and the conditions of life of the groups that are posited as the primary audiences for those textual regimes.

A classic example is Tania Modleski's attempt to explain the nature of women's pleasurable and affirmative investments in soap operas by suggesting a homology between the narrative organization of soap operas and women's daily routines. The fact that soap operas are potentially endless narratives, she thus suggests, resonates positively with the experience that "women's work is never done." The distracted pleasures women derive from soap opera, Modleski goes on to argue, embody women's resistance to – and prefigure a narrative system beyond – what she posits as the repressive and patriarchal narrative regimes of classic film in its impetus toward speedy narrative resolution and closure (see Modleski, 1982).

The most obvious problem with such hypothetical-deductive approaches is that the same means can be used to arrive at sharply contrasting, but equally convincing (or unconvincing), constructions of the reader and the nature of her or his pleasure. Radway, for example, forges quite a different connection between textual regimes and the conditions of life of her sample of romance readers in attempting "to infer from the women's conscious statements and observable activities other acknowledged significances and functions that make romance reading into a highly desirable and useful action in the context of these women's lives" (Radway, 1984: 9). Thus, in this, the hypothetical-deductive moment of her analysis, Radway also construes romance reading as incipiently resistive of patriarchy. It is so, however, for reasons which are diametrically opposed to those which Modleski advances. Reading romances, Radway suggests, is prompted by women's intense interest in and demand for narrative resolution, an interest which she sees as expressing a resistive, proto-political demand for time on one's own free from interruptions.

There is, of course, no reason why women readers should not take pleasure in different textual forms for different reasons. What is clearly impossible, however, is that such contradictory pleasures should be accounted for in essentially the same terms and be accorded the same anti-patriarchal effects: at least, not unless such readers are to be judged capable of having their resistive cake and eating it too! Yet, in truth, the reading that is at issue in such analyses is less that of the readers described in the discussion than that of those addressed by it. The former constitute, in effect, a rhetorical device whereby the latter might be inducted into a particular way of reading the textual regime concerned. The "over-active reader" thus serves as a prop whereby real flesh and blood readers might be activated into resistive reading practices in embodying a set of exercises and orientations whose emulation will – theoretically, at least – open up the textual regime under discussion to new forms of use and contextualization.

The pertinent questions to put to such constructions of reading thus concern less their empirical reliability than their technological effects; less whether they accurately describe the practices of real flesh-and-blood readers than what they allow, incite, or encourage such readers to do. Viewed in this light, the "over-active reader" occupies the same place and performs the same function as that figure of the reader it is constructed against: the "under-active reader" which informed the practices of textual commentary associated with earlier mass culture critiques or theories of patriarchy. Modleski's housewife thus occupies the same *type* of relation and performs the same *type* of function in relation to daytime soaps as did Richard Hoggart's "juke-box boys" in relation to what he dubbed the "newer mass art" of "comics, gangster novelettes, science and crime magazines" (Hoggart, 1969: 247). The politics of the positions are, of course, dissimilar. Modleski's housewife serves both to valorize soaps and as a performative prop for, and as a means of legitimating, emulative readings whereby real readers are to derive an enhanced resistive value from such texts. Hoggart's "juke-box boys," by contrast, serve as a means of denigrating the texts of mass culture while also organizing, and legitimating, a disdainful practice of reading whereby we disentangle ourselves from and lift ourselves above what such texts do to their unfortunate victims.

I shall not, here, attempt to evaluate the kind of reading practices – or habits – which this way of figuring the reader serves to promote. It does seem clear, however, that its main legacy has been a series of ideal readers – Modleski's daytime soaps fan, Fiske's and Watts's video games player (Fiske and Watts, 1985) – which might best be described as populist inversions of the hapless dupes who formed their erstwhile mass/male culture counterparts. In view of this, reading practices modeled on such figures are likely to tend toward the self-indulgent, politically lazy end of any given set of reading possibilities.

My main purpose, however, has been less to decide between different approaches to audiences and readers than to establish that the field of discourses in which audiences and readers appear is not a unitary one. To the contrary, existing approaches to audiences and readers exhibit vast differences with regard to the means they deploy of accessing and representing audiences and readers. They also differ with regard to the kinds of practical issues that are implicated in their concerns and the ways in which those issues – and the agents involved in them – are addressed. It is only by foregrounding such practical concerns, I want to suggest, that different approaches can be discussed and assessed on grounds that are appropriate to them.

Notes

1 My position is, in this respect, slightly different from Radway's in that she suggests that the modern extension of the term "audience" to refer to readers, viewers, listeners, and so on, rests on the presumed naturalness of face-to-face speech as a model for all forms of communication. This, in turn, leads Radway to suggest that the audience's conception as passive derives from the assumption of the relations of full presence – and hence the transparency of meaning – which, pre-Derrida, were mistakenly held to characterize the sphere of speech communication. My contention is rather that the deferential position mapped out for the audience derives not from the sphere of speech communication as such but from the historical weight and analogical force of the specific hierarchical sets of socio-verbal relations with which the term was originally associated.

2 I shall not, here or elsewhere, attempt to identify all the sources relevant to the different schools of audience theory I am concerned with. Several excellent general surveys of the field exist with full details of relevant sources. See, especially, Morley (1989) and Moores (1990). On issues specifically to do with the active audience, see Allor (1988), Morley and Silverstone (1990) and Nightingale (1989).

3 For a discussion of the respects in which the literary text's undecidability or unfathomability might be regarded as an artifact of the relations of correction and supervision which characterize modern literary education – rather than as an essential attribute of its literariness – see Hunter (1988a). For a related discussion of the application of these protocols of literary reading to the domain of history, see the final chapter of Bennett (1990a).

Part II   Culture, Governance, and the Social

Chapter Four   Culture and Governmentality

In assessing how Foucault's perspective of governmentality has influenced the concerns of the social and political sciences, Mitchell Dean suggests that its main effect has been to substitute what he calls an analytics of government for a theory of the state. What he means by this is clarified in the definition he gives for the expanded concept of government that the perspective of governmentality entails:

> Government is any more or less calculated and rational activity, undertaken by a multiplicity of authorities and agencies, employing a variety of techniques and forms of knowledge, that seeks to shape conduct by working through our desires, aspirations, interests and beliefs, for definite but shifting ends and with a diverse set of relatively unpredictable consequences, effects and outcomes. (Dean 1999: 11)

As such, he suggests, and in contradistinction to the typical focal concerns of theories of the state (the sources of state power, who possesses it, the role of ideology in the legitimation of power), an analytics of government is more concerned with the mechanisms of government, with its routines and operations, paying particular regard to four sets of questions:

1 characteristic forms of visibility, ways of seeing and perceiving;
2 distinctive ways of thinking and questioning, relying on definite vocabularies and procedures for the production of truth (e.g. those derived from the social, human and behavioral sciences);
3 specific ways of acting, intervening, and directing, made up of particular types of practical rationality ("expertise" and "know-how"), and relying upon definite mechanisms, techniques, and technologies;
4 characteristic ways of forming subjects, selves, persons, actors, or agents. (Dean, 1999: 23)

What is striking here is the extent to which formulations which, in other contexts, would be treated as a part of culture are included in this definition of government (to the extent that it works through "our desires, aspirations, interests and beliefs") and in the check-list of the mechanisms through which government is said to operate ("ways of seeing and perceiving," "ways of thinking," "characteristic ways of forming subjects, selves, persons, actors or agents"). Two points follow from this: first, that, questions concerning the analysis of culture are accorded a more significant role within an analytics of government than they are within theories of the state; and second, that the place they occupy within such an analytics is a radically different one in being conceived as central to the mechanics – the operations and procedures – through which governmental forms of power work rather than, as in typical constructions of the state–ideology relation, legitimating power in ways that are not immanently tangled up in its exercise. Dean notes as much himself when, in discussing the forms of rule associated with neo-liberalism, he notes the extent to which these center on "the task of cultural reformation" (Dean, 1999: 172).

This is, however, an argument in which what might be meant by "culture" is taken pretty much for granted; however central cultural mechanisms might be to the mechanisms of government in general, and to those of neo-liberalism in particular, Dean does not offer any extended consideration of the concept of culture or of how its role within an analytics of government might best be theorized. The same is true of Nikolas Rose who, indeed, writes disparagingly of what he refers to as the "amorphous domain of culture" (Rose, 1998: 24) as a concept whose use has now become so generalized and diffuse as to seriously weaken any analytical value it might once have had, or have again.

Somewhat contrary to what might have been expected, then, the concept of culture has not been effectively knitted into the concerns of those who have most consistently, and most influentially, elaborated the perspective of governmentality. While the relevance of cultural questions is clearly acknowledged, there has been no systematic attempt to think through what the perspective of governmentality might mean for earlier understandings of the concept of culture or how these might need to be revised in order to find a place within, and contribute to the development of, an analytics of government. I imply no criticism of either Dean or Rose here, for their main interests clearly lie elsewhere. The problem is rather that the passage – still uncertain and faltering – of the perspective of governmentality into the concerns of cultural studies has not occasioned any major revision of the concept of culture on the part of those working at the interfaces of questions of culture and government. Nor has it yet occasioned an adequate review of the legacy of earlier theories of culture of a kind that might then be imported back into the broader concerns of an analytics of government.

This is not to deny the value of the work that has been done through the application of the perspective of governmentality to particular cultural processes or in the analysis of particular cultural technologies. Yet the passage of that perspective will always be to some degree an obstructed one unless, rather than being approached as a perspective that has simply to be added and stirred to the already somewhat over-volatile theoretical brew that cultural studies has become, it is seen as one that entails a significantly different approach to our understanding of the relations between culture, society, and the social.

This is not, let me say immediately, a question that is likely to prove susceptible to a quick fix. To the contrary, it will require a sustained re-examination of the ways in which this relationship has been posed as a problem within post-Enlightenment social and cultural theory. While this cannot be attempted here, some pointers as to the direction such an inquiry might take can be offered by looking a little more closely at the respects in which the theoretical vocabularies of culture and governmentality are most obviously at odds with one another and at the reasons for this. I shall do so by considering the different ways in which Stuart Hall and Nikolas Rose draw on the Foucauldian concept of discourse. For it is in their contrasting uses of the Foucauldian lineage that we can see the effects of gratingly incompatible ways of replacing earlier questions concerning the relations between culture and society with ones centered on the relations between culture and the social.

The "Cultural Turn" and the Linguistic Construction of the Social

First, though, a little background is in order if we are to place both bodies of work in the context of broader transformations in recent approaches to the relations between culture, society, and the social. These have been registered principally in the form of a series of departures from, or adaptations of, Marxist constructions of culture/society relations as ones of dependency and determination. For Raymond Williams, from *Culture and Society* (1958) through to *Marxism and Literature* (1977), the central task was to insist, against idealist conceptions, that culture was both dependent on and determined by the social relationships of class arising from the organization of economic production while also – in retaining a Romantic stress on the role of creativity – setting limits to such relations of dependency. Similarly, the insistence, in Althusserian parlance, on the "relative autonomy" of culture and ideology countered, without overcoming, the stress that had previously been placed on economic, social, and political relationships as having a more primary force and influence in determining the make-up and developmental trajectory of a social formation.[1] Within both formulations, however, the concepts of society and social formation (while differing significantly in other respects) referred to a totality that was definable in terms of relatively fixed and knowable properties, and one that might be called on to account for the cultural forms it generated.

The direction of more recent debates, by contrast, has tended to dispute the value of an analytical topography that lays out the relations between culture and society for examination in these terms. This has reflected the tendency, commonly referred to as the "cultural turn," to accord an increasingly formative role to culture by imbuing it with the capacity to actively shape and organize – to constitute from within – a whole range of economic, social, and political relationships and practices. For Hall, the "cultural turn" thus constitutes "a paradigm shift in the humanities and social sciences" and, as such, consists in the contention that culture is "a constitutive condition of existence of social life, rather than a dependent variable" (Hall, 1997: 222). Its constitutive role in this regard derives from the fact that – in this account – culture functions like a language. It is, essentially, a meaning-making mechanism whose operations, while working at a higher level of signification, replicate the diacritical structure of language associated with the findings of post-Saussurean linguistics. Meaning is lodged not in things themselves but in the varying constructions of the relations between them that arise from different languages or systems of classification:

> The "cultural turn" is closely related to this new attitude towards language. For culture is nothing but the sum of the different classificatory systems and discursive formations, on which language draws in order to give meaning to things. The very term "discourse" refers to a group of statements in any domain which provides a language for talking about a topic and a way of producing a particular kind of knowledge about that topic. The term refers both to the production of knowledge through language and representation and the way that language is institutionalised, shaping social practices and setting new practices into play.
>
> The "cultural turn" expands this insight about language to social life in general. It argues that because economic and social processes themselves *depend* on meaning and have consequences for our ways of life, for who we are – our identities – and for "how we live now", they too must be understood as cultural and discursive practices. (Hall, 1997: 222)

Having thus given culture "a determinate and constitutive role in understanding and analysing all social relations and institutions" (Hall, 1997: 223), Hall goes on to qualify this argument by setting limits to culture's sway over the social. Clearly aware of the risk that extending culture's role in this way can result in an analytical stew in which "everything is 'culture' and 'culture' is everything" (Hall, 1997: 225), Hall argues that culture supplies only *one* of the constitutive conditions for other spheres of practice. Economic, political and social practices all have their own distinctive conditions and effects, but they are also constituted in and by the culturally organized relations of meaning and identity through which social agents come to take up particular subject positions and to act accordingly.

The question is: does this qualification do the trick? Does it, as Hall would want, allow him to respect the autonomy of economic, social, and political practices and relations while also insisting on their cultural constitution? At one level, yes: Hall has no difficulty, on the basis of this qualification, in arguing that each of these practices interacts with and conditions the others while also, of course, influencing the conduct of cultural practices. At another level, no: there is an asymmetry in the relations between culture and other regions of practice to the degree that the former exercises less a role of determination in the last instance (the role reserved for the economy in Marxist formulations) than one of constitution in the first instance. Culture, that is to say, is always there, and there first, immanent within economic, social, and political practices, organizing them from within, while it can itself be affected by such practices only to the extent that they supply external conditions for the operation of cultural practices which – since they too are language-like in their organization – are themselves, of course, always also cultur-ally structured from within.

What this means becomes clearer in Hall's more theoretically developed discus-sions of the relations between cultural and ideological practices and the organiza-tion of the social.[2] Two aspects of these discussions are relevant to my concerns here. The first consists in Hall's displacement of the concepts of society or social formation in favor of a conception of the social as a set of relations between the discursively constructed positions of meaning and identity which individuals – through mechanisms that are both semiotic and psychoanalytic – come to occupy. The second concerns the respects in which, in accordance with the requirements of post-structuralist conceptions of language, the relations between these positions are understood as ones of difference and deferral – or, in Derrida's sense, of *différance.* They are, that is to say, positions that are defined in relation to each other as specific forms of raced, classed, gendered, sexed, regional, or national identities which, in their complex interactions, define the plane on which social relations are organized – but never in permanently fixed forms. The relations between different discursive positions are articulated in different ways at different historical moments depending on how cultural and ideological struggles align them to, or disconnect them from, one another.

I do not want to question here the value of the work that has been made possible by bringing these formulations to bear on questions of race and ethnicity or, for that matter, of class and gender. To the contrary: Hall's contribution to the debates through which questions of difference and identity have been de-essentialized has been of inestimable importance, especially in the critiques of identity politics that it has made possible. The construction of the relations between culture and the social that emerges from these formulations does, however, generate a number of difficulties, less because it dissolves social relations into cultural relations of meaning than because it leaves the realm of culture peculiarly empty of any definite content of its own. It is not, that is to say, the application of the linguistic model to social relations that matters so much as its prior application to culture. For it is this, the linguistic paradigm on which the "cultural turn" ultimately rests, that makes it difficult to theorize culture in terms of its own set of distinctive properties except of a most general, trans-historical and anthropological kind. What culture is, and how it works: these questions are answered in advance of their being put in relation to the operation of cultural practices in any specific set of historical relations. Culture, always and everywhere, consists of a set of language-like oper-ations through which specific relations of meaning and identity are organized. Culture, to recall Hall's formulation, is "nothing but the sum of the different classificatory systems and discursive formations on which language draws in order to give meaning to things." And it works, always and everywhere, through the mechanisms of language and representation to shape social relations by organizing the frameworks of meaning which govern the conduct of social agents.

There is little scope here for any definition of, or attention to, culture that would specify its operations in terms of distinctive institutional or technical relations and processes. There is, similarly, little scope for any variable conception of the nature of the social. For the organization of this, too, is given in advance of the analysis of any specific set of circumstances by the assumption that culture acts on the social through its role in endowing social agents – whether as individuals or as groups – with the means of making their experience meaningful and intelligible. It is through this double move – the first through the notion of the linguistic construction of the social, and the second through the post-structuralist destabilization of the relations of meaning through which the social is thus constructed – that the earlier conceptions of society and social formation are called into question. And what takes their place is a concept of the social as the product of a mobile set of relations of signification whose "fixings" of the social through the relations between different discursive positionalities that they effect is always provisional, incomplete, and on the way to being unfixed again. The social, in this view, is similar to sociological accounts of the plane of social interaction; but it is also, in registering the effects of deconstruction, unlike such accounts in the inherent slipperiness that it builds into the socio-semiotic relations through which social interrelation is said to take place.

Governmentality and the Technical Construction of the Social

It is, I think, this aspect of Hall's position – or ones like it – that Nikolas Rose has in mind when he argues that "*the relations* that human beings have established with themselves," while "constructed and historical," are "not to be understood by locating them in some amorphous domain of culture" (Rose, 1998: 24). For Rose, an adequate account of subjectification – that is, after Foucault, of our relations to ourselves – is not available via a generalized mechanism in which, for example, the self is formed as an identity that is diacritically structured in relations of difference. Rather, what is needed, Rose argues, is an examination of the role played by historically specific techniques in organizing particular kinds of person and, equally important, shaping commensurately particular configurations of the social. Here is how he puts the matter:

> Subjectification is not to be understood by locating it in a universe of meaning or an interactional context of narratives, but in a complex of apparatuses, practices, machinations, and assemblages within which human being has been fabricated, and which presuppose and enjoin particular relations with ourselves. (Rose, 1998: 10)

The perspective informing these concerns derives from a different reading of Foucault's work. As we have seen, for Hall, the epistemological claims of the "cultural turn" are buttressed by aligning a Foucauldian concept of discourse with the role that language plays, in both structuralist and post-structuralist thought, in re-routing the constitution of the social through the systems of meaning that inform social actors' perceptions of themselves and of their relations to others. Rose, by contrast, interprets the Foucauldian concept of discourse in the light of the role it plays in Foucault's account of governmentality where it refers to the distinctive apparatuses and programs of governing which, working through particular regimes or games of truth, aim to involve us actively in the government, management, and development of ourselves. Discursive practices, as Foucault puts it, do not simply generate discourses as representations: "They take shape in technical ensembles, in institutions, in behavioural schemes, in types of transmission and dissemination, in pedagogical forms that both impose and maintain them" (Foucault, 1997: 12).

Expertise plays a crucial role in this definition of discursive practices and in understanding their relations to government as "an activity that undertakes to conduct individuals throughout their lives by placing them under the authority of a guide responsible for what they do and for what happens to them" (Foucault, 1997: 67). For it is centrally involved in the mechanisms through which the truth claims of particular discourses are organized and connected to particular apparatuses and programs of government. As Rose puts the matter in connection with the role of expertise in psychology:

> By expertise is meant the capacity of psychology to provide a corps of trained and credentialed persons claiming special competence in the administration of persons and interpersonal relations, and a body of techniques and procedures claiming to make possible the rational and human management of human resources in industry, the military, and social life more generally. (Rose, 1998: 11)

It is through the deployment of particular forms of expertise, in particular relations of government, that particular ways of speaking the truth and making it practical are connected to particular ways of acting on persons – and of inducing them to act upon themselves – which, in their turn, form particular ways of acting on the social. Persons, in this approach, are just as much constructed or made-up entities as they are in Hall's. There are, however, significant differences in the manner and form of their composition. These derive from Rose's contention that discourse, to become effective, must pass through the mediation of the technical. Eschewing the temptation of a general account of the ways in which experience is made meaningful – such as that of the role accorded discourse-as-language in the "cultural turn" – Rose opts instead for a more differentiating and particularizing history of the various "devices of 'meaning production' – grids of visualisation, vocabularies, norms, and systems of judgement" – through which experience is produced and organized to yield historically specific forms of relating to others and acting on the self:

> These intellectual techniques do not come ready made, but have to be invented, refined, and stabilised, to be disseminated and implanted in different ways in different practices – schools, families, streets, workplaces, courtrooms. If we use the

term "subjectification" to designate all those heterogeneous processes and practices by means of which human beings come to relate to themselves and others as subjects of a certain type, then subjectification has its own history. And the history of subjectification is more practical, more technical, and less unified than sociological accounts allow. (Rose, 1998: 25)

What Rose means by "technical" here emerges more clearly when, a little later, he elaborates on Gaston Bachelard's notion of science as a "phenomenotechnology": that is, a means for acting on the objects it constructs through the instruments in which its theories are materialized. Viewed in this light, he argues, the reality of psychology has to be understood as neither cultural, in the sense of comprising a particular system of meanings, nor as discursive if this is understood as a synonym for representation. Its reality, instead, is technological in the sense that it comprises:

> ... an ensemble of arts and skills entailing the linking of thoughts, affects, forces, artifacts, and techniques that do not simply manufacture and manipulate, but which, more fundamentally, order being, frame it, produce it, make it thinkable as a certain mode of existence that must be addressed in a particular way. (Rose, 1998: 54)

In the tradition of work that Rose represents, then, the make-up of the person emerges as what can perhaps best be described as artifactual: that is, as the contingent outcome of an ad hoc assemblage of particular technical forms and devices. It places the stress on the historical description of these forms and devices and the surfaces of their operation rather than on a general account of the role which language plays in forming identities in the midst of a linguistically patterned tissue of social differences. These differences of emphasis are, in turn, related to different conceptions of the social. For Hall, as we have seen, the social is constituted in and by the cultural representations through which relations of meaning and, as a part of these, differentiated social identities are formed. In Rose's approach, by contrast, the social has no such general characteristics but rather takes the form of a set of relations and conducts that have been problematized in particular ways with a view to being acted on with specific governmental aims in view. It is these relations and conducts – arising out of particular games of truth, the social apparatuses in which these are inscribed and the governmental programs to which they are attached – that constitute the surfaces to which particular forms of expertise are to be applied through the diversity of the technical forms they have devised for acting on and shaping conduct. It is thus that the social may mutate from one historical form to another: from its social welfarist forms in which the provision of social insurance and security stave off the threat to social solidarity arising from a conception of the social as immanently conflict-ridden to the communal structure of the social which, for both Rose and Dean, characterizes contemporary forms of neo-liberal government in the importance they accord programs of cultural management in staving off the social instabilities that might arise from colliding identities.

The advantage of Rose's formulations, then, is that they allow for a greater degree of historical variability in their account of the processes of subjectification and the construction of the social, and of the relations between the two. They also, as I argue later, allow the concepts of the social and society to be usefully distinguished from one another. The implacability of his opposition to accounts of the formation of persons that are couched in terms of the role of culture is, however, somewhat puzzling. For there is no need to theorize culture in the form, as Rose puts it, of an "amorphous domain." It, too, can be approached as consisting of a range of particular forms of expertise arising out of distinctive regimes of truth that assume a range of practical and technical forms through the variety of programs for regulating "the conduct of conduct" that they are, or have been, attached to. The expertise of the literary critic within literature's distinctive regimes of truth;[3] of the art gallery and museum curator; of the community arts worker; of broadcasters and journalists; of censors and media regulators: these are all forms of expertise subjected to particular forms of validation and translated into particular technical forms through their inscription within particular technical apparatuses. It is, moreover, important that the realm of culture should be theorized in this way if questions concerning the relations between culture and governmentality are not to become – as they tend to do in Dean's formulations – a loose and general description for governmental programs which work, through whatever means, to bring about a change in norms, beliefs, and values. For this is simply to call on the existing concept of culture and knit it into the perspective of governmentality without asking what differences that perspective might enjoin for the ways in which the concept of culture and its relations to the social should be approached. Instead, then, we need to ask: How does the concept of culture need to be approached if it is to be effectively integrated into an analytics of government? And what difference does it make to place governmentality between culture, society, and the social?

Culture, Governmentality, Society and the Social

I find myself, faced with the prospect of raising general questions of this kind about the concept of culture, agreeing both with Raymond Williams, when he said he wished he had never heard of the damned word, and with James Clifford when he remarked that, although the concept is a deeply compromised one, we cannot yet do without it.[4] Adam Kuper, in reviewing the recent trials and tribulations of the term, offers a useful reminder of some of the more conspicuous difficulties that have attended its extended anthropological usage (culture as a whole way of life) while also cautioning that it would be unwise to pin too much on the prospect of a more circumspect and exact usage. His own preference, he records, would be to "avoid the hyper-referential word altogether, and to talk more precisely of knowledge, or belief, or art, or technology, or tradition, or even ideology" (Kuper, 1999: xi). While I shall not follow him in this, his discussion does provide a broader setting for considering the currency of the "cultural turn" by tracing the parallels between its recent formulations in cultural studies and the tradition of post-Parsonian US anthropology represented by writers like Clifford Geertz and Marshall Sahlins. For what becomes clear from his account are the respects in which, for all that they purport to overturn deterministic accounts of the relations between culture and society, both traditions are nonetheless committed to a similar kind of theoretical enterprise to the extent that what both aim for remain general accounts of the culture/society relation that will apply to all cultures and all societies.

Victoria Bonnell and Lynn Hunt touch on my point here when they note that, with the "cultural turn," culture and society in effect swapped places with regard to which of these was assigned the role of *explanandum* and which the role of *explanans*. "The social," as they put it, "began to lose its automatic explanatory power" once social categories "were to be imagined not as preceding consciousness or culture or language, but as depending upon them" (Bonnell and Hunt, 1999: 8–9). Of course, this reversal of emphasis is neither a trivial nor an inconsequential matter. However, it matters less, from the point of view of my concerns here, that the "cultural turn" inverts the order of explanatory priority between these two realms, than that what is still at issue is a theoretical procedure – a mode of reasoning – that aims to arrive at some general theoretical intermediation of the relations between culture and society. For, from this perspective, however much they might differ in other respects, all such accounts can be placed on a spectrum according to the relative degree of precedence they accord to culture or society or the ways in which they account for their co-constitutive intermingling.

One of the casualties of debates couched in these terms has been the implicit merging of the concepts of society and the social. The literature on governmentality has registered a distinction between these in accounting for the emergence of the social as a distinctive field of problematic behaviors that are to be defined, managed, and regulated in certain ways and for the parallel emergence of the object of society within sociological discourse as a means of observing and accounting for regularities of conduct in ways that would help render the social governable.[5] Instead, in passing over from *explanans* to *explanandum*, society, in the "cultural turn," usually reappears "on the other side" in a different guise in being equated with a different sense of the social as the socio-semiotic ground on which the relations between social actors (individual and collective) takes place.

How, from the perspective of an analytics of government, can questions concerning the relations between culture and the social be placed on a different footing? Let me advance four arguments which, while far from answering this question satisfactorily, might point out some directions for its further exploration.

The first is to suggest that the problem does not concern the decipherment of any general set of relations between two realms – as if, in the terms of Roger Chartier's formulation, it were a matter of in some way sorting out and reconciling the relations between practices and representations.[6] The issue, rather, concerns the relations between culture and the social within different strategies of rule. This means attending to the ways in which cultural techniques and technologies are expected to act on the social to bring about specific kinds of changes (or stabilities) in conduct where the social is interpreted as a specific constellation of problems – of attitude and behavior – arising out of distinctive strategies of rule.

The second is to suggest that what is at issue here are historically specific relationships in which neither side of the equation is to be regarded as a constant. This is a necessary adjustment to the degree that the concept of governmentality specifies a historically distinctive form of rule whose development is tied up with the emergence of the notion of population as the object and end of government. There can, then, be no question, if the concepts of culture and governmentality are to be aligned with one another, of treating the former as an anthropological constant that has to be so defined as to allow its relationships to the social to be theorized in an invariant and uniform manner across all historical and contemporary societies. What has rather to be attended to are the ways in which there emerges, alongside the emergence of governmental forms of rule, new constellations of relations between what were hitherto diverse practices so as to allow them to be conceived and operationalized as an integrated ensemble brought under the heading of culture as, precisely, a new effective reality. This is to suggest that the analytical task is to account for what we might call "the cultural" developing, alongside the emergence of "the social," as a particular set of instruments – technologies – for acting on the latter with specific ends in view.

Let me offer two asides to amplify what such a perspective might mean.

First aside: we might think of "the cultural" in the terms suggested by Foucault's discussion of the relations between technologies of sign systems, technologies of power, and technologies of the self. It would belong within, as Foucault characterizes them, those "technologies of sign systems, which permit us to use signs, meanings, symbols, or signification" (Foucault, 1988: 18), but it would not be co-extensive with this domain. It would not, that is to say, comprise the totality of such technologies, only those which – from the perspective of an analytics of government – it would be intelligible to group together because of their mode of functioning in relation to, as Foucault defines them, specific "technologies of power, which determine the conduct of individuals and submit them to certain ends or domination, an objectivising of the subject" (Foucault, 1988: 18) and through which their specific mode of relation to the social would be effected. As such, "the cultural" would operate through the mechanisms of (to cite Foucault one more time) "technologies of the self, which permit individuals to effect by their own means or with the help of others a certain number of operations on their own bodies and souls, thoughts, conduct, and way of being, so as to transform themselves in order to attain a certain state of happiness, purity, wisdom, perfection, or immortality" (Foucault, 1988: 18). Again, "the cultural" would be no more co-extensive with the totality of such technologies of the self than it would be with the totality of technologies of sign systems. Rather, for example, than subsuming the psy-complex into such a redefinition of "the cultural," the logic of an analytics of government would require the identification of a "culture complex" operating alongside the psy-complex but by different means, deploying different forms of expertise, translating these into technical forms in different ways, bringing about specific ways of relating to the self whose characteristics relate to the specific kinds of self-management and development that are prompted by specific forms of governmental alignment of the relations between the "culture complex" and the social.

Second aside: a different historical perspective would be required to account for the emergence and development of "the cultural" and the "culture complex" in the sense sketched above. Different, but not entirely new: we already know, from a number of accounts, how the historical emergence of the concept of culture in the third of Williams's three senses ("the independent and abstract noun which describes the works and practices of intellectual and especially artistic activity") (Williams, 1976: 80) was made possible by the re-assembly, in new institutional and discursive spaces, of practices which had hitherto been dissociated from each other and – as something which had also previously been lacking – by their conscription for governmental purposes in the reformatory tasks they were assigned in relation to the newly constructed field of "the social."[7] We also know that it was also over roughly the same period that the second of Williams's three senses of culture ("a particular way of life, whether of a people, a period, or a group") (Williams, 1976: 80) began to emerge, albeit that its full development was to await the twentieth century. It is customary to account for the emergence of this sense of culture as a democratic extension of its earlier restricted definition as, in essence, the elite arts. From the perspective of an analytics of government, however, this development presents itself in a different light: that is, as a result of the incorporation of ways of life within the orbit of government and, thereby, the production of a working interface between culture and the social. Roger Chartier, in considering how to think historically about cultural forms and practices, suggests that it is always necessary to specify the relations between two senses of the term "culture":

> The first designates the works and the acts that, in a given society, concern aesthetic and intellectual judgement; the second aims at the ordinary practices – the ones "with no qualities" – that weave the fabric of daily relations and express the way a community lives and reflects its relations with the world and with the past. (Chartier, 1997: 21)

It is in relation to the first of these two senses of culture that, in the late eighteenth and nineteenth centuries, particular forms of expertise and regimes of truth were constituted and translated – to recall Rose's earlier formulation – into varied "devices of 'meaning production' – grids of visualisation, vocabularies, norms, and systems of judgement" through which culture, in the second sense, was to be acted upon in accordance with varied aims and programs. And it was through the way in which culture in this second sense – the field of everyday conduct and behavior – was conceptualized that culture, in the first sense, was able to be brought into a productive connection with "the social" which, hitherto, it had lacked entirely. But, of course, when looked at in this way, these two different senses of culture and their relations to the social are not locked into unchanging relationships with each other. Rather, given that the ways in which they are aligned in relation to each other depends on how they are inscribed within historically mutable governmental programs, then changes in the latter are likely to re-order the relations between them. It is clear, for example, that the division between the two senses of culture that Chartier posits above has become progressively blurred as the relations between commercially produced forms of mass culture and ways of life have, from a governmental perspective, displaced the significance of aesthetic-ally-grounded nineteenth-century programs of cultural reform.

But I must leave this aside aside! My point is that to place governmentality between culture and the social means that we have to think of the history of relations between them in new terms. But this leads nicely into my third argument, for it is clear that, if we are to do this, it is necessary to subsume the concept of culture within that of discourse rather than, as the move which sustains the "cultural turn," the other way round. For what I have suggested above, in following Rose's specification of the concept of discourse, is a way of treating culture as discourse which, rather than tending to merge the relations between culture and the social by construing the former as constitutive of the latter, retains a distinction between them. It does so by representing culture as a distinctive set of knowledges, expertise, techniques and apparatuses which – through the roles they play as technologies of sign systems connected to technologies of power and working through the mechanisms of technologies of the self – act on, and are aligned in relation to, the social in distinctive ways.

And this brings me to my final argument – or, more accurately, counter-argument – which is to anticipate at least some of the objections that might be raised in relation to the line of reasoning briefly sketched above. For there is, admittedly, something awkward and unwieldy about the vocabulary of govern-mentality which – with all its references to expertise, the technical, apparatuses, and the like – sits ill at ease with the vocabularies of culture as these have been developed within the varied, but intersecting histories, of sociology, literary stud-ies, anthropology, and cultural studies. This often results in shadow debates which arise from translation difficulties more than anything else – as when, for example, post-Foucauldian uses of the notions of expertise and the technical are misaligned with the role that these play in Habermas's account of the relations between system and lifeworld.[8] The question I want to address here, however, is a more directly political one. For doesn't speaking of the relations between culture, government, and the social in the ways I have suggested rule out the prospect of a critical politics by making it impossible to offer any account of resistance and agency?

I have to say: no, I don't think so, not if we take care to remember that, for Foucault, the concept of government is not to be confused with that of the state but refs to the much broader sphere of practices in which claims to particular forms of knowledge and authority are invoked in the context of attempts to direct "the conduct of conduct." And if we remember also to disentangle the questions of resistance and agency. Rose is especially helpful here. For if by resistance, he argues, "one means opposition to a particular regime for the conduct of one's conduct" (Rose, 1998: 35), this requires no general theory of agency of the kind that seeks to locate in individuals or particular social groups inherent capacities to strive for emancipation that "exist prior to and are in conflict with the demands of civilisation and discipline" (35). Why not? Simply because those demands do not have a unified and coherent form emanating from some single organizing center of power. We live our lives, Rose argues, in constant movement across different practices that seek to mold and form us in different ways, and it is the contradictory effects that this generates that give rise to specific forms of agency – not agency in general – as we take issue with, say, an economic system that generates inequalities in the light of those practices (humanistic or religious) which endow us with a sense of the equal worth and dignity of all human beings. Or, as an example more pertinent to my theme, it is surely clear that if the promotion of cultural diversity now stands as one of the most pressing challenges for contemporary cultural policies, this is because of the extent to which the homogenizing strategies of nationalist cultural policies have been questioned by the representatives of both indigenous and diasporic formations – not because of some general capacity for resistance that indigenous and diasporic peoples have and others don't, but because of the different knowledges, traditions, authorities, technologies, and temporal and spatial coordinates that are involved in the production of indigenous and diasporic identities and persona. If we look at the matter in this way, it just might prove possible to escape from those political topographies that Foucault took issue with, but which have proved so resilient, which polarize the political field between the power of government descending from above and that of resistance emerging from below to consider, instead, the more complex intersections between different ways of making up persons and regulating the relations between them which, while unequal in terms of their social weight and influence, operate through mechanisms which are broadly similar.

Notes

1 Yet the Althusserian construction placed on these questions did register a significant advance on earlier Marxist formulations in allowing a greater degree of flexibility and open-endedness regarding the relations that might obtain between economic, social, political, and cultural or ideological practices in any particular moment. The matrix role of determination that was assigned the economy in the context of this structural theory of causation meant that the relative importance attributed to these different forms of practice could be allowed to vary from one set of historical circumstances to another (Althusser and Balibar, 1970). Althusserian formulations also lent a greater degree of

specificity to the argument that cultural and ideological practices were characterized by distinctive properties that were peculiar to them.

2 See, for example, Hall (1986a) and Hall (1996).

3 See, for an earlier discussion of this, chapter 10 of Bennett (1990a).

4 See Kuper (1999), pp. 1 and 212.

5 I draw here on the formulations in Dean (1999) and Rose (1999).

6 See Chartier (1988): my reference here is to both the title of the book and the dominant theoretical refrain that runs through it.

7 The influential essay by R. G. Saisselin (1970) is especially suggestive in this respect. I have briefly discussed its implications elsewhere: see Chapter 5 of Bennett (1998b).

8 This is a significant flaw in Jim McGuigan's assessment of the relations between the literature on governmentality and the Habermasian tradition. See, for a more detailed discussion of this, Bennett (1999).

Chapter Five Acting on the Social: Art, Culture, and Government

One of the most distinctive recent tendencies in sociology has been the influence of the so-called "cultural turn."[1] This has consisted less in the renewed significance that has been accorded the study of culture when compared with, say, industrial sociology or political sociology than in the new place that has been organized for culture in relation to the social. The most obvious casualty of this development has been the marked decline in the influence of earlier Marxist topographical conceptions of the relations between culture and the social.[2] Within these, culture, no matter how much its relative autonomy might be stressed or how much emphasis is placed on the mediated nature of its relationship to the social, is always accorded a relay role in which its action is accounted for as an effect of the social on itself. This is evident in theories of hegemony in which culture appears as an effect of the structure of class relations, but one endowed with a capacity to react back on those relations. When this capacity is looked at more closely, however, the scope for culture's action is usually limited to its role in moderating the ways in which forces and relationships arising out of the organization of the social are able to react back on themselves. This might be to reinforce the relations of class power arising from the social relations of production, or, when the underlying movement of the economy generates moments of crisis, to contribute to the undoing of prevailing relations of class power. Either way, what is not in question in these conceptions is the existence of the social as a realm of conduct and interrelationships that exists independently of culture.

It is in challenging this assumption that the "cultural turn" in sociology has fashioned a new place for culture and a new form of action for it in relation to the social. This consists, in essence, in the importation of culture into the fabric of the social as a consequence of the role that is accorded it in organizing the identities of social agents and the forms of their interaction. The social, as a consequence, is denied any existence independently of the cultural forms in which it is constituted, while the action of culture consists in the role it plays in structuring the discursive ground on which social interaction takes place. There is little doubt that this has been a productive move: its role in disabling earlier hierarchical conceptions in which the action of culture is always secondary and derivative in relation to the social is especially to be welcomed. There is, however, a potential downside to the "cultural turn" which, in some formulations, renders the realms of culture and the social so permeable in relation to one another that it runs the risk of making them virtually indistinguishable.[3] Where this is so, the result is, so to speak, a "culturalization of the social" in which both terms of the equation tend to lose any distinctiveness of character and effect.

The move I want to propose here is therefore one in which, by adding a historical twist to the "cultural turn," culture, far from being imported into the social, is explicitly distinguished from it but in a manner which stresses the historically specific and artifactual character of both. The nineteenth-century emergence of the social as a historically-formed surface, comprising a realm of problematic conducts and interrelationships to which remedial action of varying kinds is to be applied, has been examined in detail in the literature that has followed in the wake of Jacques Donzelot's *The Policing of Families.*[4] Somewhat less attention has been paid to the ways in which, over roughly the same period, hitherto dissociated forms of cultural activity were cohered together as a sphere of activity with an identifiably separate identity as "culture," or to how these were fashioned into a means for acting on the social through the capacity attributed to them of being able to transform ways of life.[5] It is the second aspect of this historical process that I want to explore here. I shall do so by looking at some of the different programs in which art has been enlisted for the purposes of governing over the past hundred and fifty years and at how, in the process, it has been shaped to act on the social in different ways.

The role that was accorded art as a means of curbing drunkenness in the reforming programs of Henry Cole offers an appropriate point of entry into these concerns. In 1867, in the context of the extension of the suffrage to significant sections of the male working classes, Cole urged the need to "get these people who are going to be voters, out of the public-house," saying that he knew no better way of doing so than "to open museums freely to them" (Report, 1867: para. 808, p. 730). In 1875, in an address to the Liverpool Institute, he proposed that museums should "go into competition with the Gin Palaces" (Cole, 1884: 363), reflecting his confidence that the museum would prove an efficient moral reformatory, one amongst many forms of action – cultural and sanitary – that governments needed to take in order to lead the working man away from a life of drunkenness and imprudence. In the closing image of his address, Cole evokes a scene in which – if they were allowed to open on Sundays – museums would help make God's day of rest "elevating and refining to the working man." They would lead him to "wisdom and gentleness," bonding him with his wife and family while also detaching him from the life of "brutality and perdition" that would remain his lot if he were left "to find his recreation in bed first, and in the public-house afterwards" (Cole, 1884: 368).

Cole was by no means alone in entertaining expectations of this kind. They formed a part of the terms in which the benefits to be derived from opening art museums to the public were regularly posed and debated in the second half of the nineteenth century. When the Sheepshank Gallery of the Victoria and Albert Museum was opened in 1858, a contemporary magazine was in no doubt that this would be of immediate benefit to the working-class household:

> The anxious wife will no longer have to visit the different taprooms to drag her poor besotted husband home. She will seek for him at the nearest museum, where she will have to exercise all the persuasion of her affection to tear him away from the rapt contemplation of a Raphael. (cit. Physick, 1982: 35)

There is also a longer history to the advocacy of museums as a possible antidote to vicious and demoralizing entertainments. This was, however, usually as part of a tactics of diversion, in which the museum was to provide the working man with an alternative way of spending his free time, rather than as part of a strategy of reform. The difference I have in mind here is evident in the assessment – quoted above – of the good that the Sheepshank Gallery would do. For what is envisaged here is not merely that the art gallery will supply an alternative form of entertainment to the taproom. Rather, the scene that is conjured for our contemplation is that of a working man who is not only not drinking but who has been so transported to a higher plane of existence that he has lost the desire to do so. This was, for nineteenth-century liberal reformers like Cole, the acid test of art's reforming capacities. As such, it rested on a belief in art's capacity to bring about an inner transformation of a kind whose more general effect would be that of changing the working man into a self-regulating moral agent capable of managing and subduing his passions in developing a commitment to a way of life based on prudential principles of self-restraint.

To us now, of course, it seems improbable if not downright fanciful to expect that art might induce the working man (or anyone else for that matter) to shun the demon drink. My first concern, then, will be to perform an act of historical recovery that will help make the benefits that were sought through creating new public contexts for art's exhibition intelligible rather than a historical curio. My second concern will be with the more lasting effects of this – to my mind – formative moment in the development of a distinctively modern set of relations between art and liberal forms of governance. This consisted in the construction of art as an instrument for acting on the social whose mechanism depended on its ability to effect an inner moral transformation that would give rise to changed forms of behavior. The specifics of this mechanism have long since fallen by the historical wayside as have the conceptions of the social as a problematic set of working-class conducts that are to be regulated – in a gendered logic that will become clear – by enhancing the self-regulatory capacities of the working man. Nonetheless, the view that art can be fashioned as a means of acting on the social remains very much a part of contemporary art and art-museum practice. This is true of what is now the most distinctive nexus of relations between art and liberal forms of government. This consists in the proliferation of programs which construct the social in the form of a set of differentiated communities which, when acted upon by art – seen, now, as a means of community empowerment – are to be rendered self-managing and self-sustaining as collectivities while also functioning as important sites for the identity formation of their individual members. My concern here, then, is with the respects in which the enlistment of art for such purposes comprises a mutation within, rather than a departure from, the relations of art, government, and the social that were developed in the context of the reforming programs of nineteenth-century liberalism.

My third concern will be to identify the implications of these perspectives on the relations between art, government, and the social for the terms in which the history of the modern art museum should be written. The most influential tradition here, in a line which runs from Theodor Adorno (1967) to Douglas Crimp (1993), views the modern art museum as an institution which – in bringing together works of art which originally had their roots in a diversity of social contexts – abstracts art from life, disconnecting it from any effective attachments to, and involvement in, the world. There can be little doubt regarding the productivity of this tradition and the richness of the insights it has generated. It is at best, however, only half the story. For the history of the modern – by which I mean post-Enlightenment – art museum has also been one in which the works of art collected together in the art museum have been reconnected back to the social world in a diversity of ways in the very process of being wrenched from the earlier social contexts in which they had originally been set.

These worldly connections have been comprised by the programs – of artists, curators, education officers, and arts bureaucrats – in which works of art have been deployed with a view to acting on the social by involving a range of agents (the working man, communities) as voluntary participants in their own management and regulation. In this aspect of its practices, moreover, the modern art museum has comprised the very model of the new forms of cultural administration required by liberal forms of government. For, in eschewing the impositional logic of earlier forms of rule based on the principle of *raison d'état*, these have typically relied on means of acting on the social which respect the freedom and autonomy of individuals (or communities), seeking to govern them at a distance, and indirectly, by involving them as active agents in the processes of their own transformation and self-regulation.[6] The construction of art as a means of self-reform has provided government with a means of intervening in the regulation of social life while also keeping its distance from it. I shall suggest, in arguing this point, that such relations of art and government comprise a form of culture's action on the social that can best be understood from the perspective of the historical twist to the "cultural turn" within sociology that I have outlined.

Governing at a Distance: Art and the Working Man

Let's go back to Cole. The concern to find a way of influencing the conduct of the working man in a manner that would respect his autonomy and freedom is clear from the alternatives that he rehearses before alighting on the art museum as an appropriate cultural means for the task of combating male drunkenness. Whereas the poor had previously had access to the fine arts – "the handmaidens of religion and gentle culture" – through churches, abbeys, and cathedrals, Cole warns his Liverpool audience that it is no use looking to religion as a cure for drunkenness as the "millions of this country have ceased to be attracted by our Protestant churches and chapels, and the law cannot compel them to attend" (Cole, 1884: 368). Similarly, the experimental town of Saltaire, where public houses were banned by the simple diktat of its owner, did not offer a generalizable solution to the problem of drunkenness precisely because it depended on the exceptional and arbitrary power of a despotic individual. "But Sir Titus Salt," as Cole puts it, "is a burly despot, as his very name proves, and he makes his people healthy, happy, and godly without drink" (Cole, 1884: 366). That Cole is in search of an inner mechanism that will avoid the need for exterior forms of compulsion is clear when he goes on to say that his aim is "to make every place more attractive than the public-house, and to encourage the feeling of responsibility among all classes that it is a disgrace to get drunk, even in a public-house" (Cole, 1884: 366). The desirability of intervening directly in the working-class home, by-passing the male head of household, is also entertained. Cole clearly believes that the circumstances warrant such intervention even though it would be at odds with the principles of liberal government. At the same time, though, he recognizes that, in fact, it would exceed the scope of action granted the liberal reformer:

> I have little hope for the class of people, forty years of age, that lay on straw drunk. I do not know what can be done with them; but if I were potent enough, I would take from their wages something for their wives and children before they had spent all, though that would be interfering with the liberty of the subject. (Cole, 1884: 365)

The limits that government must not trespass beyond are clear. It may go so far as the working man's front door, but no further; it may provide contexts in which behavior will be changed through the voluntary actions of free and sovereign individuals, but it cannot compel any specific change of conduct. If this much is clear, we shall need to look elsewhere to explain why, for Cole and other liberal reformers, the working *man* was consistently singled out for such special attention. This was attributable, ultimately, to the influence of Malthusianism and the unique focus this brought to bear on the morality of the working man in the new forms for the administration and relief of the poor that were introduced by the 1834 Poor Law Amendment Act.[7] Directly inspired by Malthus's work, this Act aimed to establish a close connection between morality and poverty in tying the provision of material support for the poor to measures that were intended to bring about the moral transformation of the working man. Within the merciless logic of Malthusianism, forms of pauper support which allowed the improvident poor to breed without restraint merely aided the geometric growth of population. The prospect of an accelerating increase in numbers, always outstripping the arithmetic growth of the means of subsistence, transformed eighteenth-century utopian conceptions of progress into the dystopian visions of a society destined for misery, mass starvation, and civil strife that dominated nineteenth-century thought (see Young, 1985).

The only way of avoiding this seemingly inexorable fate that Malthus left open was the possibility that the exercise of prudential restraint in the conduct of conjugal relationships might avoid the threat of overpopulation. This was a demand, however, which, as Mitchell Dean (1991) has shown, bore uniquely on the male head of household. For given an economic theory which still took the household as its basic unit and a legal context in which, with some exceptions, the head of household was male, the male head of household served as the sole point of connection between the household, the market and, beyond that, the unremitting scarcity of nature. Only he, accordingly, was in a position to interpret the effect of nature's scarcity – mediated via the market – and to translate this lesson into a voluntary and self-imposed program of prudential restraint that would rescue the household from a remorseless descent into brute poverty and starvation. This was reinforced, of course, by the legal entitlement to the exercise of their conjugal rights that men still enjoyed.

For a complex conjunction of reasons, then, the morality of the working man was placed on the line in a manner that was not true previously and that has not been paralleled since. The new poor laws sheeted home this responsibility inexorably in denying able-bodied males, their wives and children – whether living with him or not – any forms of poor relief outside the disciplinary alternative of the workhouse. In the midst of these pressures, the morality of the working man was opened up as a new zone of individualized responsibility. Whether or not the specter of overpopulation, and of the vice and misery that would be attendant on it, could be averted was seen to depend on whether or not the working man could develop a capacity for self-restraint in his conjugal relationships. This, in turn, was connected to his ability to develop a capacity for self-regulation in all the other areas of his life. Male drunkenness occupied a special place within this nexus of concerns. It was related to fears of working-class promiscuity as drunkenness decreased the likelihood of a restrained male sexuality. The public nature of drunkenness also meant that it functioned as the most visible sign of the limitations of the working man's moral capacities when compared with what was asked of them. Male drunkenness also posed a threat to the moral economy of the new forms of poor relief through its association with improvidence and with a carelessness for family obligations. Women and children, who were ineligible for any direct forms of public support so long as they were married to an able-bodied male, were entitled to receive such support in their own right on the death of their husbands. Those who drank themselves to death would therefore impose a burden on the public or philanthropic purse even in departing the world. Cole makes the problem graphically clear:

> Now, if you want to see sights in Liverpool that reduce men to the nature of aborigines, you will see people that are allowed to get as drunk as they can, starve their wives and children, looking to others in the end to find coffins for themselves and feed them in the workhouse beforehand. (Cole, 1884: 364)

It was because Malthusianism and the new systems for administering the poor to which it gave rise made the inner life of the working man an object of attention in new ways that art and culture came to occupy an important role in the newly-emerging strategies of liberal government. "The evil attendant upon the principle of population," Mitchell Dean argues in summarizing the cultural logic of Malthusianism, "is thus the force which promotes civilising conduct and institutions" (Dean, 1991: 89). Of course, the ways of life of the laboring classes had been an object of concern in association with earlier forms of poor relief administration. The ale-house, in eighteenth-century debates, was seen as a threat to the requirements of a productive economy and there was no shortage of proposals for legislative mechanisms and forms of surveillance that would rescue the laborer from the ale-house and save his unwasted body, spared the ravages of alcohol, for a life of productive industry. There was also – and this is a part of Cole's argument too – a ready appreciation of the need to provide alternative and attractive forms of popular entertainment to help lure the working man away from the temptations of drink. However, this was a tactics of diversion which lacked a strategy of reform that either sought to effect or relied on an inner mechanism of moral restraint. Just as important, it provided no opportunity for practicing a capacity for ethical self-regulation that would be of more general use. Yet, as we have seen, the concern to encourage thrift and self-reliance while leaving improvidence unrewarded that characterized the post-1834 system of poor relief placed considerable stress on the cultivation of just such a capacity. If, then, in the liberal programs of cultural reform which, in the mid-century period, are most conspicuously symbolized by the development of the South Kensington museum complex, the accent is placed on art's role in helping to form a working man who will not *want* to drink, this is because it was also important to help cultivate those capacities that would make the working man *want* to save, *want* to practice sexual restraint, and *want* to work.

If Malthusianism supplied the need, Romantic aesthetics promoted the belief that the work of art might serve as a means of meeting that need. Yet Cole's relationship to Romanticism was a complex one. On the one hand, his conception of the South Kensington Museum as the center of a national system of schools of art and design that would help improve the standards of British design and manufacturing constituted an instance of the very kinds of "practicalization" and commercialization of art that Romanticism pitted itself against. Ruskin, for example, thought that Cole "corrupted the system of art-teaching all over England into a state of abortion and falsehood from which it will take twenty years to recover" (cit. Alexander, 1983: 152). Cole was also at odds with many of his contemporaries in stating that any art, not necessarily of the highest quality, would assist the purposes of reform so long as it started the working man off on a course of aesthetic and, thereby, moral self-cultivation.[8] On the other hand, his belief that exposure to art might help the working man to acquire powers of self-inspection and self-regulation depended on the ways in which Romanticism had fashioned a space within the artistic text in which the subject could be inserted and initiate a program of self-improvement in contemplating the distance between the ideal forms of perfection embodied in the art work and the imperfections and inadequacies of the empirical self. For it was in the perception of this gulf that the individual might be prompted to commence a program of self-cultivation designed to bridge the gap between the two.[9]

It is in thus opening up a moral surface within the individual as the interface through which art acts on the social that the distinctive accomplishment of Cole's rich and complex mixture of liberalism, Malthusianism, utilitarianism and Romanticism consisted. For the view that art might serve as a "moral technology" (Levin, 1982: 54) was a central perception of the Enlightenment and one that was put into effect in the aftermath of the French Revolution by the use of art in festivals (see Ozouf, 1988) and museums (see McClellan, 1994) as a means of cultivating civic virtue. The mechanisms at work here, however, were mainly emulative as the citizen was invited to model his conduct on the exemplars of national and civic virtue that the art museum, in its republican conception, was to make visible and commemorate. What the mid-nineteenth-century mix I have been concerned with added to this was a mode of relation between the individual and the work of art which made it possible for the latter to act on ways of life, thereby vastly expanding the orbit of its possible activity.

Communalizing the Social

This concern to use cultural resources as a means of acting on the social was not restricted to the aesthetic sphere. The second half of the nineteenth century witnessed a profusion of schemes for, in one way or another, enrolling the newly-enfranchised citizens of western democracies as active participants in the task of managing themselves by bringing them into contact with the lessons of nature (whether those of a benign and harmonious Paleyism or those of a Darwinian nature, red in tooth and claw) or the lessons of evolution (whether inscribed in the history of the rocks, the development of species, or the progress of human societies from the "primitive" to the complex). A significant, although by no means the only, site for these endeavors was that comprised by the new collecting institutions – museums of natural history, geology, and ethnology – that were developed in this period. These, together with public art museums, constituted a highly distinctive set of contexts in which a new class of experts (specialist curators in anthropology, natural history, and art history) contrived to manage a range of cultural resources (paintings, sculptures, bones, costumes, stuffed species, tools, rocks, minerals) in such a way as to enable them, when exhibited publicly, to function as the props and occasions for various forms of civic or moral self-management.

It would be wrong to attribute any unity of design or purpose to these. The reforming schemes of this new class of scientific showmen varied according to the particular positions they took up within the scientific controversies of the period (Darwinists versus Owenites, liberal Darwinists versus eugenicists) as well as the configuration of the field of the social in different national contexts. The migrant child was an obsessive object of attention in the United States in ways that had no ready parallels in Britain whereas, in Australia, fears centered on the Australian-born or larrikin child. That said, these reforming programs had in common a conception of the social as a field of conducts defined principally in class terms. In being put to work to act on the social, art and culture were envisaged as means for bringing about changes in working-class ways of life in order to avert whatever catastrophe otherwise threatened: the Malthusian nightmare of overpopulation if the working man carried on drinking to excess; revolution if the political implications of Darwin's message of evolutionary gradualism were not heeded; degeneration if the unfit continued to outbreed the fit. It is also true that in most cases these programs aimed to achieve their effects through the mechanism of the individual, acting on the social indirectly through changes in ways of life that were to be brought about as a result of individuals having learned to act on themselves, and to regulate their own conduct, in new ways.[10]

The legacy of the ways in which nineteenth-century liberalism brought art (and, indeed, culture more generally), government, and the social into new forms of contact with one another is still a part of the horizon in which cultural resources are managed. The belief that ways of life can be acted on through the governmental deployment of artistic and cultural resources still informs the practices of both public and private cultural institutions as well as the policy agendas of governments. The most obvious difference, however, is that it is no longer the classed individual that is targeted as the primary surface to which the actions of art and culture are to be applied. Rather, art's object, the surface on which it is to act, is now more typically that of community as it is increasingly assigned the task of empowering communities. This involves the use of artistic resources as a means of building strong, self-reliant communities that are capable of managing themselves and of producing a strong, but not exclusive, sense of identity and belonging for their members while also contributing to the resolution of social problems at the community level. The Artskills project at Merseyside provides a convenient example. In offering a training in arts skills, it aims to bring disaffected young people back into the mainstream through the route of community involvement while also using arts training as – in the words of its coordinator, Fiona Cameron – a means of "raising young people's awareness of the different ways they can help themselves in every aspect of their lives" (cit. Hilpern, 1998: 8).

This change of focus had its first dress-rehearsal in the Community Art Centre program of the New Deal whose initiatives were often resurrected, albeit in different form, in the post-war cultural policy initiatives of the US, Britain and Australia (Gibson, 1997). The formative role of these initiatives is also acknowledged in the title of the Blair government's New Deal for Communities program. The Community Art Centre program was, however, very much a transitional form in promoting the cultures and values of specific communities – sometimes identified in regional terms, and sometimes in racial terms – as the route through which to rebuild what was seen as a fragmented community at the national level. Its purpose was to reconstitute American society as the sum of a set of non-antagonistic differences in which identification with the national whole was routed through its, ideally, harmoniously constituent communities (see Harris, 1995). The purposes for which, today, art, culture and community are most distinctively brought together are different. For the focus is now typically on the organization of self-regulating and self-managing communities which are, in some respects, disconnected from the larger wholes of nationally defined societies or, in the case of diasporic communities, cut across them.

This is not, however, a development restricted to the cultural sphere. The project of "governing through community" is, in the assessment of Nikolas Rose, part of a significant mutation in the forms and methods of liberal governance. There are two issues here. The first concerns the relationships of government, individuals, and communities. These have been significantly transformed in the respect that it is now no longer the freedom and autonomy of individuals as such that is to be respected, but the freedom and autonomy of individuals only insofar as they are members of communities. The second issue concerns the relationships between community and nation. These, too, have been transformed to the extent that the primary surface on which government is called on to act is no longer that of a nationally unified society but the differentiated and often deterritorialized field of communities. Rose's concern here is to chart the effects of the criticisms of earlier forms of liberal government that have been mounted, since the 1960s, by civil rights activists, libertarians, and new social movements in the context of the emergence of new forms of identity politics and empowerment. These criticisms questioned earlier understandings of the role of the subjects of government as "a relation of obligation between citizen and society enacted and regulated through the mediating party of the State" (Rose, 1996: 330). Emphasizing instead the need to involve individuals more actively in their own governance, they substituted "a relation of allegiance and responsibility to those one cared about the most and to whom one's destiny was linked...one's family, one's neighbourhood, one's community, one's workplace" (Rose, 1996: 331) for the formal bonds of civic obligation. In their critique of earlier identification projects centered on organizing an unmediated relationship involving "the socially identified citizen" as "a member of a single integrated national society," these critical movements, Rose suggests, have resulted in a new conception of the forms of identification into which individuals should be enlisted:

> The subject is addressed as a moral individual with bonds of obligation and responsibilities for conduct that are assembled in a new way – the individual in his or her community is both self-responsible and subject to certain emotional bonds of affinity to a circumscribed "network" of other individuals – unified by family ties, by locality, by moral commitment to environmental protection or animal welfare. Conduct is retrieved from a social order of determination into a new ethical perception of the individualised and autonomised actor, each of whom has a unique, localised and specific tie to their particular family and to a particular moral community. (Rose, 1996: 334)

Much of this is familiar ground. Rather more important for my concerns here is the spin Rose puts on these observations when he goes on to suggest that these communitarian and libertarian arguments should be seen as parts of a process through which the norms, forms, and strategies of liberal government – far from having been abandoned – have been reconfigured:

> ...community is now something to be programmed by Community Development Programmes, developed by Community Development Officers, policed by Community Police, guarded by Community Safety Programmes and rendered knowable by sociologists pursuing "community studies." Communities became zones to be investigated, mapped, classified, documented, interpreted, their vectors explained to enlightened professionals-to-be in countless college courses and to be taken into account in numberless encounters between professionals and their clients, whose individual conduct is now to be made intelligible in terms of the beliefs and values of "their community." (Rose, 1996: 332)

This is a veritable swarming of new forms of expertise based on new objects of knowledge and connected to strategies of governing which work, essentially, by organizing communities as points of emotional investment and identification in order that they might become self-governing as collectivities and capable of managing the activities of their members. This embodies a redistribution of responsibilities from the centralized mechanisms of the state and their dispersal across and through the overlapping networks of community. This is so whether these are defined as territorial communities grounded in a particular place, as diasporic communities comprised in networks which span national boundaries and encompass territorially displaced populations, or as virtual communities based on a shared lifestyle or common political interests: the gay and lesbian communities, for example. At the same time that it is central to this new conception of governing, however, community has constantly to be rescued from its imminent disappearance or, since the perceived need for community often precedes its existence, to be organized into being:

> Each assertion of community refers itself to something that already exists and has a claim on us: our common fate as gay men, as women of colour, as people with AIDS, as members of an ethnic group, as residents in a village or a suburb, as people with a disability. Yet our allegiance to each of these particular communities is something

that we have to be made aware of, requiring the work of educators, campaigns, activists, manipulators of symbols, narratives and identifications. (Rose, 1996: 334)

Here, then, is a broader context in which to place the various forms in which art and community have been brought together over the last quarter of a century or so: in community arts, community cultural development, cultural diversity, and cultural maintenance programs; in community museums or ecomuseums or in the community galleries of larger museums.[11] These new spaces and forms in which art has been made active have also, of course, been accompanied by new forms of knowledge and expertise. These typically focus on organizing and managing community-based processes of dialog and consultation. The forms of expertise associated with community arts and development officers are the most obvious case in point. But so, too, are curators being increasingly called on to act as cross-cultural mediators managing – in the terms proposed by James Clifford (1997) – the "contact zones" between "settlers" and indigenous communities or, in different contexts, other cross-cultural boundaries. No single unifying purpose underlies these new relations of art, government, and the social: the objectives to be achieved may range from the empowerment of specific communities through the promotion of cross-cultural dialog between differentiated communities to the role of art in ensuring the cultural survival of particular communities. Nor is there a single politics in play here. Rather, the political values invested in community may range from those of radical identity politics through social-welfare constructions of community to the understanding of community as a force for moral and religious reformation which characterizes conservative forms of neo-liberalism. The community renewal strategies of the "Third Way" in which culture is to play its role in reviving lost forms of civility provides yet another variant of the community theme (see Giddens, 1998: 87). Whichever the case, though, what is at issue is the role that artistic and cultural resources are able to play through the manner in which they are organized to act upon the social by organizing, maintaining, and developing community-based ways of life. That this is not Henry Cole's world is clear. It is equally clear, though, that the contemporary articulation of the relations between art, government, and community is an adaptation of, rather than a total departure from, the coordinates for deploying works of art as instruments within a liberal program of governance that Cole and his generation established.

Art, Museums, and Walls

How we might most usefully view the modern art museum in the light of the perspectives outlined above will depend, ultimately, on how we see the relationships between art, museums, and walls. The critique of the museum which sees it as responsible for disconnecting art from the world interprets the museum's walls as essentially enclosing in their function, separating art off from the museum's outsides in order that it might become an object of cultic veneration. This tradition, as I have already suggested, is not without point, especially when viewed in the light of the tendency – undeniably still with us – for art museums to function as socially exclusive institutions in which their *habitués* accumulate marks of distinction by virtue of the social distance which participation in the art museum establishes for those whom it includes from those whom it excludes. Even so, this is not the truth and nothing but the truth so far as the history of the modern art museum is concerned. This rather consists in the pull between this tendency, in which the museum's walls function as an impermeable divide, and the counter-vailing tendency in which the museum's walls are viewed as surfaces on which to so arrange art that its effects – however they might be construed – will be carried back out into the world and be enabled to act upon it.

This tension may be present in many ways. It may exist within the space of a single institution in the tugs-of-war which often characterize the relationships between specialist curators and education departments. It may take the form of a different set of priorities between, on the one hand, major metropolitan museums and, on the other, regional galleries and their relations to community arts projects. It may also, in some contexts, take the form of a tension between the professional staff of art museums and the representatives of the local elites which often dominate their boards of trustees. The complex and contradictory nature of these institutions – when looked at not just singly but as parts of a network – comes to light, however, only when we keep both aspects in view.

But there's another point at issue here too. For if it is important to restore to the art museum that aspect of its history in which it has, so to speak, constantly striven to breach its own walls – to devise a means for art to connect with the world outside in order that it might be effective in and on the world – this is because this tendency always dethrones art, always embroils it in a muddy and tangled set of realities, in a manner that disavows the special status that is required for it to function as the marker of a privileged zone of social exclusivity. When Henry Cole, in his address to the Liverpool Institute, discussed the reformatory role he envisaged for art museums, he did so alongside a discussion of many other things – efficient sewerage systems and supplies of clean water – which might have con-tributed to the same end of combating male drunkenness. This was a general characteristic of the speeches and writings of liberal reformers: at the same time that the reforming capacity derived from art's Romantic idealization was extolled, art was also brought down to, and discussed on a par with, a whole series of practical remedies tending to the same end. The enlistment of art in the service of community has the same effect: it "practicalizes" art, placing it on the same footing as a whole series of other initiatives (community development programs, AIDS awareness programs, the promotion of cultural diversity, the maintenance of indigenous communities) with similar characteristics.

These, I think, are the debates that matter: that is, how, through the contexts of its deployment, art can be brought into contact with the social in order to have good and useful effects. How these are to be defined, though, is, of course, a matter for political struggle and contestation – struggles which, today, revolve in good part around the meaning that is to be given to the politics of community in both civil life and public policy. For, if, in its relationships to identity politics, to community empowerment, to cultural diversity, and to social and political movements, art is connected to community through its "good" side, we can also see how, in the new right's attempts to reconstitute an authoritarian moral or virtuous community, art can be attached to community through its "bad" side. In these respects, the cultural wars of our times are very much about the ways in which cultural resources are to be deployed and managed – how they are to be socially harnessed – in the context of these, and other, competing versions of community. These struggles will be more effectively engaged in, however, when it is acknowledged that the art museum has not been solely a place of art's seclusion "where art was made to appear autonomous, alienated, something apart, referring only to its own internal history and dynamics" (Crimp, 1993: 13). There needs also to be an active recognition of, and engagement with, the ways in which the art museum has, at various times in a range of contexts, been tied – discursively and institutionally – to a variety of governmental programs aimed at bringing about changes in ways of life.

It is equally clear, though, that a cultural politics of this kind requires that the action of art and culture, and the nature of their relationships to the social, should be reviewed along the lines proposed at the beginning of this chapter. From the perspective of Adorno or Crimp, the work of art is disabled if it is detached from the social and historical conditions in which it originated or if it does not remain connected to them by an effective continuity of tradition. When deprived of these anchoring points, it is unable to connect with and act on the social except in ways that are axiomatically negative. From the perspective of the "cultural turn" in sociology, the work of art is compressed into the social as one amongst many signifying practices helping to constitute the identities of social actors and the discursive ground of their interactions. When the "cultural turn" is given a historical twist along the lines I have suggested, however, works of art emerge as being successively connected to the social in different ways. Their relation to the social does not have a general theoretical character but depends on different discursive and institutionalized forms of culture's action on the social within which they come to be inscribed and through which their historically varying forms of effect are organized. Culture, rather than being superimposed on the social as a relation of meaning in a general manner which reflects, ultimately, the influence of linguistics, has rather to be thought of as standing off from the social in a manner which allows us to see the historically variable ways in which it is then connected to it in different strategies of governing.

Notes

1   This is a general tendency evident, *inter alia*, in the work of Stuart Hall (1997), the project of the journal *Theory, Culture and Society*, and, more recently, the work of Fredric Jameson (1998).

2   I draw here and in other parts of this opening discussion on an earlier engagement with related issues: see Bennett (1997c).

3   Hall recognizes the difficulties here clearly enough when he notes the danger that the "cultural turn" can become a new form of cultural idealism in which the sense of any distinction between what is, and what is not, culture is lost. See Hall (1997: 225). However, Hall's response to these difficulties is different from the one I want to pursue here.

4   The literature here is now abundant. However, the editorial programme of *Ideology & Consciousness* was perhaps the most influential early route through which these ideas connected with English-speaking debates, although the role of *Economy and Society* in this regard has proved more enduring.

5   See, however, Brewer (1997) for a suggestive account of the respects in which earlier courtly practices of culture were reassembled, alongside emerging forms of commercial culture, in new relations of use and effect in the course of the eighteenth century. Brewer suggests that it was as a consequence of these developments that culture, as a distinctive and separate sphere, first became recognizable as such. Therborn's account of the relations between Marxism and sociology (Therborn, 1976) and the role accorded cultural and moral factors within the latter as a means of acting on the social is also instructive as an example of the late-nineteenth-century tendency to harness the cultural sphere to governmental tasks. Therborn's discussion is also a useful reminder that aspects of the 'cultural turn' in sociology embody a return (but in different theoretical and political form) to the stress on the role of culture that characterized the classical period of sociology. Hall also makes this point: see Hall (1997: 224).

6   My arguments here are derived from Foucault's comments on liberal government and the now extensive literature that has developed in their wake. For two central sources of reference, see Burchell, Gordon and Miller (eds.) (1991) and Barry, Osborne and Rose (eds.) (1996).

7   I draw here on a discussion of these matters in an earlier essay. See Bennett (1995c), republished in Bennett (1998b).

8   See, for example, Cole's testimony to the 1867 Select Parliamentary Committee Report on the Paris Exhibition. I have discussed this aspect of Cole's position elsewhere: see Bennett (1992b).

9   The apparent contradiction between Romantic constructions of art and the use of art as an instrument of government is, I would argue, akin to that which Bourdieu notes in suggesting that it was the organization of an aura for art that established the conditions for its commercial circulation (see Bourdieu, 1993a: 113–14). In both cases, aesthetic conceptions which seem to provide for art's distancing from the world in fact provide the necessary conditions for specific forms of its worldly deployment.

10 The major exception was that comprised by eugenic programs which often proposed direct forms of intervention directed at specific social groups that were defined, usually, in racial terms.

11 For examples of different forms of art/community relationship, see Nancy Fuller (1992) for an account of the use of art in an ecomuseum community empowerment program, and Gay Hawkins (1993) for an account of the community arts programs of the Australia Council. I have also addressed these issues elsewhere: see Bennett (1997f).

Part III   Museums as Civic Machineries

Chapter Six   Archaeological Autopsy:
Objectifying Time and Cultural Governance

The current state of relations between the concepts of culture and governmentality is largely unsatisfactory. I say this, first, because it is clear that the conceptual inheritance that is put into play whenever the concept of culture is invoked needs to be carefully sifted if the concerns of earlier approaches to cultural governance are to be reframed in ways that are compatible with the perspective of governmentality, and, second, because it is equally clear that this has not yet happened. The question is not one that concerned Foucault, and while governmentality theorists such as Mitchell Dean and Nikolas Rose constantly stress the importance of culture within the new forms of self-rule associated with contemporary forms of neo-liberalism, their accounts depend on off-the-peg sociological versions of culture as a set of norms, beliefs, and values which sit ill at ease in their new theoretical surroundings.[1] There is, as a result, little attempt to work through how the perspective of governmentality and the assumptions on which it rests – its understanding of the relations between the activity of government and the organization of the social, for example – might enjoin the need for rethinking the concept of culture and the role that it has played in social thought. This means that there is, in turn, little sense of the distinctive place which an appropriately refashioned account of culture might play within the concerns of governmentality theory more generally.

I have argued elsewhere (Bennett, 2002b) that progress on these questions requires that at least two conditions be met. The first is that the analytical issues that are posed in relation to the concept of culture should be disconnected from the endeavor – which has characterized much of cultural studies and a good deal of sociology – to provide a general account of the relations between two separate realms: culture and society. It does not matter how these relations are finally construed: as ones of the determination of culture by society, as ones of the reciprocal intermediation of culture and the social, or – and we find this in some formulations of the "cultural turn" – as ones in which social relations are constituted in the relationships between

103

the identities produced by cultural or discursive practices. It is, I believe, the very enterprise itself that is mistaken and, from the point of view of the concerns of governmentality theory, unproductive in detracting from the respects in which the social – when understood as the result of specific governmental problematizations of conduct – can have no general form of the kind that such sociological accounts require as a condition of their intelligibility. The second condition is that, as a response to this difficulty, what is meant by culture within the perspective of govern-mentality needs to be more circumscribed, limited to the operations of those institutions comprising the "culture complex" within which particular kinds of knowledge and expertise translate and organize cultural resources into ways of acting on the social – in the sense that I have given above – with a view to bringing about particular changes, or stabilities, of conduct. Art galleries, libraries, museums, and heritage sites are examples of what I have in mind here. These are all similar in bringing specific forms of knowledge to bear on the classification, arrangement, exhibition, and distribution of cultural resources and materials arising from other practices.[2]

But there is a third condition, too: that of being able to account for the ways in which the distinctive forms of knowledge and expertise that characterize the "culture complex" translate the resources with which they work into technical forms that make particular governmental programs practical and operable. Eschewing the logic that culture works by some general mechanism (of ideology, representation, or hegemony) means that attention must be paid to the varying ways in which different kinds of cultural knowledge are translated into the varying technical forms through which new realities are produced and sustained, and brought to bear on the regulation of conduct. Yet it is here that the Foucauldian legacy is limited. It has long been clear within science studies that Foucault was better at theorizing the outcomes of particular *savoires* than he was at accounting for how these were translated into particular technical forms in particular institutional settings in and through the working practices of scientists.[3] The contributions of actor-network-theory to these concerns have, on the whole, been more influential. It is, then, to actor-network-theory that I shall look, in what follows, for both theoretical and methodological guidance in seeking to identify how particular cultural knowledges are translated into particular technical forms in the context of specific programs of government. I do so by examining the role played by what Alain Schnapp calls "archaeological 'autopsy' " (Schnapp, 1996: 181) – that is, techniques for reading material artifacts as evidence of prehistory – within the governmental programs of late nineteenth-century museums of ethnology and natural history.

The Ancients and Moderns Revisited

Suzanne Marchand provides a useful point of entry into these questions in suggesting that it is to the changing practices of nineteenth-century museums that we should look for the final chapter in the debate between the ancients and moderns. The context she has in mind is Germany where, initially in local museums and then later, toward the end of the century, in the major national collections, museums served as the incubators for new forms of knowledge that were to prove crucial in the eventual victory of an anthropological view of culture over an older, more aristocratic view. Marchand characterizes these new knowledges (her list is historical geography, ethnology, art history, folklore studies, prehistory, archaeology, and paleontology) as "the ethnological sciences" on the grounds that they "all aspired, in one way or another, to convert material evidence into historical narratives, and usually expended their energies on the study of more or less exotic societies and eras with little in the way of written records" (Marchand, 2000: 181). Her contention, in brief, is that the increasing prominence of the artifact-based ethnological sciences contributed to a relative decline in the cultural authority of the text-based humanities. Acting like a Trojan horse, these sciences undermined the principles of classification that had underlain museums centered on the classics owing to the stress that they placed on the typical – that is, on traits shared by large numbers of artifacts – over the beautiful, or the uniquely distinguishing qualities of singular aesthetic objects. As a consequence, the older notion of culture as "acquired refinements" gave way before the ascending influence of the anthropological view of "culture as a complex of traits and styles" (Marchand, 2000: 181).

Broadly similar processes were at work in British museums over the same period. Here, too, the closing decades of the nineteenth-century witnessed a flurry of new museums – most of them provincial or local – focused on geology, prehistoric archaeology or ethnology. And here, too, there were signs, by the end of the century, that the major national institutions – the British Museum, for example – were, however grudgingly, re-arranging aspects of their collections to accord more significance to the typological principles of display that had been developed in the fields of prehistoric archaeology and ethnology.[4] But it is also clear that, in Britain, this chapter in the struggle between the ancients and the moderns did not solely concern a change in the relative influence of two different understandings of culture. For this has itself to be seen as part of a contest between two different programs of cultural governance reflecting fundamentally different conceptions of the kinds of cultural resources that would prove most relevant in the context of the newly-developing forms of mass public instruction that characterized the period, and of the ways in which those resources might best be deployed to foster new forms of self-governance.

However, it will be necessary, in developing this argument, to qualify Marchand's thesis to take account of two respects in which the configurations of the intellectual field in Britain at this time differed from those in Germany. The first has to do with the distinctive, albeit short-lived, fusion of concerns and methods that characterized the relations between the sciences Marchand describes as ethnological and developments in natural history in the post-Darwinian development of evolutionary theory.[5] This means that, at the very least, developments relating to natural history museums have to form a part of the picture in view of the very close associations – in personnel, intellectual orientations, and political dispositions – that existed between these and museums based on ethnological, paleontological or prehistoric archaeological collections. The second qualification is more substantial. It concerns the adequacy of the label "ethnological" as a way of describing the distinctive concerns and orientations of this group of sciences. For this occludes the respects in which natural history, geology, paleontology, ethnology and prehistoric archaeology saw themselves not just as object-based rather than text-based sciences but also as practicing a distinctive kind of historical reasoning in view of their shared concern to reconstruct pasts (whether of the history of the earth, of life on earth, or of primitive civilizations) stretching back beyond the reach of written records.[6]

The nub of the matter at issue here concerns the relations between this group of sciences and the eighteenth-century paradigm of conjectural history. So called because it relied on retrospective speculation rather than experience or eye-witness accounts, conjectural history (a term coined by Dugald Stewart in 1790) was essentially concerned, in Mary Poovey's formulation, with "how 'rude' societies became 'civilised' " (Poovey, 1998: 215). This was a project which necessarily relied on conjecture given that, as Poovey again puts it, "one could not see, or read accounts of anyone who had seen, the transition from hunter-gatherer to agricultural society" (Poovey, 1998: 221). At odds with the forms of authority that had been constructed for the experimental sciences with their reliance on verification by authoritative witnesses,[7] conjectural history fell out of favor in the early nineteenth century. It was, however, revived in the latter part of the century, mainly, as Russell McGregor notes, owing to the influence of evolutionary theory (McGregor, 1998: 21). This was, however, not simply a revival. The conjectural paradigm, in its late nineteenth-century form, operated in a much broader intellectual context as a set of procedures that were applied across the human and natural sciences to account not merely for the transition from rude to civilized societies but also for the history of the earth and of life on earth.[8] One consequence of this was that questions concerning the origins of society were relocated by being placed in the contexts of these longer histories. The conjectural paradigm was also able to claim a new authority that was closer, in some respects, to that which had earlier been claimed for the experimental sciences. For when viewed in the light of the equation of distance from Europe with the prehistoric past that characterized evolutionary thought, the rock formations, flora and fauna, and human inhabitants of colonized territories – and their cultures – seemed to embody the possibility that the pre-recorded past might be reconstructed not just conjecturally but with the added credibility of eye-witness accounts of its continuing presence within the present.

It is, however, not just for the sake of contextual accuracy that I think it preferable to describe this group of knowledges, in their British formation, as "the historical sciences". An appreciation of their distinctive mode of historical reasoning is also crucial for understanding their role in organizing a new logic of culture and governance. For this depended on replacing the splittings of the self associated with aesthetic culture and the kinds of work on the self that these encouraged with a historical splitting of the self into its archaic and modern components and the new kinds of developmental work on the self that this division made possible. There are, however, a couple of intermediate stages in the argument that need to be filled in before this contention can be sustained. I turn first to the ways in which the historical sciences organized a new network of relations between human and non-human actors in the process of making the prehistoric past.

Making Prehistory

In his discussion of Louis Pasteur's memoir on lactic acid fermentation, Bruno Latour is keen to distance his account of how science produces new objects from the relativist implications of those accounts of social construction which imply that fabricated entities are in some way artificial, not "really real". This is true, for example, of those versions of the "cultural turn" which view society or the social as being constructed by and through the linguistically derived relations of meaning which necessarily imbue all forms of social relation and interaction. For, in such formulations, the autonomy of society or the social is reduced to the degree that, the more culturally constructed it is, the more it seems to be indistinguishable from the cultural representations within and by which it is constructed. Latour seeks to distinguish his concerns from accounts of this kind by comparing the process through which Pasteur fabricates lactic acid fermentation – making it visible and articulable with other human and non-human actors – to that of "*designing an actor*" (Latour, 1999a: 122). In doing so, he contends that, with each test that Pasteur sets it, the strength of lactic acid fermentation as an actor is enhanced. This leads him to the general conclusion that the autonomy of the entities produced by science and their force as actors increases in proportion to the work that goes into their fabrication.

How might similar perspectives be applied to the concerns of the historical sciences and their relations to the prehistoric past that was shaped into being through their labors? It is here, I think, that Alain Schnapp's notion of "archaeological 'autopsy' " is suggestive. For it calls attention to the respects in which the reality and autonomy of prehistory and its constituent actors were increased in proportion to the degree of success with which new archaeological modes of reading challenged literary-based methods of historical interpretation. Relying more on sight and touch than on the principles of philological analysis, the methods of "archaeological 'autopsy' " comprised a series of moves through which the signs comprised by visible marks on the buried remains of earlier civilizations were read as material evidence for pasts beyond writing. Although seventeenth-century antiquarians had developed a rhetoric in praise of the primacy of the object, seeing in coins and inscriptions on archaeological finds more enduring, less corruptible, and more direct forms of evidence than literary ones, it was not until the early eighteenth century that the rudiments of a systematic method for reading the past on the basis of the physical qualities of its artifactual remains were developed. These comprised early versions of what would later be called the typological or comparative method which allowed objects to be assigned to particular territorial cultures on the basis of common design traits while also providing for their arrangement in historical sequences – from the simple to the complex – through the development of techniques designed to detect the progress of design traits through time.

The work of Christian Jürgensen Thomsen was especially important here. By using techniques for relative dating (seriation) that were specific to archaeological material and interpreting similar technologies as evidence of societies exhibiting comparable levels of cultural development, Thomsen's work resulted in the "creation of a controlled chronology that did not rely on written records" (Trigger, 1989: 73). His three-age system (the stone, iron, and bronze ages) translated this into a mechanism for classifying, managing, and exhibiting artifacts. The contribution, in France, of Boucher de Perthes was to provide, in 1847, a means of integrating the sequential ordering of human technologies with the techniques of stratigraphical analysis developed in the sphere of paleontology, thereby connecting human time with geological time and the time of natural history. This proved important in the establishment of human antiquity – finally achieved through the discovery of human remains at Brixham Cave a little more than a decade later – in providing a common chronology for flora, fauna, and human artifacts which, by equating depth with age, overcame the objections that had earlier prevented human remains found in the same strata as extinct species from serving as proofs of human antiquity.[9]

Schnapp indicates how, once human prehistory had been fabricated in these ways, the principles of "archaeological 'autopsy' " which had made this possible continued to be developed, in the second half of the nineteenth century, in a manner which related these developments in archaeology to collateral developments in other historical sciences:

> The scholars of the second half of the nineteenth century were staggered by the discovery of the great antiquity of man. Attracted by the progress made in the natural sciences, they wished to lay the foundations of a scientific archaeology free from the burden of antiquarian traditions. Typology freed archaeology from the tutelage of text; technology liberated it from the nature/culture dilemma; and stratigraphy from the local/universal paradox. Typology places the object in an identifiable time-frame and renders it useful as historical evidence. Attention to technological features, by establishing the "natural" and "cultural" components of each product, allows each object to be assigned its particular function. Stratigraphy adds another dimension: the object was buried by the action of depositional phenomena at the same time local and universal. Every object and every monument is destined to find its place in a general process of stratification which is linked to the history of the planet. (Schnapp, 1996: 321)

This, then, is an abbreviated account of the processes through which – like Pasteur's lactic acid fermentation – new entities were fabricated through the procedures of the historical sciences. These gave rise to a whole series of new relationships between humans (primitives, moderns, ancestors rather than ancients) and non-humans (fossils, relics, missing links) which, through what Latour calls the mechanism of delegation, made it possible for the actions, long past, of dead actors to become active in the present. And this, in turn, made it possible for institutions in the present to "mobilise forces set into motion hundreds or millions of years ago in faraway places" (Latour, 1999a: 189).

Latour's contention in an earlier study that each science works through "a cycle of accumulation that allows a point to become a *centre* by acting at a distance on many other points" (Latour, 1987: 222) will help to amplify this point while also connecting it to my more specific concern with the relationships between the entities fabricated by the historical sciences and the practices of museums. This aspect of Latour's work has informed recent approaches to early nineteenth-century natural history museums in which the objects of natural history, increasingly disconnected from the collecting practices of gentlemen virtuoso, were reassembled in new and more systematic configurations as parts of colonial networks of science and government.[10] The accumulation, in metropolitan centers (London, Paris, Berlin, New York), of flora and fauna from a variety of distant places and their assembly in new contexts and combinations permitted the development of abstract and totalizing frameworks of knowledge. This made it possible for those metropolitan institutions to function as "centers of calculation", acting at a distance on a variety of peripheral locations by providing the intellectual frameworks within which the activities of agents in those locations could be organized. The paradox here then (and it is one writ large in the history of geology, too)[11] is that centers of calculation devalue the knowledge that is located at sites of collection – that is, the places from whence objects are taken – in making a knowledge of objects dependent on an appreciation of their place within abstract systems of relationships which are only visible from those centers.

George Cuvier's elevation of the sedentary naturalist over the field naturalist offers an early and influential example of the logic at work here. The field naturalist, he wrote in 1807, may observe objects and living things "in their natural surroundings, in relationship to their environment, and in the full vigour of life and activity", but he lacks the means of drawing comparisons between them with the result that his observations are "broken and fleeting" (Cuvier, cited in Outram, 1996: 259–60). The sedentary naturalist, by contrast, may labor under the disadvantage that his knowledge of "living beings from distant countries" is a secondary and mediated one so that a "thousand little things escape him … which would have struck him if he had been on the spot" (Cuvier, cit. Outram, 1996: 260). But there are compensating advantages:

> If the sedentary naturalist does not see nature in action, he can yet survey all her products spread before him. He can compare them with each other as often as is necessary to reach reliable conclusions … He can bring together the relevant facts from anywhere he needs to. The traveller can only travel one road; it is only really in one's study (*cabinet*) that one can roam freely throughout the universe … (Cuvier, cit. Outram, 1996: 261–2)

The *Muséum national d'Histoire naturelle*, under Cuvier's direction, performed an analogous function for the public: it provided for the public witnessing of nature's order by bringing together "in one place the whole range of the natural order, which, in the 'real world', would never be found together in one space" (Outram, 1996: 256). However, this also meant, Outram adds, "that the visitor to the Muséum could see not only the denizens of many different parts of the earth's surface together in one spot, but also the products of many different *eras* of the earth's history" (Outram, 1996: 256). This anticipated a significant aspect of the later development of evolutionary museums. It is true of all museums that what Frederick Bohrer calls "the presentness of the artifact" (Bohrer, 1994: 199) strives to overcome both temporal and spatial distance, rendering present that which is absent because it occurred long ago or is located far away. In the "strategies of presence" which organized the exhibition practices of late-nineteenth-century ethnological and natural history museums, however, the "long ago" and the "far away" were superimposed on one another through the network of assumptions which equated what was distant from Europe with its prehistory. This manoeuver, whose operations in anthropological discourse have been traced by Johannes Fabian (1983), also applied to geology and natural history in the expectation, for example, that the maritime exploration of the Pacific would allow Europeans to overcome both space and time in bringing back the past – the living past of forms of life that were extinct in Europe – from far away. The most famous example of how the colonial structure of natural and human times overlapped in this respect is John Lubbock's contention that "the Van Diemaner and South African are to the antiquary, what the opossum and the sloth are to the geologist" (Lubbock, 1865: 336). However, we can also see this structure at work in the system of equivalencies that was established between the fossils found lying on the surface in the "far away" of Australia with those excavated, through coal-mining, from the deep past of Europe (Desmond, 1982: 14–15, 148–9).

It is, however, the lamination on top of one another of the temporal-spatial coordinates produced by the different historical sciences that I am most interested in here. At a later point in *Science in Action*, Latour suggests that to suppose "that it is possible to draw together in a synthesis the times of astronomy, geology, biology, primatology and anthropology has about as much meaning as making a synthesis between the pipes or cables of water, gas, electricity, telephone and television" (Latour, 1987: 229). From the perspective of contemporary science, this is no doubt so. However, the closing decades of the nineteenth century were characterized by precisely such a synthesis in which these historical sciences – whose development had hitherto proceeded along more separate lines – were compacted, temporarily, into a close and cohesive unity. The result, as Henry Pitt Rivers put it, was "a band of union between the physical and cultural sciences which can never be broken" in which "history" is "but another term for evolution" (cited in M. W. Thompson, 1977: 40). It was in this context that the typological method inherited from Scandinavian archaeology, but interpreted more expansively, played a key role in stabilizing, managing, and administering the relationships between the pasts that had been produced by the coordinated labors of these sciences.

Administering the Past

The two main defining principles of actor-network-theory, John Law has argued, are those of *relational materiality* and *performativity*. The first, as he elaborates it, applies the semiotic principle of the relationality of entities to all materials rather than only to those that are linguistic. If this principle entails that entities acquire their reality from the relations within which they are located, this also means that "they are *performed* in, by, and through those relations" with the consequence that "everything is uncertain and reversible, at least in principle...never given in the order of things" (Law, 1999: 4). The principle of *performativity*, accordingly, is concerned with how, in practice "things get performed (and perform themselves) into relations that are relatively stable and stay in place" (4). Latour attributes a key role to institutions in the processes through which entities are stabilized (albeit without ever becoming permanent) since, as he defines the term, "institutions provide all the mediations necessary for an actor to maintain a durable and sustainable substance" (Latour, 1999a: 307).

While there have been several attempts to apply the principles of actor-network-theory to museums,[12] David Jenkins's discussion of the relations between field-work, classification, and labeling comes closest to describing the role played by museum practices in fabricating, stabilizing, and administering new entities. The labeling of objects at the site of collection, effecting their archival inscription from the outset; the translation of objects into a two-dimensional visual grammar through the drawings that are made of them as they are accessioned; and their translation into a classified inventory recording the provenance of each object: these processes, Jenkins contends, have two main consequences. The first consists in "a reduction of the empirical world to new, more easily manageable objects that are, in Latour's phrase, 'mobile...immutable, presentable, readable and combinable with one another'" (Jenkins, 1994: 254). And the second arises from the relations between these different stages in the processing of the museum object. "Each step – field collection, proper labelling, archival systematisation, and museum display – was," Jenkins argues, "apparently linked to the prior step, ensuring the authenticity and stabilising the meanings of ethnographic collections" (Jenkins, 1994: 255).

The case he has in mind are the systems developed for the processing and systematization of ethnographic artifacts developed in the late nineteenth century, paying particular attention to the typological method which, Jenkins argues, allowed those artifacts to be arranged in terms of criteria that were simultaneously evolutionary and bureaucratic. Under the influence of Henry Pitt Rivers and, subsequently, Otis Mason at the Smithsonian Institution, the typological method – which arranged all artifacts sequentially along a linear axis of development from the simple to the complex – had been developed from its Scandinavian origins into a universal means for the evolutionary calibration of all cultures. It provided, as Edward Tylor summarized it, "a set of object lessons in the development of culture" (Tylor, cited in Rudler, 1897: 57). This is not to suggest that it was the only method for arranging evolutionary displays: Mary Bouquet (2000) has drawn attention to the continuing influence of genealogical trees in providing a point of connection between earlier biblical genealogies and evolutionary thought. The significance of the typological method, however, was precisely that it provided a means of breaking with scriptural or, more generally, text-based histories to the degree that it was conceived as functioning analogously to the taxonomies governing natural history displays.[13] It played a crucial role in this respect in translating new forms of intellectual authority based on experimentation, observation, and verification into technical mechanisms capable of challenging the sway that text-based forms of knowledge had previously exercised over the organization and interpretation of the artifactual field. And it was through this, its technical form, that the typological method provided a new set of principles for administering the relationships between objects and, thereby, rendering those relationships relatively stable and durable.

The administrative or, in Jenkins's terms, bureaucratic virtues of the typological method derived from the transformation it brought about in the status of the museum object. For it was no longer, as it had been in traditional museum disciplines, the object's singularity or uniqueness that counted but its substitutability – that is, its ability to stand for other objects of the same type representing a stage within a developmental sequence. To the degree that it was now both movable and repeatable, the museum object was able to take on a new role as part of an expanded network of museums in which otherwise dissimilar objects were – in Law's terms – so performed that they were able to perform the same function of representing equivalent stages of development. By according objects, no matter what their cultural provenance, the role of representing stages within universal evolutionary sequences, the typological method established a system of equivalencies between otherwise dissimilar objects which allowed them to circulate between collections and, by filling in the gaps in order to make up complete evolutionary series, to make good the deficiencies that would otherwise occur.[14]

The typological method thus introduced into the cultural field principles of repeatability and substitutability that had previously been associated exclusively with natural history and geology museums.[15] It functioned, in this respect, as the museum equivalent of the invention of movable typeface. Henry Balfour realized this when comparing the relative advantages and disadvantages of geographical versus typological principles of display for ethnological collections. While the former might serve best for large museums with extensive collections relating to particular localities, Balfour was in no doubt concerning the value of the typological method for smaller collections. By allowing objects not regionally connected to be placed in the same sequence to illustrate evolution, it allowed museums to draw on objects from unrelated collections in order assemble the prehistoric past and illustrate its evolutionary momentum. Nor was he in any doubt as to the virtues of the typological method from the point of view of the development of a national museum system. It provided new principles of exchange to govern the circulation of objects between museums to the degree that one museum might buy or borrow objects from another to fill up gaps in its evolutionary sequences, just as another museum might be willing to part with such objects to the degree that it already possessed a surfeit of objects which (however dissimilar they might be in other respects) were, typologically speaking, substitutable. His reasoning was, in these respects, tellingly similar to those deployed by museum geologists in their concern to reform local collections so that they might provide educational series whose gaps would be filled by drawing on central repositories (see Knell, 1996).

The typological method thus served to so perform objects that they could perform their function of making the new pasts of prehistory, and their direction, visible realities. It did so, moreover, in a way that made it possible for those pasts to be duplicated and multiplied to fuel the rapid proliferation of new museums of ethnology and natural history that characterized the closing decades of the nineteenth century owing to the importance that was attached to them as machineries of popular instruction intended to carry the messages of the historical sciences to the masses.[16] The Horniman Museum offers a good example of how the functioning of objects was transformed as a result of a scientific rationalization of the museum environment. Originally established as a private museum, the Horniman Museum's collection was initially arranged as an assemblage of national and colonial curio reflecting the personal interests and obsessions of its owner, the tea-merchant Frederick Horniman (see Levell, 1997). Once the Museum passed into the ownership of London County Council in 1901, however, it was subjected to a rigorous and extended program of rationalization in order to transform its collections into evolutionary displays with both an ethnological and a natural history focus (see Coombes, 1994: 115). The description, in the 1908 *Annual Report*, of the rearrangement of the relations between the Museum's departments gives a clear idea of the principles underlying this rationalization:

> The most important change in this department during the year has been the removal of the Egyptian collection from its former position in the Natural History Hall. The mummies are now conveniently placed in the South Corridor, and most of the other Egyptian antiquities are in the section of Magic and Religion, to which they properly belong. The space left vacant by the Egyptian collection is being filled up with the specimens upon which the future section of Physical Anthropology will in part be based. In this section it is proposed to illustrate the zoological affinities of man by means of specimens and preparations of allied animals (apes and monkeys), and to give the outlines of the more important external and skeletal differences that exist between the various races of man. (6)

The rearrangement described here made possible a programmatic approach to acquisitions and exhibition planning of a kind that had not previously been possible. And it did so precisely because the commitment to arranging evolutionary series allowed gaps to be identified where, in an earlier collection philosophy that stressed the singularity of the object, none had previously existed. Equally, though, those gaps could then be filled by judicious acquisitions in which it was not the individuality of the object that mattered but its ability to be fitted in the place prepared for it. This aspect of the typological method is made especially clear in a report prepared by Henry Balfour in 1890 in which he advised, in connection with his work on the Pitt Rivers collection, that "it has been and would be in the future possible to greatly improve the existing series by filling up gaps in their continuity, or to add a new series, and so to advance greatly the educational value of this unique collection" (Balfour, 1890: iii). Lee Rust Brown notes the operation of a similar principle in the late eighteenth-century arrangement of the *Muséum national d'Histoire naturelle* in which Enlightenment classification allowed a space to be reserved for everything as yet awaiting discovery to complete its microcosmic assembly of the world. "The Museum," as he puts it, "could afford to welcome all new facts precisely because it was sure that every new fact would disappear into one *lacune* or another, and bring its encylopedic representation of the world a step closer to perfection" (Brown, 1997: 103). The typological method operated with a different set of relations between objects and spaces in which the latter were to be filled by the former only to the degree that they could connect two points in a line of evolutionary development. But the principle remained the same – with the significant difference that the typological method applied this principle to the field of cultural artifacts as well as that of natural and geological specimens.

Evolutionary Showmen, Culture and Time Management

These, then, are among the procedures through which the new entities of pre-scriptural pasts were fabricated, brought into relation with one another, stabilized, and – in museums – organized into networks of human and non-human actors. There was, however, another key stage in this process. In his discussion of Pasteur, Latour notes how, toward the end of his experimental scenography, Pasteur autonomizes the lactic acid fermentation that his experimental labors have produced by presenting this as an entity that has now simply to be observed ("we have before our eyes a clearly characterised lactic fermentation"). "The director," as Latour glosses this passage, "withdraws from the scene, and the reader, merging her eyes with those of the stage manager, *sees* a fermentation that takes form at centre stage *independently* of any work or construction" (Latour, 1999a: 132). In a similar way, the new entities fabricated by the historical sciences were, in being translated into museum displays, ushered forth in their own right, set free from the labor of their construction. In his proposals for the contexts in which natural history specimens would best be displayed, Thomas Huxley envisages an equivalent act of withdrawal on the part of the curator: "The cases in which these specimens are exhibited must present a transparent but hermetically closed face, one side access-ible to the public, while on the opposite side they are as constantly accessible to the Curator by means of doors opening into a portion of the Museum to which the public has no access" (Huxley, 1896: 128). On one side of a hermetically-sealed glass divide, the curator lays out his specimens in accordance with the principles of evolutionary science, giving them a reality of their own by remaining wholly back-stage; on the other side, the public, denied access to the back-stage area in which the curator organizes the *mise-en-scène* for his specimens and determines what roles – of narrative and representation – to accord them, observes what has been placed clearly before its eyes (see Figure 6.1).[17]

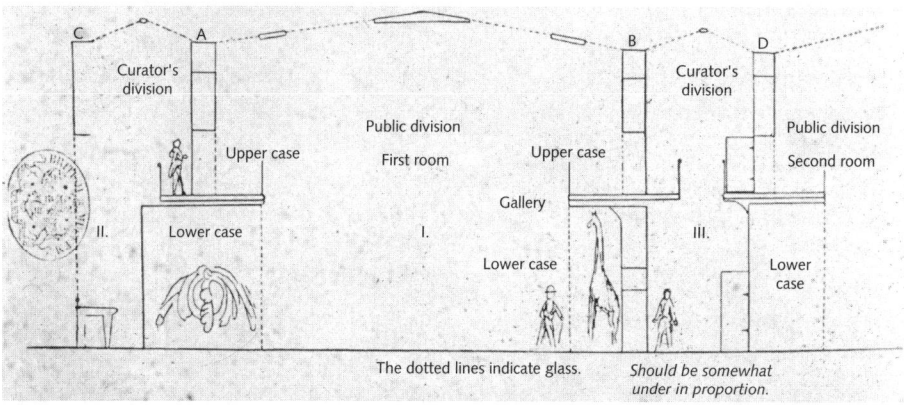

Figure 6.1 A map of what Thomas Huxley suggests is the best way for a curator to organize his exhibit

It was through practices of this kind that the public was installed in its place to absorb the lessons of the evolutionary sequencing of a series of newly-fabricated pasts as objects that had hitherto served different functions (fossils, human and animal remains, tools, weapons, etc.) were now performed as new entities in which, to borrow a term from Norbert Elias, they served as key markers of a new "temporal conscience". Elias coins this term to describe how "the external compulsion coming from the social institution of time" is converted "into a pattern of self-constraint embracing the whole of life of an individual" (Elias, 1987: 11). This is precisely what E. P. Thompson (1967) was concerned with in his classic essay on the emergence of time–work discipline in the clocked time of the factory and whose central insights Graeme Davison extends in his perception that the "the clock on the wall or in the waistcoat pocket is but the metronome for a soul already singing to the music of modernity" (Davison, 1993: 6). There is, however, another aspect to the temporal conscience that was fashioned under the influence of late nineteenth-century modernizing discourses, one that operated through the partitioning of the modern self into a division between its newly-discovered archaic and primitive components and – given the threat of degeneration – the fragility of its progressive and modernizing components. And it was in their attempts to convert this division into a site for a progressive working of the self on self that the historical sciences aimed to convert the new realities they had fabricated into instruments for new forms of self-governance consistent with the principles of liberalism, that could – recalling my earlier theme of the struggle between the ancients and moderns – challenge the claims of aesthetic education in these regards.

These claims were initially developed, Poovey suggests, in the context of the collapse of absolutism that gave rise to a need for new ways of rendering individuals "thinkable as governable subjects" (Poovey, 1998: 147). In place of strategies aimed at rendering the population knowable through abstract and impersonal forms of calculation monopolized by the sovereign authority, and in place of government by decree and a reliance on coercive means of securing obedience, the emerging forms of liberal government operating in the relations of the market and civil society depended increasingly on new forms of self-rule. The discourses of aesthetics – crystallizing into an identifiably distinctive formation in the course of the eighteenth century – played a significant role in relation to these new forms of self-government in laying out the self in the form of a set of divisions between its cultivated and uncultivated components which allowed new forms of internal action of the self on the self to emerge. While originally forming a part of a renovated culture of civic humanism and, as such, restricted to the cultivation of virtue on the part of the landed and mercantile classes, this aesthetic technology of a multiply-divided self was subsequently grafted onto forms of self-governance with – at least in aspiration – a broader social reach and circulation. It was an active component in the eighteenth-century culture of taste which provided for a work of self on self through its influence on the organization of practices of consumption just as it was later to prove influential, in its Romantic version, in providing the moral vectors for programs of popular schooling.[18] And it was also, of course, caught up in the history of the art museum, providing, the discursive ground on which – in its nineteenth-century conception – the public art museum was to discharge its obligations as a reformatory of public morals and manners.[19]

By the late nineteenth century, however, the labors of the historical sciences had supplied the conditions for the development of a different organization of the self. This provided the vectors for an alternative program of self-governance in the division it established between the self's primitive and archaic components on the one hand and the progressive momentum it derived from the impetus of earlier phases of social development on the other.[20] We are perhaps more familiar with this architecture of the self from its subsequent history in the context of Freud's work and its translation, there, into a set of psychoanalytic techniques of self-management (see Otis, 1994). There is, however, little doubt that the emergence of this "archaeological structure of the self" was first associated with the historical sciences and their attempts to marshal this, in the context of both popular schooling and museums, as part of programs of liberal government that would serve as an aid to social progress by producing and managing the tension between the self's archaic and progressive components in favor of a dialectic of development in which the latter would gain sway over the former.[21]

A brief discussion of the role played by culture in Huxley's understanding of the architecture of the self will help to make my point here. For Huxley, in *Evolution and Ethics*, the self is governed by a vertiginous division between two layers in which "the innate aggressive impulses of the ancestor" are moderated by "the acquired social restraint of the cultured being" (Huxley, 1893: 20). It is only by putting the accumulated results of culture into play within the self, and thereby equipping it in each generation with the means of advancing rapidly to the highest levels of civilization, that social development – as a process with an ongoing and incremental logic – is made possible. As is the case with Matthew Arnold, these formulations stress the place that culture should play in mediating the relations between the separate components of a divided self. The difference, however, is that the Huxleyan self is divided by the temporal coordinates constituted by the historical sciences rather than by the a-temporal structure of the aesthetic relations that mark the division between Arnold's better and lesser selves. Both conceptions, it is true, provide a justification for state action in the cultural sphere as the means by which the struggle that takes place within the self might be reconciled in favor of its civilized, and civilizing, components. Nonetheless, the coordinates within which this struggle is set are different to the degree that relations of historical time are not centrally implicated in the organization of the Arnoldian self or the kind of work of self on self that it enables. Relations of time are, however, central to the coordinates within which the Huxleyan self is formed as they are also to the role that culture plays in mediating the relations between its divided components. The logic of this divided self, and of its inscription in the programs of "evolutionary self-management" that characterized Darwinian liberalism, is, in these ways, a by-product of the fabrication of prehistory that had resulted from the work of the historical sciences.

Some Conclusions

If the main drift of my argument in the foregoing holds true, there are good reasons for doubting that simply adding and mixing available sociological accounts of culture to the perspective of governmentality will yield either a properly theorized account of the relationships of culture and governance which characterize "modern societies" or a satisfactory means of engaging empirically with the analysis of those relationships. At the same time that it disqualifies the logic of earlier sociological problematics in which culture and society are presented as two separate-but-connected realms whose separation/connection requires some general theoretical specification, the perspective of governmentality opens up the field of changing governmental problematizations of the social as an alternative theoretical setting for the concerns of cultural analysis. It does not itself, however, provide the means of rethinking how those concerns should be pursued within such a setting or of translating them into new and distinctive programs of inquiry.

In proposing a corrective to this, I have suggested, first, that an analytical engagement with changing governmental problematizations of the social requires a theoretical focus centered on the activities of the "culture complex" consisting of those institutions in which specific forms of knowledge and expertise are invoked in attempts to organize cultural resources in ways that will allow them to be brought to bear on the regulation of conduct with specific ends in view. I have also suggested that the methods that have been developed within actor-network-theory for studying how entities are fabricated offers a useful model for examining how the application of specific forms of knowledge and expertise to the cultural field produces new entities and renders these into technical forms that allow them to function as key cultural operators in governmental programs which aim to work on the social through the regulation of the self. Bringing these two perspectives together in this way has the additional advantage of moving the ground of cultural analysis clearly away from the logic of separation/connection characterizing those sociological approaches to culture/society relations in which – whether by symbolizing or legitimating them – culture's role is seen as supplementary in relation to processes and forms of power deriving primarily from the dynamics of society. For in both actor-network-theory and the perspective of governmentality – and in the intrication of their concerns that I have proposed here – power is theorized as being immanent to the processes and relations in which it is produced and exercised.

That said, it is important to place limits on what might be expected from the intermixing of these two perspectives. For what I have proposed does not amount to a totalizing account of culture that can substitute for or displace the full range of issues that might be addressed under the headings of the sociology of culture or cultural studies. Its remit is the more limited one of providing a means of engaging with the specific issues that are posed when cultural resources of particular kinds become tangled up with particular kinds of knowledge and expertise in the context of specific governmental programs. It is with this in mind, as well as the similarity of the moves that I have proposed to those that have characterized the history of science studies, that this specific nexus of concerns might best be explored under the heading of "culture studies". This, however, is an argument whose fuller development will have to await another occasion.

Notes

1 See, for example, the role that culture plays in the accounts of neo-liberalism offered in Dean (1999) and Rose (1999).

2 The distinction proposed here is not a watertight one: the activities of the "culture complex" also have significant consequences for how those cultural practices on whose products they work are themselves conducted. Phillip Fisher's account of the respects in which the modern art gallery organizes contemporary artistic production is a case in point: see Fisher (1991).

3 I draw here, for this assessment, on the perspectives developed in Golinski (1998).

4 See, for example, the account offered by Ian Jenkins (1992) of the extent to which aesthetic conceptions were eventually obliged to yield some quarter to the increasing influence of archaeological conceptions of the typical in the sculpture galleries of the British Museum. See also Caygill and Cherry (1997) for a detailed account of the faltering progress made in rearranging the British Museum's collections in accordance with the principles of the typological method during the period of A. W. Franks's influence.

5   Huxley was an important figure here, especially in crossing the boundaries between natural history and ethnology – serving, for a while, as President of the Ethnological Society (see Edwards, 2001: 134).

6   Huxley's definition of ethnology as an umbrella term for the study of the physical characters, languages, civilizations, and religions of imperial subjects also indicates that, in the British context, the term was not defined as a specific methodology of the kind that Marchand identifies in Germany. See Edwards (2001: 134–5).

7   See Shapin and Schaffer (1985), Shapin (1994) and Eamon (1994).

8   A key line of transmission for these concerns is from Cuvier, who, in his conception of himself as 'a new antiquarian' (see Rudwick, 1997: 183), explicitly drew on the vocabulary of conjectural history in describing his famed reconstructions of past forms of life, to Huxley who viewed the methods of natural history as a version of conjectural history (see Huxley, 1882).

9   See, for the most detailed accounts of these developments, Grayson (1983), van Riper (1993) and Rupke (1983).

10 See, for example, Gascoigne (1994) and a number of the essays collected in Miller and Reill (1996).

11 David Oldroyd has applied Latour's perspectives to the social relations of nineteenth-century geology, showing how the British Geological Survey functioned as a center of calculation in allowing successive generations of geologists to visit distant collecting sites with a better knowledge of regional geological formations than local residents because of the accumulating information system produced by the Survey. See Oldroyd (1990: 340–52).

12 See, for example, Hetherington (1999).

13 See, for a discussion of this understanding of the typological method in the work of both Pitt Rivers and Henry Balfour, Coombes (1994: 118–19).

14 By the same token, however, this procedure made the individuality of specific cultures invisible. This was the nub of Franz Boas's objection to the effects of the typological method as deployed in Otis Mason's displays at the Smithsonian Institution: see Stocking Jr (1999: 171–2).

15 But not, it has to be said, with notable long-term success. It is, Carla Yanni notes, precisely because museums based on cultural artifacts tend to stress the singularity and uniqueness of their collections that they occupy a more important position within tourists' itineraries than do natural history collections. Visitors to Cairo go to the Egyptian Museum to see the mask of King Tut, she observes, or to Rome to see the Sistine Chapel "but few out-of-town visitors in Cairo or Rome wander into the museums to look at stuffed sparrows" (Yanni, 1999: 10).

16 David van Keuren has estimated that, of the 71 new museum collections established in Britain in the 1870s, 1880s, and 1890s, 28 were natural history collections and 5 ethnological collections – a figure which compared with 3 such collections established in the whole of the preceding part of the century (van Keuren, 1982: 155).

17 For a discussion of the background to this aspect of Huxley's proposal, see Yanni (1999: 144ff).

18 See, on the first of these questions, Brewer (1995), and, on the second, Hunter (1988a).

19 I have discussed this elsewhere; see Bennett (1995c).
20 For a good example of the case that was made for the role that the historical sciences had to play in liberal education – and for an advocacy of their virtues *vis-à-vis* those of the classics and aesthetic education – see Huxley (1868).
21 I have explored these issues more fully elsewhere: see Bennett (2001d and 2002d).

Chapter Seven   Civic Seeing:
Museums and the
Organization of Vision

From the early modern period, museums have been places in which citizens – however they might have been defined – have met, conversed, been instructed, or otherwise engaged in rituals through which their rights and duties as citizens have been enacted. They have also been, from roughly the same period, primarily institutions of the visible in which objects of various kinds have been exhibited to be looked at. The issues I want to explore in this chapter are located at the intersections of these two aspects of the museum's history. They concern the respects in which the functioning of museums as civic institutions has operated through specific regimes of vision which, informing both the manner in which things are arranged to be seen and the broader visual environment conditioning practices of looking, give rise to particular forms of "civic seeing" in which the civic lessons embodied in those arrangements are to be seen, understood, and performed by the museum's visitors. Or at least by those visitors who are included in the museum's civic address. The rider is an important one. For while, since the French revolution, public museums have been theoretically committed to the service of universal citizenries, the practice has usually proved to be somewhat different with, at various points in time, women, children, the working classes, the colonized, and, in many western countries still (Dias, 2003), immigrants simply not being addressed by museums in ways that have enabled them to occupy the optical and epistemological vantage points which particular programs of "civic seeing" both require and make possible. Indeed, as we shall see, it is often through the forms of "civic seeing" that they effect that different kinds of museums have organized the distinction between citizens and non-citizens as precisely one of differentiated visual capacities.

As it will prove difficult to address these issues comprehensively in a chapter of this scope, I shall, instead, opt for a number of symptomatic examples which, ranging across different types of museum, will offer an insight into the civic assumptions informing some of the more distinctive "visual grammars" that have been developed in association with museum displays from the early modern period to the present. I look first at the regimes of vision associated with public art museums, and especially at how these have operated as a means for enacting social distinctions in ways that have run counter to art museums' claims to speak to and for all citizens. I then look at some of the contrasting ways, from cabinets of curiosity through to evolutionary museums, in which a civic importance has been attached to seeing nature and the relations between different cultures in a proper light. In doing so, I also consider how questions of "civic seeing" relate to those concerning other forms of sensory involvement in museum displays and, indeed, to the more general forms of civic comportment associated with the museum's conception as a key site for "civic rituals" (Duncan, 1995).

This prepares the ground for an examination of the respects in which "civic seeing" in the museum is always posed relationally as a project requiring that seeing be regulated in ways that are designed to offset the influence of other practices of seeing, usually those associated with commercial forms of popular visual entertainment, which are said to lure the eye into civically unproductive forms of visual pleasure. I shall then come, finally, to consider some of the key ways in which questions of "civic seeing" are posed in relation to contemporary museum practices. These include debates about the extent to which the tension between museums and commercial forms of visual entertainment have now collapsed to such a degree that the ability of museums to shape distinctive forms of "civic seeing" is called into question. They also include attempts to move away from the directed forms of vision that have dominated western museum practices since the Enlightenment in favor of more dialogic practices of seeing which, in enabling a greater degree of visual give-and-take between different perspectives, might prove more conducive to the requirements of "civic seeing" in culturally diverse societies.

Divided Seeing: Visual Competence and the Art Museum

In a series of pamphlets he published in the final years and immediate aftermath of World War I, John Cotton Dana, the founding director of the Newark Museum, outlined his vision for a new museum, one which, escaping the influence of the old museums of Europe – and those American museums modeled on European examples – would become useful civic instruments for a young, democratic, and industrious nation. An important part of the set of rhetorical contrasts between old and new museums that he organized for this purpose consisted in the different ways in which they addressed the eye. New museums, he argued:

> are not to be storage warehouses, or community attics, or temples of dead gods, or copies of palaces of an extinct nobility, or costly reproductions of ancient temples, or grand and elaborate structures which are of service only as evidences of conspicuous waste by the rich and as ocular demonstrations of the unwise expenditure of public funds. (Dana, 1917b: 18)

Instead, he argued, they should aspire to be Institutes of Visual Instruction if they were to engage the eye in a lively and useful civic fashion that would dispel what he had earlier called "the gloom of the museum" (Dana, 1917b). Returning to the same theme three years later, the ethos of visual instruction to which the new museum should aspire was highlighted by his condemnation of America's existing art museums as mere "gazing museums" (Dana, 1920: 13).

In the event, Dana's voice was not to prove the most influential in determining the future path along which American art museums would develop. While the 1920s and 1930s, especially in the context of the New Deal, did witness a significant stress on the public educational and civic role that museums should play in relation to the general population (see Adams, 1939), and while Dana remained an active and influential contributor to these debates until his death in 1929, the practices of art museums over these years were, in Andrew McClellan's assessment, more in tune with the curatorial philosophy of Benjamin Ives Gilman at Boston's Museum of Fine Arts (McClellan, 2003). As heir to the civic value that Victorian theorists of art had invested in aesthetic education as a means of ordering persons and adjusting them to their place in an ordered society, Gilman continued to stress the special responsibility of the art museum to cultivate an appreciation of beauty by exhibiting the classical and modern canons of painting and sculpture. For Dana, by contrast, it was precisely this prejudice that had to be broken in favor of an active engagement with the standards of beauty enjoying widespread use and circulation in the objects of everyday life if the museum were to become a "living, active and effective institution" (Dana, 1917b: 23).

As Theodore Low (1942) was to note with regret, however, the tide was running against Dana, and against Gilman too, in favor of a conception in which, far from being a place for generalized forms of "civic seeing," in which the lessons to be derived from art's improving qualities were to be made equally available to all visitors, the art museum was to function as a space governed by what Pierre Bourdieu (1996b) called "the pure gaze" of the connoisseur. This had been evident earlier in the century in the so-called "battle of the casts." This pitched the inimitable quality of the original prized by the connoisseur against the educational value that had been placed on casts in earlier Victorian conceptions of the art museum's function. The battle was resolved largely in favor of the former tendency at both the Boston Museum of Fine Arts and New York's Metropolitan Museum of Art (Wallach, 1998: 49–56). This tendency was, moreover, significantly strengthened and generalized through the US art museum sector as a result of the influence of the course in museum studies that Paul Sachs ran at Harvard from the 1920s through to the 1950s. Focused on cultivating "the most exacting standards of an elite," this course promoted the interests of a "narrow cult of collectors, critics and fellow museum professionals" (McClellan, 2003: 22) at the expense of the public in ways which, as Dana had warned, resulted in a complete absence of any engaged civic purpose or usefulness.

The tension that is traced here between the art museum as "an elite temple of the arts" and as "a utilitarian instrument for democratic education" (Hooper-Greenhill,

1989: 63) has, however, a longer history, one in which the forms of "seeing" that the museum is to organize, and for whom, have constantly been points at issue. While the French revolution had opened the Louvre to the public, and celebrated its capacity as a venue for new forms of "civic seeing" in which the virtues of a republican citizenry would be strengthened, the actual practices of the museum assumed a public that was much the same as that which had informed pre-revolutionary plans for both the Louvre and the Luxembourg Gallery. There was no attempt to instruct the museum's new public on how to read and interpret the art displayed any more than the Louvre was opened to popular arts rooted in the everyday lives of the people. "Theoretically one," as McClellan puts it, "the museum public was divided by degrees of visual competence" (McClellan, 1994: 9). The connections between these divisions of visual capacity and contemporary social divisions were evident in a continuing tradition of caricature which, satirizing those who visited art museums without the requisite forms of visual competence, confirmed a sense of superiority on the part of those whose eyes had been trained in the correct ways of seeing. Honoré Daumier's engraving, discussed by McClellan, of a rustic family unable to appreciate the non-realistic nature of

Figure 7.1 The work of art: rural literalism satirized as a new form of cultural illiteracy ("Effet de la sale des *Pietà* sur les spectateurs ruraux," *Journal amusant*, 23 July 1859)

Egyptian funerary decoration thus finds its echo, more than a half-century later, in a caricature of rural visitors who, as Dominique Poulot (1994) notes, proved unable to respond appropriately to the new forms of attention required when religious art was placed in the secular and civic context of the art museum (Fig. 7.1)

If it organized a division in class terms, the civic address of the Louvre was also uneven in terms of gender. For, whilst open to women, the Louvre only included them within its civic address indirectly and in purely auxiliary roles to the extent that, in accordance with the exclusively male conception of revolutionary citizenship, its primary concern was to inculcate the virtues of a republican brotherhood through its construction of a male pantheon of civic virtue. The same was true, nearly a century later, of Ruskin's program for the museum in which both women of all classes and working-class men were addressed through an assumed norm of the middle-class man's relation to art. The resulting relay system of looks was one in which bodily passions and manual capacities were to be directed by subordinating them to the controlling influence of male and class-centered ways of seeing (Helsinger, 1994).

Seeing and Enacting Nature's Civic Lessons

Although most conspicuously foregrounded in the practices of art museums and the debates to which these have given rise, questions concerning how best to arrange the visual environment so as to promote specific civic values have also been centrally implicated in the development of other types of museum. And, as in the case of the art museum, such debates have concerned more than the regulation of sight. As key sites for the performance of civic rituals, the organization of seeing that museums aim to effect has to be seen in relation to the more general ordering of the forms of self-presentation, social interrelation, and civic comportment that they construct as normative ideals for their visitors. Indeed, it is only in the context of this broader set of concerns that the specific civic value that is placed on seeing as such can be properly appreciated. For the privileging of sight in relation to the other senses that this represents is a relatively recent phenomenon and, since there are ample signs that the attention that is accorded to speaking, hearing, and touching in contemporary museum practices are now challenging the primacy of the visual, one whose historical rim may well now be in view. It is, indeed, precisely because this is so that there has been a marked revival of interest in those pre- or early-modern practices of collection and exhibition in which civic issues were posed in relation to a broader mix of the senses, rather than solely to vision in isolation.

Paula Findlen's work has been important in this regard, tracing the respects in which the development of museums as civil and, later, civic spaces depended on a series of transformations in their socio-sensory environments. Modeled initially, in early humanist conceptions, on the monastic *studium*, the museum was seen as a solitary and contemplative space sequestered from the noise of the world. "*Museum* is a place where the Scholar sits alone," John Amos Comenius wrote in 1659, "apart from other men, addicted to his Studies, while reading books" (cited in Findlen, 1994: 102). The movement of the museum from the inner recesses of the house into more permeable spaces that accompanied the development of the Renaissance cabinet was also a movement from silence into sound as the museum's function as a *solitarium* gave way to its new conception as what Findlen calls a "conversable space."

Providing a context in which displaying nature served as a prelude to ritualized conversational exchanges between (mainly) elite males, this space played a key role in shaping both the codes of civility and the classed and gendered boundaries of civil society through the inclusions and exclusions that it operated. The parallel transition, in royal collections, from the private and enclosed *studio* of the prince to the *galleria* also involved the construction of more permeable spaces in which the codes of civility that were cultivated through knowledgeable conversation about the collections were invested with a more public and civic significance. The Düsseldorf Gallery, while adjacent to the Elector's palace and accessible through it, thus also had separate outside entrances to which local artists, civil servants, and nobility had unrestricted access and through which, as Goethe recorded in the account of his visit to the Gallery in 1768, members of a more general public were also able to enter (Sheehan, 2000: 33).

As places for looking and seeing, certainly, but also as places for ritualized conversations, such early modern museums did not isolate and privilege seeing at the expense of other forms of sensory involvement. The practice of seeing itself, moreover, was modeled on the norms of conversational give-and-take rather than itself constituting a norm of attentiveness to which, as would later be the case, the other senses would be obliged to defer. The "polymathic cabinets of curiosity" of the seventeenth century, Barbara Stafford (1994) thus argues, served as prompts for conversation as a means of resolving the perplexities occasioned by the puzzling juxtaposition of apparently disconnected objects. Equally, far from distancing the eye before a scene of ordered vision, they enticed the spectator to enter into the system of sideways looks characterizing the cabinet's regime of visuality. "Crumbling shells, clumps of madrepores, coral branches, miniature busts, Chinese porcelain teapots, small medals, intaglio gems, pottery shards, drawn and engraved portraits, masks, carved ivory, pickled monsters, religious utensils, and multicultural remains," she writes, "cacophonously 'chatted' among themselves and with the spectator" (Stafford, 1994: 238).

The reciprocity between seeing and conversation that is evident here was intelligible where museum collections provided the props and occasions for ritual exchanges between members of a restricted civil society whose members were presumed to meet as equals. Its intelligibility, furthermore, depended on the assumption that such conversations could be conducted on the basis of the observable properties of things that were equally open to the inspection of all. These assumptions no longer held when, under the influence of Enlightenment conceptions, the museum was developed as an instrument of public instruction. Developed most influentially at the Muséum national d'Histoire naturelle, the program for the Enlightment museum installed a hierarchical relationship between curators and visitors in the form of a practice of directed vision through which the latter, by following the guidance of the former, were to be made to see the rational order underlying nature's apparent diversity.

This hierarchical relationship was both social and epistemological. The curator and visitor were placed on opposite sides of a line separating those who had been trained to see the invisible order subtending nature's rational classification and those untrained beholders who needed to be tutored into the right ways of seeing if they were to absorb the civic import of nature's lessons correctly. This involved, Lee Rust Emerson argues, "a special discipline of seeing" (Brown, 1997: 143) in which the exhibition of different species and *genera* in accordance with the differences in their observable characteristics was a technical device intended to lead the eye to an apprehension of the invisible logic of classification which, laying at the back of such visible differences in appearances, bore witness to a rational order underlying both nature and, as the manifestation of that order, the human mind that was also capable of understanding it. Georges Cuvier's armoires, as Brown puts it, "charted a natural world whose apparent surfaces were only an index to what could be 'seen'" (1997: 78). The economy of the relations between words and things was entirely altered in this context. Just as the eye of the visitor was distanced from the exhibited objects in order to look through them to perceive the order underlying them, so words here functioned purely descriptively as a scientific nomenclature that was superimposed on the order of things via labels which located the exhibits to which they were attached in their proper place within the rationally partitioned space of *genera* and species.

In thus making the underlying order of nature democratically visible – or, at least, making it so in principle, provided only that the citizen would subordinate his vision to the direction of the curator – the Muséum national d'Histoire naturelle affirmed the principles of revolutionary citizenship by serving as a place "where citizens could behold for themselves the mutual identity of nature and reason" (Brown, 1997: 131). That, at any rate, was the theory. In practice, as well as in Cuvier's own later interpretation, the Muséum, by providing an insight into the invisible order underlying natural and, by implication, social life as well, served, in the aftermath of the political upheavals of the revolution, as an antidote to excessive political passion. "Civic seeing" here was an object lesson in order. The same was true of the civic lessons that the evolutionary museums, which flourished in the closing decades of the nineteenth century and in the early twentieth century, were meant to impart, but with the significant qualification that the order that had now to be seen and learnt was an evolutionary one governed by the principles of unidirectional and progressive time. This was, then, a developmental order which enjoined the "evolutionary showmen," who aimed to translate the principles of Darwinism into museum displays, to do so in ways that would make the lessons of evolution, and the political conclusions to be drawn from those lessons, readily perceptible.

This involved, as I have argued in more detail elsewhere (Bennett, 2004b), striking a delicate balance between two conflicting tendencies. On the one hand, the exhibition of progress needed to be arranged so as to locate viewers within developmental time in ways that would promote, as a civic task, an awareness of the need to contribute to the continuing progress of civilization, and thus ward off the threat of social stagnation or, worse, degeneration. The depiction of particular customs, technologies, and ways of doing things as outmoded in evolutionary terms thus served as a spur to the adoption of new forms of behavior that would further the evolutionary development of civilization, freeing it from the drag effect of unthinking habit.

On the other hand, however, in a political context in which socialist agitation was proving increasingly influential, and in which the naturally ordained orders of gender were being seriously questioned by the programs of first-wave feminism, such displays were also called on to stress the principles of evolutionary gradualism. By giving a new meaning to the old maxim that "nature makes no jumps," Darwin's account of evolution as the incremental outcome of countless unintended minor variations provided a template for late Victorian liberalism in its concern to manage progress by both encouraging and stimulating it, while simultaneously restraining it within the pre-established limits of a capitalist and patriarchal – and, of course, colonial – social order.

This resulted in a number of significant departures from the forms of "eye management" associated with the Enlightenment museum. For, since the order of things constructed by evolutionary displays was a developmental one, that order could not be revealed, as in the Enlightenment museum, by organizing the visitor's gaze to look through the objects displayed in order to provide a glimpse of the broader order of classes and *genera* into which they fitted. Yet the order of things that evolutionary arrangements aimed to render perceptible was, like its Enlightenment predecessor, still an invisible one. As the outcome of countless unintended variations, evolution, whether of species, of design traits, or of culture and civilization, was not itself directly perceptible. It could only be made visible by displaying – side by side – forms of life, or artifacts, that both resembled each other and yet were also different, and to do so in a manner that suggested that those differences had resulted from the passage of time. Evolution, that is to say, could only be seen in the relations between things and not in things themselves. This entailed that, far from looking *into* things, the visitor's eye had to be directed to look *along* the relations between them. And, even then, a correct appreciation of the direction and tempo of evolution could not be guaranteed. How to ensure that visitors followed things in the right order? How many objects to include in a sequence, given that too few intervals between the start and the end of evolutionary series would dramatize evolution, whereas too many, while getting across the message of evolutionary gradualness, would tend to clutter displays and make them illegible? These were the kinds of debates that preoccupied the directors and curators of evolutionary museums in their endeavors to make the new order of nature that the evolutionary sciences had constructed civically readable.

While clearly different from both the "pure gaze" of connoisseurship and the practice of seeing associated with the Enlightenment museum, the practice of looking along developmental series promoted by evolutionary museums was equally a form of directed seeing. As such, it gave rise to its own distinctive way of distinguishing those who could, and those who could not, properly perceive and understand its message. The structure of the "pure gaze," as we have seen, separates those who have been tutored to see art aesthetically, in and for itself, from those who have not. The penetrative look into natural history displays in order to perceive the rational order that lies behind the visible differences that mark nature's surface appearances also inscribed a division in the visiting public between those trained in the techniques of penetrative seeing and those weekend and holiday visitors who, seeing little distinction between the Muséum and the menagerie, which was also located in the Jardin des Plantes, related to both as assemblages of the curious, the marvelous, and the exotic (Burkhardt, 1997; Spray, 1997).

The differentiation of visual capacities associated with evolutionary museums was different in kind to the degree that it arose immanently from the logic underlying evolutionary displays rather than from the uneven distribution of particular visual trainings. For the meaning of evolutionary displays could only be taken in by the eye which, in sweeping along the relations between objects in evolutionary series, could also fathom their direction. This was possible only from the vantage point of the most highly developed stages of evolution. Just as, in the evolution of species, only the evolved human eye could see and understand the processes that had made its own development possible, so also only the eye that was socially and culturally evolved could properly "take in" the meaning of evolutionary displays of cultural artifacts, peoples, and ways of life. This vantage point was most evidently socially marked in its racialization: since their undeveloped state, both culturally and physiologically, was taken as axiomatic, non-white peoples and their cultures were gathered in museums only to be looked at, not to look. It was, however, also a classed vantage point, requiring that the visual practices of the working classes be subjected to a developmental program if they, too, were to see evolution correctly. In this case, as with the other examples we have considered, museum programs for "civic seeing" also involved a struggle to detach sight from the influence of popular forms of visual entertainment in view of their capacity to corrupt or misdirect the eye.

From Obstructed to Distracted Vision

The scene that Charles Willson Peale reveals and invites us to enter in his famous self-portrait before his Philadelphia museum in 1822 is, Susan Stewart (1995) argues, one of attentive viewing in which a Quaker woman holds up her hands in astonishment at the sight of a mastodon, while the attention of a father and his son are divided between the exhibits and the open book the boy is carrying as a guide, just as, behind them, another figure looks diligently at the exhibits (Figure 7.2). Seurat's *Cirque* (1891) provides a contrasting scene in which, as Jonathan Crary (2001) discusses it, the audience is distracted into a state of

Figure 7.2 The museum as a scene of attentive viewing. Charles Willson Peale, *The Artist in His Museum*, 1822. Oil on canvas. Size: 103¾ × 79⅞ in [263.5 × 202.9 cm]. Courtesy of the Pennsylvania Academy of the Fine Arts, Philadelphia. Gift of Mrs Sarah Harrison (The Joseph Harrison, Jr Collection)

trance-like immobility and disengagement from the scene of simulated movement represented by the circus performance: note, for example, the two men talking to one another on the row near the back (Figure 7.3). The painting thus reworks contemporary concerns, which were as evident in responses to early cinema as they had been in debates about earlier visual technologies such as the magic lantern, of an audience stunned into a numb, and numbing, inattentiveness as the perceptual assault of the new visual media complemented the shock of the new that was the hallmark of modern city life.

By contrast, on the cover of the April 1891 edition of *Frank Leslie's Popular Monthly*, the magic lantern is shorn of its associations of visual trickery in a depiction of a lecture at the American Museum of Natural History in which the look of the audience is subjected to the authoritative guidance of the lecturer. The same was true, later, of the conditions on which film entered into the museum. Although the American Museum of Natural History was one of the first museums to experiment with film, its distrust of the medium was reflected in the delay of

Figure 7.3 Distracted vision. George Seurat, *Cirque*, 1891. (Paris, Musée d'Orsay. Photo RMN/© Hervé Lewandowski)

fifteen years between the invention of the kinetoscope in 1893 and its first film screening. Even then, film was admitted only in carefully regulated contexts: films were to be used only in lectures where their meaning could be mediated via the scientific authority vested in the lecturer, and where the risk of distracted forms of inattentiveness could be minimized (Griffiths, 2002).

My purpose in juxtaposing these scenes of spectatorship is to highlight the respects in which museums have pitched themselves against what have been variously construed as the clouding, diverting, hynoptic, dazzling, numbing, or shock effects of more popular visual technologies in their concern to promote those forms of visual and, more broadly, perceptual attentiveness that are needed if visitors are to take part in the forms of civic self-shaping that the modern public museum has been concerned to promote. If the images I have selected here are all nineteenth-century ones, there are both earlier and more recent versions of similar tensions in the social organization of vision that have defined the countervailing forces with which museums have had to contend in their endeavors to lend a civic direction to the eye. The earliest version of these tensions is traceable to the growing epistemological and social gap that emerged, early in the eighteenth century, between the practices of wonder and those of curiosity. By the time of

Diderot's *Encyclopédie*, Lorraine Daston and Katharine Park argue, curiosity had cast off its reputation as a somewhat idle, undisciplined form of seeing to be ranked as a noble pursuit demanding sustained attention of a kind that only a few could achieve. Wonder, by contrast, had come to be regarded as a form of gawking, "a low, bumptious form of pleasure" that "obstinately refused to remedy the ignorance that aroused it" (Daston and Park, 1998: 328).

These terms in which curiosity and wonder were contrasted played a significant role in articulating the distinction between the elite and the vulgar as a distinction of visual practice and sensory comportment within the developing class dynamics of early capitalism. We can also see their lingering influence well into the nineteenth century. In Figure 7.4, the difference between, on the one hand, disciplined and knowledgeable looking and, on the other, ignorant gawking is depicted as a division within the group assembled before an exhibit at the 1876 Centennial Exhibition in Philadelphia. Joy Kasson, in discussing this image, draws attention to the difference between the knowledgeable and focused attention of the well-dressed couple at the left of the group and the other spectators who "stand amazed, mouths agape" in an "awkward posture (hands in pocket, necks craning upward)" which "marks them as visually unsophisticated, while their clothing suggests that they are probably poor and from the country" (Kasson, 1990: 38).

A similar social division informed the terms in which, at the end of the nineteenth and start of the twentieth century, the distracted attention attributed to film audiences – who were strongly associated, prior to the introduction

Figure 7.4 Wonder as gawking. "Lost in wonder." Norton, *Frank Leslie's Historical Register of the United States Centennial Exhibition*, 54

of narrative cinema and respectable exhibition venues, with the unruliness of the urban working masses – served as a negative counterpoint to the ideal of the rational, attentive, well-ordered museum-going public. And it is true still of the terms in which the relations between museums and television audiences are posed when, as in a 1996 article in *The Daily Telegraphy*, a visit to the museum is invoked as an antidote to the culture of the "couch potato," the late-twentieth-century embodiment of distracted vision, who, it is said, "sits back on the sofa, his face vacuous and dumb, and stares at the television screen, and shovels popcorn, crisps, chocolates into his agape mouth while programmes reel by" (cited in Michael, 2000: 106). For Seurat's *Cirque*, we could now substitute a typical scene from the UK television series *The Royle Family* in which a roomful of couch potatoes eat, drink, gossip, fight, and make love before the box that is never able to claim more than half of their attention.

Yet, instructive though they are, these parallels across a two-century period can prove misleading if attention is not also paid to the role of different theories of vision and the accounts these offer for the failed or distorted vision of the popular classes. The ways in which distinctions of visual capacity mark, and are marked by, social distinctions, that is to say, have to be understood as being also conditioned by different accounts of the mechanisms of seeing. As Jonathan Crary's work has shown, the transition from the geometric optics which governed European accounts of vision in the seventeenth and eighteenth centuries to the physiological optics which governed nineteenth-century accounts of vision played a key role in redefining the terms in which class anxieties associated with the politics of vision were posed. Within geometric optics based on the Cartesian model of a detached and decorporealized observer, the challenge for museums and other rational forms of visual instruction was to counter the influence of popular visual entertainments whose effect was seen as one of clouding or obstructing vision by placing an irrational filter between the eye and the world. The challenge for the museum here was to provide a clear and transparent rational alternative to such obstructed vision.

Within physiological optics, by contrast, vision was viewed as rooted in the physiological structure of the body and, thereby, emerged as simultaneously sub-jective (different from one person to another) and social (to the degree that the body is affected by the social conditions in which it is formed). This meant that the reform of vision to attune it to the requirements of "civic seeing" was a develop-mental rather than a restorative project in the sense that it had to take account of the embodied nature of the visitor's visual capacities and the ways in which these might be affected by specific social conditions (Bennett, 2004b: ch. 7). For Henry Pitt Rivers, accordingly, it was not enough to simply arrange evolutionary displays to teach the working man the lessons of progress; account had also to be taken of the specific circumstances, rooted in working-class occupations, that limited or impaired working-class vision so as to put in place a developmental program of visual instruction that would counteract those influences.

Account has also to be taken, so far as contemporary debates are concerned, of the changed relations between museums and commercialized forms of popular visual entertainment. If the incorporation of television, video, touch-screen computer displays, and Imax theaters into museums has undermined the distinction between museums and other contemporary forms of audiovisual culture, the increased importance of blockbuster exhibitions has also undermined the distinction between museums and the field of commercialized cultural production. There are, indeed, those who, like Paul Virilio (1994) and Jean Baudrillard (1982), have argued that these distinctions have now been eroded to such an extent that museums have themselves become "distraction machines." Such postmodernist perspectives typically overlook the variability of museum experience arising from the practices of different types of museum and variations in the social characteristics of their visitors. They also, Nick Prior suggests, miss the respects in which museums are now typically obliged to negotiate and balance the needs and interests of different audiences to meet government requirements that they both enlarge and diversify their visitor profiles. This means, he argues, that "the contradictory tensions that once might have threatened the idea of the museum are now permanent fixtures within it" (Prior, 2003: 67).

The tension between the museum as civic educator and the negative pull of distracted vision is thus often enacted *within* museums as forms of "civic seeing" compete with distracting visual technologies within the museum space. This tension is, indeed, sometimes playfully foregrounded in exhibits whose primary *raison d'être* is to engage with the organization of museum space as a form of meta-commentary on the conditions of museum practices. Duane Hanson's *Tourists* (1970) – two figures located in one of the galleries at the Scottish National Gallery of Modern Art – is a case in point (Figure 7.5). Gaudily dressed in casual holiday clothes, cameras at the ready, shopping in hand, these two life-like figures, installed unmarked in the middle of the gallery, catch the visitor unawares. Their verisimilitude is so strong that it takes a while to realize that they are not really other visitors, but an exhibit which, in occupying the position of spectator, foregrounds the question of the visitor's look. Are they knowledgeable visitors? Ignorant ones? Are they puzzled? Attentive? Or just bluffing? And what kind of visitor am I? How do the other visitors see me? As like these? Or as different? There is not really any way of answering these questions which, nonetheless, are insistently raised, injecting a restless tension into the museum space as the visitor is caught between self-recognition and identification as also a tourist and an uncertainty regarding just how best to play the role of spectator which, forced by the exhibit into self-consciousness, is thereby made problematic, no longer habitable on a purely spontaneous basis.

Yet these figures also point to something of broader significance by calling attention to the importance of point of view within the museum space. Throughout the greater part of the eighteenth and nineteenth centuries, seeing civically was a practice to be undertaken from the singular and fixed spectatorial position that museums sought to arrange as the ideal vantage point from which to see and understand the logic underlying the exhibition arrangements. The key developments in the twentieth century, particularly during its later decades,

Figure 7.5 The spectator as exhibit. Duane Hanson, *Tourists*, 1970. (Courtesy of The Scottish National Gallery of Modern Art, Edinburgh)

worked to pluralize the optical – and, thereby, also the epistemological and political – vantage points that visitors might take up within, or bring with them into, the museum space. This was, and continues to be, partly a matter of the development of interactive displays which, freeing visitors from the tutelary grip of earlier, more directive forms of curatorial authority, leaves them more scope for constructing their own forms of engagement with the museum environment. No longer addressing a detached observer placed before an exhibition arranged for his or her contemplative inspection, interactive displays also often dislocate the eye from its controlling position in favor of more multi-sensory forms of engagement in which sight, hearing, and touch interact to produce a more embodied, active, and participatory relationship to the museum, and to other visitors.

These transformations, Andrew Barry argues, have, in turn, to be understood in relation to the shift from earlier, more corporate models of citizenship to those of neo-liberalism. If interactivity promotes the development of more active forms of self-direction, less reliant on the authoritative guidance of others, this reflects a

135

change in the role of public authorities from one of directing the citizen to one of establishing the conditions in which citizens can become more active in, and more responsible for, their own government (Barry 2001: 135). It is, however, in response to the politics of difference and the influence on museums of the emerging agendas of cultural citizenship in their commitment to the recognition of differentiated cultural rights and entitlements that demands for museums to develop more plural forms of "civic seeing" have been most insistently pressed.

Seeing Differences Differently

Museums have, of course, always, at least in their modern forms, been places for making differences – whether natural, social, or cultural – visible. They have done so, however, mainly to and for a controlling point of view which, while theoretically universal, has, in fact, in accordance with the restricted understandings of citizenship prevailing at different historical moments, been restricted to white, middle-class men only, to white men only, to white men and women only, or to men only. Their depictions of difference have also usually been hierarchically arranged, especially, in the context of museums' varied roles in relation to colonial histories, in racialized hierarchies – whether they be those of the developmental series of typological arrangements, cranial exhibitions, or exhibitions resting on Orientalist assumptions (Dias, 1998). The first significant challenges to such hierarchical visualizations of cultural difference came, in the United States, from Franz Boas's development of the life group in its commitment to reconstruct the totality of a culture as something to be understood on its own terms and, in France, from the similar exhibition forms developed at the Musée de l'Homme by Paul Rivet and Georges-Henri Rivière and, subsequently, the *ensemble écologique* developed by Rivière at the Musée des Arts et Traditions Populaires (Dias, 2003). While these new visual technologies proved important as a means for equalizing the relations between exhibited cultures in the museum space, they proved problematic in other regards, seeming to fix the cultures they depicted in a condition of static timelessness (Dias, 1994). Their chief limitation from a contemporary perspective, however, is that they did little to challenge the assumption that there was one, and only one, point of view for the visitor to occupy.

By contrast, the terms in which questions of "civic seeing" are now posed typically stress the need for exhibitions to be arranged so as to allow multiple possibilities in terms of how they are both seen and interpreted. The demands of indigenous peoples, of diasporic communities and minority ethnic groups of longstanding, of women, and of minority sexualities for recognition within the museum space have thrown into high relief the socially marked nature of the supposedly universal, singular point of view museums had earlier constructed as the sole one from which their civic lessons might be correctly seen and interpreted. At the same time, new approaches to difference, whether of ethnicity, sexuality, or gender, which stress their unfixed, relational, constantly mobile nature, have called into question the taxonomic approaches to difference which characterized museum practices throughout the nineteenth century and well into the twentieth.

This stress on the relationality of difference – the view, as Kevin Hetherington (2002: 196) puts it, "that we all differ from one another because of gender, class, ethnicity, age, sexual orientation, etc. and not that just some differ from an unmarked norm" – has led, in the steps that museums have taken to translate public-policy agendas of cultural diversity into practical and material forms, to access strategies that are posed in terms of "multiple optics rather than a singular trained one" (Hetherington, 2002: 192). And this, in turn, has led to a significant renewal of interest in exhibition practices from the pre-Enlightenment period when the eye was not so singularly addressed or so authoritatively regulated. James Clifford's (1997) influential conception of museums as "contact zones" – as places where the perspectives of different cultures can mix and mingle, entering into dialogic exchanges that are not subordinated to a controlling point of view – has thus been connected to a notable increase in the attention paid to cabinets of curiosity both for the possibility they hold out of a more flexible, varied, and dialogic organization of the visitor's lines of sight and as a reminder of exhibition contexts in which seeing was accompanied by reciprocal relations of conversational give-and-take.

It is, however, in programs intended to make museums accessible to the visually impaired that the continuing optical bias of museums is most revealingly thrown into high relief. The visually impaired, Hetherington argues, constitute a special case for the museum as "they are not just another category of difference demanding that they be recognised and catered for, from the start they are Other to the principles of the museum as a space of vision and conservation" (Hetherington, 2002: 195). Examining a number of initiatives, from the Tate's first touch tour for the blind in 1976 to the 1998 tactile display and book produced by the British Museum to make the Parthenon Frieze accessible to the visually impaired, Hetherington usefully draws attention to the respects in which they reflect a continuing optical bias. The tactile book prepared for the Parthenon Frieze, for example, aimed to make available to touch an impression of the frieze as it might be seen, thus functioning as a sight-centered organization of touch in a context where actually touching the frieze itself was not allowed. It was, as Hetherington puts it, "an optical prosthesis in which the hand (secondary) can become like the eye (primary)" (Hetherington, 2002: 199). It is a useful example in underlining how far museum practices would need to change if the eye-centered programs of "civic seeing" that have dominated the museum's post-Enlightenment history were to be developed into places for more pluri-directional civic exchanges that engage a broader range of the visitors' senses.

Part IV   Intellectuals, Culture, Politics

Chapter Eight Intellectuals, Culture, Policy:
The Technical, the Practical, and the Critical

There are now ample signs that cultural policy is emerging as an increasingly important area of theoretical and practical engagement for intellectuals working in the fields of sociology and cultural studies. This has occasioned a good deal of debate concerning the roles of intellectuals and the relationships they should adopt in relation to the bureaucratic and political processes through which cultural policies are developed and put into effect. It is with these debates that I engage here with a view to distinguishing the light that might be thrown on them by different accounts of the social roles and distribution of different kinds of intellectual function.[1] My concerns here will center on the relations between two traditions of social theory.[2] The first derives from Jürgen Habermas's classic study of the public sphere (Habermas, 1989) and theorizes the role of intellectuals in terms of the distinction between critical and technical intellectual functions which characterizes Habermas's construction of the relationships between different forms of rationality. The second comprises the tradition which, following in the wake of Michel Foucault's essay on governmentality (Foucault, 1978), has concerned itself with the roles of particular forms of knowledge and expertise in organizing differentiated fields of government and social management.

My starting point will be with the Habermasian tradition. The concept of the public sphere is, of course, one that now need no longer be constrained by its Habermasian lineage. In its post-Habermasian history, moreover, the concept has made positive contributions to both the theory and practice of cultural policy. It has supplied the language through which governments have been called on – with some success – to develop forms of media regulation that will inhibit the oligopolistic tendencies of media industries by providing for at least some semblance of democracy and diversity in the role of the media in the organization and circulation of opinion.[3] The differentiation of Habermas's singular public sphere into plural public spheres – feminist and indigenous, for example – has also been important in legitimating claims on the public purse which have helped in winning new forms of public, and publicly educative, presence for groups excluded from the classical bourgeois public sphere.[4] My concerns, however, are less with these adaptations of the Habermasian concept than with Habermas's own account of the public sphere and the role it has played in subsequent debates, when viewed in the light of the splitting of intellectual work between the differentiated functions of *critique* and *praxis* which he proposes.[5]

My engagements with this tradition of work will be of three kinds. First, I shall argue that Habermas's polarizing procedures do not offer us a cogent basis for debating and assessing the politics of contemporary intellectual practice. Their main weakness is that of dividing reason into two without then being able to offer any means of reconnecting its severed parts except through the endlessly deferred mechanism of the dialectic. Second, I shall argue that Habermas's account of the development and subsequent deterioration of the bourgeois public sphere seriously misunderstands the role that the main institutions of public culture have played in the development of modern practices of cultural governance. A Habermasian theoretical world-view, to come to my third concern, also fails to see how the roles played by the personnel of culture in managing cultural resources involve attention to questions of a technical kind in ways that do not automatically entail that such personnel should be cast in the role of critical reason's bureaucratic other.

The vantage points from which I pursue these three concerns are ones supplied by different branches of the post-Foucauldian literature on governmentality. In developing the first argument, I draw on work which stresses the ethical comportment which characterizes the conduct of bureaucratized intellectual functions. This aspect of my argument serves to undercut the view that the exercise of practical intellectual functions within bureaucratic contexts can serve as an "ethics-free zone" in counterpoint to the ethical purity of the critical intellectual. The second point is developed by looking again at Habermas's historical account of the public sphere through the lens of post-Foucauldian inquiries into the development of modern forms of government and culture. In developing my third argument I draw on Foucauldian perspectives on the relationships between expertise and government to identify the wide range of functions performed by the personnel of culture as parts of governmental programs aimed at deploying cultural resources as a means of acting on the social.

The Critical and the Practical

Jim McGuigan's *Culture and the Public Sphere* offers a convenient point of entry into the first set of issues. This closes in posing two questions: How can critical intellectuals be practical? And how can practical intellectuals be critical? By critical intellectuals McGuigan has in mind intellectuals whose work is academic in the sense that the conditions in which it takes place disconnect it from any immediate practical outcomes for which those intellectuals can be held responsible. The problem for such intellectuals, then, is that the opportunity for critically reflexive work which such conditions make possible is purchased at the price of a loss of any immediate practical effectivity. The practical intellectuals McGuigan refers to are cultural workers "engaged in some form of communication and cultural management" in practical contexts where, as he defines them, "the possibilities of critical knowledge...have already been closed off" by the need for "recipe knowledge" (McGuigan, 1996: 190). Two kinds of intellectual, then, each of whom, at least at first sight, seems to lack what the other possesses. It becomes clear on further inspection, however, that the relations between these different categories of intellectual are not, and cannot become, relations of exchange. Rather, they take the form of a one-way street in which the task enjoined on the critical intellectual is that of dislodging the forms of reasoning – the "recipe knowledge" – which govern the contexts in which practical intellectuals do their work. The most that can be asked of practical intellectuals – parties to a gift relationship in which they can only be receivers – is that they should be prepared to jettison those forms of reasoning which spontaneously characterize their work in favor of the essentially different forms of reasoning represented, and selflessly donated, by critical intellectuals.

How is that these lowly servants of a mere "recipe knowledge" find themselves placed on the opposite side of a divide separating them from the realms in which critical intellectuals operate? This separation is the local manifestation of a more fundamental division between critical and instrumental reason which has its roots in Habermas's account of the division between system and lifeworld and their opposing principles of rationality. In the latter, where communication is relatively undistorted by uneven relationships of power and where there is a common interest in shared horizons of meaning arising out of shared conditions of life, communicative rationality is orientated to mutual understanding. By contrast, the instrumental rationality which characterizes the world of system is one which displaces questions of human value and meaning in favor of a means-end rationality whose direction is dictated by existing structures of class and bureaucratic power. This opposition between system and lifeworld is most economically represented in the terms of Habermas's distinction between *praxis* and *techne*. The first of these, as Habermas glosses it, is concerned with the reasoned assessment of the validity of norms for action whereas *techne* is concerned solely with the rational selection of the best instruments for achieving particular outcomes once the normative goals for social action have been determined (Habermas, 1974: 1–3).

When these broader aspects of the argument are taken into account, it is clear that the form of mediation that McGuigan proposes for overcoming the separation of critical and practical intellectuals would extend the sway of *praxis*, whose spokesperson is the critical intellectual, beyond the lifeworld into the world of system where it would ideally displace, or provide a superordinate context for, the application of *techne*. At the same time, however, the prospects of this actually happening are not good to the degree that the conditions of work of intellectuals located within the world of system predispose them to focus exclusively on narrowly technical forms of reason and action. Thus lessons of *praxis*, since they do "not tell us *directly* what to do," will "always be regarded as unsatisfactory by those who prefer to act without thinking; in effect, those who want recipe knowledge but not critical thought, information but not ideas" (McGuigan, 1996: 187). McGuigan seems not to notice the paradoxical effects of a body of theory which, on the one hand, holds out the possibility of universally valid norms of communication and mutual understanding arising out of the shared conditions of the lifeworld while, on the other, dividing reason into two antimonial realms – *praxis* and *techne* – whose separation, once established, cannot be overcome except by imposing the values of one on the other. What is perhaps more harmful, however, is the mapping of this opposition between different kinds of reason onto the relations between different kinds of intellectuals working in different contexts.

The dubious value of this procedure is all the more evident when it is considered that, in most other regards, the differences between these so-called critical and practical intellectuals would seem to be so slight. From everything that we know of the demographic characteristics and shared occupational cultures of academics and cultural intermediaries and policy professionals, it might have been thought that they would be able to communicate effectively with one another on matters of common practical and intellectual concern from the perspective of a shared horizon of professional, social, and cultural understandings. Indeed, I would contend that this *is* so, except in the world of the dualities generated by critical reason where it *cannot* be so. For even assuming that they deign to do so, once critical intellectuals take it upon themselves to connect their work to the realm of system, the democratic norm that all parties to any communicative interaction should be treated as equal is abandoned as the critical intellectual assumes a discursive position – a capacity for critical independence and detachment – that is, by definition, superior to that of the purely technical competence of the administrator or manager. This superiority is invested with further normative significance in the related assumption that the "culture of dissatisfaction" that results from the restlessly self-reflexive persona of the critical intellectual is the sole source of progressive change within the administration of culture, and one that is pitched constantly against the inertia and conservatism of the agencies and personnel that are actually responsible for the development and implementation of cultural policies. As McGuigan puts it:

> The culture of dissatisfaction is the perpetual bugbear of any official cultural policy: the very officialness of governmental policy, in effect, makes it conservative, the upholder of the status quo, from the point of view of a restless dissatisfaction with the way things are presently constituted ... The new ideas and most important issues are always engendered by a sense of dissatisfaction coming from outside the currently official system. Official institutions and practices of cultural policy are like authoritarian states ultimately doomed when they are closed to the constant pressures exerted by cultural dissatisfaction.' (McGuigan, 1996: 50)

It is easy to see how the dualities informing this passage have an element of self-fulfilling prophecy built into them. For if McGuigan's purpose really is to build bridges between critical and practical intellectuals, the Habermasian spin he gives to this task makes him a poor diplomat in his own cause. For what are the chances that the communications and cultural managers who *do* read his book might feel parties to an open and unconstrained dialog in which the positions, perspectives and experiences of intellectual workers situated in different contexts might be regarded as matters for genuine debate? Not strong, I'd have thought, given that they have been defined in wholly negative terms as the source of a lack owing to their incapacity for critical or independent thought.[6]

This is a pity, and especially so as there are no good reasons for taking the virtues of *critique* so much for granted. There is now a substantial body of work which, far from taking *critique* to be a transcendent and self-subsistent norm – and so being above criticism, so to speak – historicizes and relativizes it in ways which seriously question its ethical, epistemological, and political credentials. A significant case in point is Bruno Latour's recent questioning of emancipatory rhetorics. Contending that the prospect of revolutionary simplifications of the social has now ceded place to the challenge of "coexistence between totally heterogeneous forms of people, cultures, epochs and entities," he argues that the complexities this entails mean that the arrow of time can no longer run from "slavery to freedom" but only from "entanglement to more entanglement" (Latour, 1999a: 13–15). From perspectives of this kind, it becomes possible to read the tradition of critical sociology, to which Habermas's work belongs, as itself a powerful form of "recipe knowledge." As heir to the tradition of post-Kantian philosophy, it guarantees a continuing role for *critique* by its formulaic construction of the historical process as one which establishes divisions (in this case, between *praxis* and *techne* and its various derivatives) which have then to be overcome and reconciled with the aid of the philosopher-sociologist's critical intellectual mediation. It is by means of this operation that *critique*, as a stylized intellectual practice, is substituted for more grounded forms of critical inquiry in making an entirely predictable set of intellectual routines whose form, moves, and conclusions – in setting up oppositions and projecting their reconciliation while simultaneously regretting the factors which impede the unfolding of this ideal dialectic – stand in the place of an analytical engagement with the recalcitrant positivity and dispersed diversity of social relations and forces.

I am more concerned here, however with the other side of the Habermasian division of the sphere of reason into two. For the purely means-end rationality of bureaucratic reason can be rescued from the terms of Habermas's condemnation by recognizing that it can lay its own claims to virtue on grounds that are simultaneously ethical, critical, and historical. Ian Hunter's spirited defense of the bureaucratic vocation will serve as a good point of entry into these concerns.[7] For in restoring an appropriate degree of virtue to the bureaucrat, Hunter also calls into question the absolutist forms of authority which those who speak in the voice of the critical intellectual spontaneously and unreflectively claim as their own. In doing so, he strips *critique* of its pretensions to universality in both circumscribing the spheres in which it can operate while also severely limiting the kinds of influence it can exert on the practical conduct of human affairs.

Hunter takes his initial bearings from those ways of depicting the persona of the bureaucrat which project it "as 'one side' of a full moral personality, the other side of which is represented by the 'humanist intellectual' " who is the mirror image of the bureaucrat in espousing "a commitment to substantive values" while lacking the "technical means for realising them" (Hunter, 1994: 146). While this division of the world of reason into two rests on Weber's neo-Kantian distinction between instrumentally rational and value-rational forms of social action, Weber's position differed from Kant's in refusing to make the humanist intellectual the ultimate arbiter of value-rational action. Weber's stance was rather pluralistic and sociological, regarding the ends of value-rational action as being multiple and specific to particular spheres of life and giving rise to distinctive ethical disposi- tions and capacities. This included, Hunter is shrewd to note, an assessment of the bureaucracy's commitment to instrumentally rational action as itself constituting a distinctive ethos of office requiring particular ethical capacities rather than figuring as a sphere of moral vacuousness and critical emptiness.

This leads Hunter to suggest that what Habermas devalues as mere *techne* is the result of a specific ethical training rather than a form of ethical lack. The bureau, he says, is not something that has been separated off from critical reason as a result of some split in the lifeworld or the opening of some historical chasm in the organization of public life. Rather, it is the site for the formation of a distinctive ethical persona in the sense that "the office itself constitutes a 'vocation' (*Beruf*), a focus of ethical commitment and duty, autonomous of and superior to the holder's extra-official ties to kith, kin, class or, for that matter, conscience" (Hunter, 1994: 156). The construction of this persona and the associated routines of office, Hunter suggests, need to be valued as "a positive organizational and ethical acquisition, involving an important augmentation of our technologies for living" in view of their capacity "to detach governmental decisions from personal loyalties and religious passions" (Hunter, 1994: 155). From this perspective, to denounce the instrumentalism of bureaucracy for its apparently amoral indifference to qualita- tive ends is to fail to appreciate the historically distinctive form of morality which such an ethos of office represents:

> The ethical attributes of the good bureaucrat – strict adherence to procedure, acceptance of sub- and super-ordination, *esprit de corps*, abnegation of personal moral enthusiasms, commitment to the purposes of the office – are not an incom- petent subtraction from a "complete" (self-concerned and self-realising) comport- ment of the person. On the contrary, they are a positive moral achievement requiring the mastery of a difficult milieu and practice. (Hunter, 1994: 156–7)[8]

Why, then, is the critical intellectual more likely, instead, to devalue the bureau- crat as a one-sided and incomplete embodiment of the function of reason?

In answering this question, Hunter draws on Weber's general sociological principles, treating the post-Kantian construction of the critical intellectual as a person
committed to a higher and universal sense of moral duty as itself a particular ethos
requiring analysis in terms of its relations to particular kinds of social prestige and
power.[9] When considered sociologically, "the persona of the self-reflective scholar
acting on the basis of inner conviction is no more ethically fundamental than that
of the official, whose ethos involves subordinating his inner convictions to the
duties of office" (Hunter, 1994: 163). Both represent specific moral dispositions
cultivated through the exercise of particular spiritual disciplines and routines.
Critique, however, arranges these differences hierarchically by "treating its own
status-persona – the self-reflective scholar, the 'complete' person ... – as 'ultimate'
for all comportments of the person, the bureaucrat and citizen included" (Hunter,
1994: 163). Hunter is clear in seeing this absolutizing tendency of *critique* as part of
a tactics of intellectual life through which a particular stratum of intellectuals,
while disconnected from the actual administrative forms through which social life
is organized, aspires to a distinctive kind of social influence. This is to be achieved
by cultivating the status of moral notables who, speaking to the world at large,
claim the mantle of a "secular holiness" which, as part of a practice of "world
flight," allows them to "criticise the dominant organization of social life by
practising an exemplary withdrawal from it" (Hunter, 1994: 167).

Said's *Representations of the Intellectual* provides a convenient example of this
practice of "secular holiness" and of the forms of critical intolerance and ethical
bullying it entails. For Said's strategy in elaborating his view of the intellectual as an
exile and marginal, as an amateur whose true vocation is "to speak the truth to
power" (Said, 1994: xiv), depends on trapping professionals, experts, and consult-
ants – those false intellectuals who have traded their critical independence for
wealth, power, and influence – in the contaminating mire of their associations with
worldly powers and the limitations, of perspective or of moral capacity, that these
entail. Said's "world flight" into universality is thus sustained by the role in which
the bureaucratic or managerialist intellectual is cast as the low Other against whom
the stellar trajectory of the true intellectual – the amateur whose activity "is fuelled
by care and affection rather than by profit, and selfish, narrow specialisation"
(Said, 1994: 61) – can be mapped:

> In other words, the intellectual properly speaking is not a functionary or an
> employee completely given up to the policy goals of a government or a large
> corporation, or even a guild of like-minded professionals. In such situations the
> temptations to turn off one's moral sense, or to think entirely from within the
> speciality, or to curtail scepticism in favour of conformity, are far too great to be
> trusted. (Said, 1994: 64)

But how clear-sighted is the universal intellectual when he has cut a moral trench
between himself and other intellectual workers? In truth: not very. Said, in what
he has to say about the relationships between intellectuals and government, surveys

the world through the tinted lenses of a metropolitan parochialism whose belief in its universal validity is based on nothing so much as a constitutive blindness to its own forms of limiting particularity. For when Said – speaking to and for all the world – places true intellectuals outside of government and charges them to speak the truth to power, it is clear that he imagines government always and only in the form of some branch of the US science-military-industry complex.[10] The possibility that, in other parts of the world, intellectuals might see themselves as speaking the truth to *and for* more local forms of power with a view to muting or qualifying the effects of other forms of power is simply not thinkable from within Said's elementary bi-polar construction of the relations of truth and power. I have in mind here the role that intellectuals – whether as academics, government employees or as public intellectuals – have played in the development of progressive nationalist cultural policies in contexts (France, Australia, Scotland, Wales, Canada) where this is seen as involving both setting limits and nourishing alternatives to the invasive influence of other dominant national cultures (American, English). The same is true of intellectuals who work within government as cultural workers of various kinds – curators, community arts workers, arts administrators – in cultural diversity, community or art and working life programs.

This is not to suggest that any of these contexts for intellectual work are without their ambiguities and contradictions. My point is rather that the simplified and polarized construction Said places on the politics of intellectual life does not allow an adequate recognition, let alone resolution, of those ambiguities and contradictions. More important, it eviscerates the work of the critical intellectual in sanctioning a refusal to engage with those ambiguities and contradictions. For Said, the intellectual must choose "the risks and uncertain results of the public sphere – a lecture or a book or article in wide and unrestricted circulation – over the insider space controlled by experts and professionals" (Said, 1994: 64). Yet this either/or-ism is misleading owing to its inability to distinguish the radically different forms in which – depending on the issue and the context – the relationships between specific regions of government and specific realms of public debate might be related to one another. For there are intellectuals who manage to speak into, and to influence opinion on, matters of general public concern in ways that have long-term consequences for the ways in which bureaucratic forms of social and cultural administration are exercised, while also taking account of the distinctive technical and ethical exigencies which characterize the practice of those who work in such bureaus. This is not remotely possible, however, if the realms of the critical and the technical are hermetically separated from one another at the outset in ways which require that the latter should be subordinated to the former (even though, in fact, it clearly is not).

There is a need, then, for those who aspire to be critical intellectuals to look more closely at their own practice and the conditions which sustain it. This, in its turn, will require a clearer differentiation of *critique*, as a highly specific practice – a moral technology, in effect – dependent on the discursive coordinates of post-Kantian philosophy, from the more general categories of criticism or critical thought. This is necessary if we are to recognize that intellectuals can both contribute critically to public debate about particular forms of social and cultural policy, assessing these in terms of their shortcomings when viewed from particular ethical and political standpoints, while at the same time contributing their expertise to particular areas of policy formation and learning from the other intellectuals, working within the policy process, with whom such work brings them into contact. To engage in critical thought in this way, however, does not require – and is not assisted by – any rigid separation of means-end from normative rationality of the kind proposed by *critique*. Nor does it require any elevation of the latter over the former. Critical thought, no matter who its agent might be, is most productive when conducted in a manner which recognizes the need to take account of the contributions of different forms of expertise without any a priori prejudicial ranking of the relations between them and, equally, when it takes account of the forces – social, economic, political, and moral – which circumscribe the field of the practicable.

To put the matter in this way is also to allow the possibility that intellectual work conducted within the bureaus of social and cultural administration may possess an in-built mechanism of critical self-reflexiveness. This is especially so if the issue is posed at the level of institutional practices rather than that of the mental proced-ures of individuals. Jeffrey Minson's work has been suggestive here in identifying the respects in which bureaucratic forms of management are structurally restless owing to the incorporation within them of principles of reflexive self-monitoring which make for what is often a remorseless capacity for unending change (see Minson, 1993). There are, of course, countervailing tendencies in which bureau-cratic processes function to manage political tensions by "massaging" policy processes so as to favor specific outcomes. Nor can there be any ducking the fact such processes can be applied in the pursuit of ends that are socially and politically debilitating: the literature on the functioning of bureaucratic mechanisms in the context of eugenic or fascist programs is ample proof of this. To recognize the potential critical effects of bureaucratic procedures is not to minimize the equally crucial questions concerning the social and political ends toward which those procedures are directed, and the need for these to be arrived at through open and democratic procedures.

However, this does not gainsay the point that bureaucratic procedures are a form in which the requirements of a critical self-reflexiveness are institutionalized since it is in the very nature of those procedures to interrogate their own effectiveness in accomplishing particular ends. In these ways, bureaucratic mech-anisms have built into them means of connecting with the realms of social life they are responsible for administering as well as for being corrected and revised in the light of those connections. It is here that the opposition McGuigan poses in counterposing the "culture of dissatisfaction" as the source of a restless demand for change to the closure and stasis of the bureaucratic apparatuses of government is so questionable. While the mechanisms of connection that characterize bureaucratic procedures are, no doubt, imperfect, they are a significant advance on those of *critique* which often accomplishes little more than to repeat endlessly the same moves, as it establishes sets of polarities whose mediation or reconciliation it then projects as a goal to be accomplished via its own dialectical conjuring tricks – and all of this without ever having to give an account of how this is to be done in terms of the connections it will establish with the actual forms of social and cultural administration through which social and cultural life are managed.

Yet this is the central point at issue, and one that will be greatly assisted if, rather than seeing questions of mediation as ones concerning how to overcome the apparently irreconcilable divisions which split the realm of reason into its critical and instrumental forms, poses them as questions concerning the need for new forms of *institutional and organizational* connection capable of interrelating the work that intellectual workers of different kinds do in different contexts. For there is no cognitive or, indeed, ethical gulf separating intellectuals working in government and industry centers of cultural management from those working in universities. There are, to be sure, different pressures, exigencies, and priorities bearing on these different contexts. However, these are best represented not in the form of an essential split between different mental operations but as a division between those contexts in which intellectual work is disconnected from immediate practical consequences (academic contexts) and those in which it is, and has to be, connected to such consequences (government and industry contexts). This is a significant difference, and one in which the benefits afforded by academic contexts – the latitude to canvass a broader range of issues, to bring a historical perspective to bear, to have long-term considerations in view, to take the points of view of constituencies who might otherwise be marginalized – should be valued as enabling distinctive contributions to be made to the actual, and no doubt compromised and contested, processes through which cultural life is organized and managed. However, intellectuals working in such contexts will constantly marginalize themselves and what they have to offer if they broach this task as involving haughtily hailing across a moral and cognitive divide, rather than as a matter of devising institutionalized mechanisms of exchange that will allow academic knowledges to connect productively with the intellectual procedures of policy bureaus. For these inescapably comprise an interface which academic intellectuals have to recognize as a necessary and valid, but not exclusive, point of reference for their work. Equally, of course, there is need for reform on the "other side" of this exchange: more open policy processes, less "control freakery" and, so far as the culture and media industries are concerned, better ways of mediating the relations between commercial advantage and public interest that are involved in their own research activities. But these are not questions that require the epistemological mediation of different intellectual faculties.

To approach them productively, however, will require that we review our sense both of where public spheres are and the nature of our relations to them. This requires a cautious assessment of the value of Habermas's work on this subject. This is not to gainsay the role it has played in providing the primary point of reference for the now extensive literature in which the concept of a public and democratic space for, and function of, intellectual life has been both elaborated and sustained within European and Anglo-American debates.[11] Its influence – although not without qualification – on debates in the Asia-Pacific region has also been strong and increasing over the past decade.[12] I want to suggest, however, that the support it has lent the view that the public sphere or spheres comprise an institutional and discursive realm which might provide a critical exterior in relation to the power effects of both state and economy is historically misleading and politically unhelpful.

Relocating the Public Sphere

The general contours of Habermas's account of the rise and fall of the classical bourgeois public sphere are well known. The classical bourgeois public sphere is understood in terms of its role in forming a public which, through reasoned debate, aspired to articulate a public will as a set of demands arrived at independently of the state or public authority and advanced in the expectation that they would need to be taken into account in the exercise of state power. The radical implications of this commitment to a critical rationality are then subsequently lost as a consequence of the increasing commercialization and bureaucratization of public communications from the mid-nineteenth century onwards. While I cannot engage here with the detail of this account, I want to propose a different way of reading the historical unfolding of the relations between government and culture. Rather than seeing the founding ideals of the public sphere as being subsequently overturned through bureaucratic forms of statism and new forms of commercial cultural production and distribution, this would trace the steps through which the institutions and practices of the public sphere have been translated into modern forms of cultural governance in which cultural resources are applied to varied tasks of social management. This is not, though, a matter of offering a history that is entirely at odds with Habermas's account. Rather, the view I wish to develop can be arrived at by means of, first, highlighting an aspect of his discussion of the classical bourgeois public sphere that has not always received the attention it merits, and, second, commenting on an equally little-remarked absence in the account he offers of the subsequent structural transformation of the public sphere.

The first point is most easily introduced via a commentary on Habermas's diagrammatic representation of the bourgeois public sphere at the moment of its emergence in the eighteenth century. His depiction is as follows:

Private realm		Sphere of public authority
Civil society (realm of commodity exchange and social labor)	Public sphere in the political realm	State (realm of the "police")
	Public sphere in the world of letters (clubs, press)	
Conjugal family's internal space (bourgeois intellectuals)	(markets of culture products) "Town"	Court (courtly-noble society)

Figure 8.1   Habermas's representation of the bourgeois public sphere. English translation © 1989 Massachusetts Institute of Technology. Reprinted with permission from The MIT Press and Polity. (Habermas, 1989: 30)

The division that most concerns Habermas is that between the sphere of public authority and the private realm: hence the double line separating the two. He accordingly approaches the manner in which the different components of the private realm interact with one another from the point of view of their common differentiation from the sphere of public authority. From this perspective, what matters most about the public sphere in the world of letters (or, as Habermas also calls it, the literary public sphere) is its role as a set of sites for forming opinions that are to be taken heed of in the exercise of state power. Similarly, the market for cultural products plays a historical role in desanctifying cultural products with the consequence that they are able to play a role in these secular processes of opinion formation. In detaching such products from their aura, the market allows works of culture to become objects of critical discussion with the consequence, first, that they become embroiled in the critique of both the state and courtly society and, second, that they become vehicles for the enunciation of new generalized rights of public accessibility: the public for culture becomes, for the first time, theoretically universal.

It is noteworthy that Habermas sees the historical emergence of culture's autonomy as a necessary precondition for the process through which culture is then enlisted as a political instrument in the formation of a public opinion critical of, and opposed to, the realm of public authority. This instrumental view of culture –

the notion, that is, that cultural forms and institutions are shaped into new instruments to serve new purposes – emerges from the language of "functional conversion" which Habermas uses to account for the detachment of the literary public sphere from its earlier tutelage to the publicity apparatus of the prince's court and its refashioning into a properly bourgeois public sphere. This bourgeois status, however, is clearly an historically acquired rather than an autochthonous attribute. The procedures and the composition of the institutions comprising the public sphere, and the role these play in allowing cultural resources to be harnessed in the cause of rational and public critique, are the results of a historical process through which earlier institutions and practices are functionally converted to new uses:

> The process in which the state-governed public sphere was appropriated by the public of private people making use of their reason and was established as a sphere of criticism of public authority was one of functionally converting the public sphere in the world of letters already equipped with institutions of the public and with forums for discussion. (Habermas, 1989: 51)

The institutions of the literary public sphere, then, comprised a site in which culture, via the new forms of critical commentary and debate through which its reception was mediated, was forged into a means of acting against the sphere of public authority. It did so in a manner that was conditioned by the role those institutions played in forging a critical and public rationality out of the differentiated interests comprising the private realm. But this does not exhaust what Habermas has to say about this new realm of public culture, or about the directions in which it faced and the surfaces on which it acted. To the contrary, he is clear that, through the literary public sphere, cultural goods became involved in new spheres of action in the relationships they entered into in connection with what Habermas variously characterizes as civil society or the sphere of the social: that is, with the institutions comprising the left-hand column in the diagram above. For if the public sphere mediated between the sphere of public authority and the social, it faced both ways in doing so with the result that the use of cultural resources within the public sphere also had a dual aspect to it. It was, at one and the same time, a means for forming a public opinion in a rational critique of state power, and a means of acting on the social to regulate it. This is made clear in the terms Habermas uses to differentiate the functioning of the modern public sphere from that of the ancient public sphere:

> With the rise of a sphere of the social, over whose regulation public opinion battled with public power, the theme of the modern (in contrast to the ancient) public sphere shifted from the properly political tasks of a citizenry acting in common (i.e., administration of law as regards internal affairs and military survival as regards external affairs) to the more properly civic tasks of a society engaged in critical public debate (i.e., the protection of a commercial economy). The political task of the bourgeois public sphere was the regulation of civil society (in contradistinction to the *res publica*). (Habermas, 1989: 52)

This dual orientation of the public sphere is reflected in the contrasting positions that the personnel of culture were obliged to adopt according to whether their activities were directed toward the sphere of public authority or that of the social. In the early stages of the public sphere's formation, the new cultural role of the art critic was thus, according to Habermas, "a peculiarly dialectical" one in view of the requirement that he serve "at the same time as the public's mandatary and as its educator" (Habermas, 1989: 41), both taking a lead from the public and directing and organizing it. The point, however, is a general one: all of the new forms of criticism (art, theatrical, musical, moral weeklies) and institutions (theaters, museums, concerts, coffee houses) Habermas is concerned with had, in the late eighteenth and early nineteenth centuries, this dual orientation. Nor, at this time, was this perceived as a contradiction: it was by acting on the social that the institutions of the public sphere formed a public opinion which was then able to act on the sphere of public authority.

Habermas associates these aspects of the public sphere with what he characterizes as "the tension-charged field between state and society" (Habermas, 1989: 141). His account of the subsequent social-structural transformation of the public sphere rests mainly on his argument concerning the tendencies which, in closing down the gap between state and society, led to what he calls a "refeudalisation of society". This resulted from two intersecting processes in which public functions were transferred to private corporate bodies (the modern firm) while, at the same time, the sway of public authority was extended over the private realm. "Only this dialectic of a progressive 'societalisation' of the state," as Habermas puts it, "simultaneously with an increasing 'statification' of society gradually destroyed the basis of the bourgeois public sphere – the separation of state and society" (Habermas, 1989: 142). Caught in the pincer movement comprised by these two tendencies, the public sphere, in its liberal form, ceased to exist. The contradictory space in which it had operated was no longer there: the autonomy of the social as an independent realm was no longer sustainable as a result of the new forms of private and public administration which directly repoliticized society in subjecting it to increasingly direct and extensive forms of control. At the same time, the development of new forms of mass consumption deprived culture of that hard-won historical autonomy that had earlier allowed it to function as an instrument of criticism through its connection to the public sphere. The forms in which the new mass culture was distributed – book clubs, for example – disconnected it from any public context of debate and criticism except for administered forms (Habermas's examples are the adult education class and the radio panel discussion).[13] The commercialization of culture which had once provided for culture's autonomy now takes it away:

> To be sure, at one time the commercialization of cultural goods had been the *precondition* for rational-critical debate; but it was itself in principle excluded from the exchange relationships of the market and remained the centre of exactly that sphere in which property-owning private people would meet as "human beings" and

only as such. Put bluntly: you had to pay for books, theatre, concert, and museum, but not for the conversation about what you had read, heard, and seen and what you might completely absorb only through this conversation. (Habermas, 1989: 164)

The shortcomings of Habermas's account of this social-structural transformation of the public sphere have been thoroughly rehearsed in the literature. These usually focus on the liability of his account to the pessimism of the Frankfurt School's mass culture critique and the considerable historical foreshortening which characterizes his tendency to treat the period from the 1870s through to the 1950s more or less indiscriminately. The issues I want to focus on here, however, concern two aspects of Habermas's account which, taken separately, might occasion no particular concern but which, when looked at together, suggest a different light in which the tendencies he is concerned with might be described and accounted for. The first concerns his characterization of the last quarter of the nineteenth century, the period in which the public sphere is structurally transformed, as marking the end of the liberal era. The second concerns the marked narrowing in the focus of his attention which results from his limiting his account of the transformation of the public sphere to the press and the book industry. The broader range of institutions which form a part of his account of the historical formation of the classical bourgeois public sphere – museums, concerts, art galleries – do not enter into his account of this later period any more than does the new institution which arguably ought to have been at the center of an account organized primarily in relation to the literary public sphere: the public library.

Habermas's perspectives on the first of these matters are drawn from what were, at the time he was writing, the standard Marxist accounts of the shift from liberal to monopoly capitalism. For Habermas, this transformation in the structure of the economy entailed a related move away from liberal forms of government and a consequent closure of the relations between state and society which he summarizes as a tendency toward the "refeudalisation" of society. This is extremely questionable. It is, of course, true, to take the British case that he dwells on so much, that the last quarter of the nineteenth century did see the introduction of a new form of liberalism which, in comparison with the "Manchester liberalism" of the earlier period, supported a stronger role for state intervention, particularly in the moral sphere. But it is equally true that the programs of liberal government that developed over this period, especially insofar as they involved using cultural resources to regulate the moral sphere, depended on – and worked to maintain – a separation between state and society. This was evident in their construction of the social as a realm which the state might intervene in only indirectly, through the mechanisms of moral reform, primarily with a view to making the members of society voluntarily self-regulating and self-directing without the need for more direct forms of state intervention. It is clear, moreover, that the programs of late nineteenth-century liberal cultural reformers and administrators were explicitly motivated by a commitment to retain the separation of state and society in opposition to the closure of the gap between the two that was involved in the panoptic and directly interventionist forms of state action implied by eugenic conceptions of the role of government.[14]

However, I shall not pursue this line of analysis further except to suggest that, to the degree that the separation of state and society was undermined in this period, this had little to do with any "refeudalisation" of state–society relations. Rather, it was an effect of the increasing racialization of relations of government as new conceptions of biopower gave rise to increasingly direct forms of state administration orientated toward the purification of the population (see Stoler, 1995). My interest here, to come to my second point, concerns the role that was accorded the institutions Habermas neglects – museums, art galleries, and libraries – in the liberal programs of cultural management characterizing this period. For, although enabling legislation for the establishment of public museums, libraries, and art galleries had existed since the mid-century period, it is not until the last quarter of the century that European governments – at both the national and local levels – begin to invest significantly in the provision of such institutions which, alongside public schooling, constituted the backbone of the public cultural infrastructure until the advent of public broadcasting. While this might accurately be described as a process which resulted in the incorporation of components of the earlier liberal or bourgeois public sphere into the state, this did not result in a closure of the gap between state and society. To the contrary, the purpose of redeploying these institutions of public culture as instruments of government was, precisely, to obviate the need for the state to exercise direct forms of social control by developing a capacity for moral self-regulation in the population at large. The realm of public culture, however much it was now integrated into and directed by the state, continued to function – as in Habermas's account of its earlier phase of development – as a means for acting on the social as a realm that was still conceived as separate from government. What had changed was not the action of culture as a set of resources deemed capable of shaping the conduct and attributes of individuals through their voluntary self-activity but the social relations within which that action was put to work. The field of "the social" to which the action of culture was to be applied now comprised not the civil society of Habermas's private realm but a set of problematic behaviors – defined mainly in class terms – that were to be managed while, just as important, this action was to be put to work in the context of institutions that were located within the sphere of government rather than in a realm outside of and opposed to it.

Indeed, from a global perspective, this location of the public sphere within the realm of government has more typically characterized its origins as well as its point of contemporary arrival. To read these institutional complexes in terms of their colonial histories proves instructive in this regard. For the late nineteenth century was also the period in which the public cultural institutions developed in western Europe first began to go global. They did so, however, as parts of histories which fall quite outside the terms of the story Habermas proposes for their European origins, early development, and subsequent transformation. Martin Prosler has written usefully on this subject, remarking that, in the case of museums, their initial spread up to and including the mid-nineteenth century was limited to white settler colonies in the Americas, India, Australia, and South Africa, and to British colonial territories in Asia (Madras, Lucknow, Lahore, Bangalore, Mathura and Colombo) (Prosler, 1996). It is clear, however, that the functioning of these institutions in these colonial contexts was sharply different from their European origins. In Australia, for example, museums were parts of a public sphere that was nurtured into existence by government rather than having an earlier history in a pre-existing and separate realm (see Finney, 1993). Their formation was, in this sense, part of a process through which a civil society was fashioned into being. Similar tendencies characterized their major period of growth in the late nineteenth century (see Kohlstedt, 1983) which, like that of the other institutions of public culture such as libraries, art galleries, and art schools (see Candy and Laurent, 1994), relied more extensively on direct forms of government support than had been true of early stages in the development of their European counterparts. There was, to put the point bluntly, no time at which these institutions had ever been developed in opposition to, or in critique of, the state in a way that would make it intelligible to view their integration into government as a structural transformation of an earlier condition. In Australia, public culture was thoroughly governmentalized from the outset. Equally important, the surface of the social on which such institutions were to act was conceived in racial as well as class terms in ways that had no parallels in Europe. Unlike their European counterparts, the civil society that was pertinent to the definitions of citizenship characterizing these transplanted institutions was defined in racial terms owing to the manner in which they were distinguished from the indigenous populations which they excluded: in Australia, Aborigines were admitted into museums only as dead specimens (see Lampert, 1986 and Turnbull, 1991). In India, similarly, museums operated to bond colonial and indigenous elites rather than relating to the population as a whole (see Prakash, 1992).

We shall similarly find, in other contexts, that, in being globalized, these institutions were shaped by different histories. Prosler notes that, outside of India and the Dutch East Indies, Asian museums were not developed until the 1870s with museums being opened in Japan (1871), Bangkok (1874), China (1905) and Korea (1908) (Prosler, 1996: 25). It is clear, however, that this was mainly a response to the spread of the museum form via the international exhibitions (see Harris, 1975 and Yoshimi, 1993). As such, it had more to do with nationalist and modernizing imperatives than with any acceptance of, or subscription to, European conceptions of citizenship or the democratic values of a public sphere. The same was true of the development of museums in Africa in this period, and especially Egypt where the role that was envisaged for imported western-style public cultural institutions was driven entirely by a modernizing imperative (see Mitchell, 1988). However, I shall not labor the point any further. Although apparently similar in form to their European counterparts, the institutions of public culture that have been translated into other settings in the context of colonial histories have always formed parts of the distinctive socio-cultural relationships in which they have been inserted and which, in turn, they have helped to shape.

The Personnel of Culture

My purpose, then, is to suggest that, with a little "tweaking," Habermas's account of the " 'societalisation' of the state" and the " 'statification' of society" can usefully be seen as addressing the same historical processes Foucault is concerned with – albeit from a different theoretical perspective; Foucault is explicit in his critique of the concept of "the *étatisation* of society" (Foucault, 1991: 103) – in his account of the "governmentalisation of the state." I do so not because Foucault's approach to governmentality or the role that it plays in his account of the emergence of liberal forms of government is without problems. There are, however, some advantages in superimposing a Foucauldian optic on the historical processes Habermas is concerned with. The first is that it becomes possible to offer a more open-ended account of how the institutions that comprised the classical bourgeois public sphere assumed new functions as a result of their subsequent incorporation into relations of government. This opens up to investigation their changing uses in the context of historically mutable relations between government and the social rather than attributing to them a generalized function of social control arising from a general historical closure of state/society relations. The advantages of this for a historical approach to cultural policy are evident. It makes thinkable a much greater variability in the relations between government, culture, and the social as a consequence of the ways in which cultural resources are organized to act on the social in different ways in accordance with shifting governmental conceptions and priorities.

A second advantage is that an account couched in these terms can help prevent a polarization of the relations between critical and practical intellectuals of the kind that Habermasian constructions tend to propose. I have suggested, in my discussion of Habermas's approach to the early formation of the public sphere, that the action of culture within this had a dual orientation in both acting on the social to regulate it while also functioning as means for forming an opinion in which state power was subjected to rational forms of critique. If my emphasis so far has fallen on showing how the transformation of this first orientation might be viewed from a Foucauldian perspective, there is also much to be gained from considering how the institutions of public culture have continued to perform aspects of the second function in spite of their having become branches of government. Indeed, it is, in some cases, precisely because they are branches of government that these institutions have assumed a function of criticism that is, now, more or less institutionalized. The translation of anti-sexist and cultural diversity policies into the exhibition practices of collecting institutions, for example, has resulted in a considerable amount of cultural effort being dedicated to depicting both past and, where they persist, present culturally discriminatory practices as unacceptable with a view to the role this might play in fashioning new norms of civic conduct. In such cases, where the institutions of public culture have comprised the cultural and intellectual spaces that have played leading roles in both developing and disseminating specific forms of social and cultural criticism, governing and criticism go hand in hand. Where this is so, it is appropriate to refer to such institutions as places in which, just as much as universities and sometimes more so, government employees – whether as administrative or creative staff or, increasingly, as staff performing hybrid functions – have operated as critical intellectuals. They have done so, moreover, precisely in and through their performance of technical functions.

This brings me back to my earlier discussion of the ways in which Habermas's distinction between *techne* and *praxis* limits our ability to theorize the varied roles and functions of the personnel of culture in envisaging the technical solely in the form of a purely means-end administrative rationality that is, by definition, critical reason's opposite. For there is then a tendency to impose this grid of oppositions on to the concept of the technical wherever it is used even though this may be contextually inappropriate. An example is McGuigan's interpretation of a suggestion I had made, in an earlier essay, that cultural studies should think of itself as having a role to play in training cultural technicians whom I defined as "intellectual workers less committed to cultural critique as an instrument for changing consciousness than to modifying the functioning of culture by means of technical adjustments to its governmental deployment" (Bennett, 1992b: 406). McGuigan, in placing a Habermasian tint on this passage, views it as a suggestion that there can be "no normative principles other than administrative usefulness" (1996) that can be drawn on either to specify the aims to which the work of such cultural technicians should be directed or to provide a perspective from which the outcomes of their endeavors might be assessed. This is only so, however, if Habermas is granted a monopoly over the use of the concepts of the technical and the critical so that the oppositional structure he posits between these is then seen as necessarily invoked whenever the two terms are used. There are, however, no good reasons for doing so, and there are plenty of reasons for not doing so if it prevents us from equating the concept of critique with the more general notion of being critical and allows the field of the technical to be thought of in a manner which does not see being technical and being critical as automatically incompatible.

For the example I gave of the ways cultural resources might be technically adjusted as a part and parcel of their becoming involved in new governmental projects was one to which these oppositions are simply not relevant. It had to do with the role that nineteenth-century Romantic aesthetics played in allowing art to be reconceptualized in a manner that made it intelligible to suppose that the activity of government might usefully be directed to the task of bringing art and the working man closer together in view of the benefits it was expected would follow from exposing the latter to the soothing, elevating, and refining influence of art: less drunkenness, a lower birth rate, lower rates of domestic violence. It was clear to contemporaries, however, that if art were indeed to serve this purpose, then a host of technical changes – and these were endlessly debated at the time – would need to be made to the ways in which works of art were exhibited: how they should be hung, how labeled, how the visitor's route should be organized, what should be said of the art exhibited, what value should be placed on originals versus copies.[15]

This is not, then, a concept of the technical that can simply be equated with the purely disinterested means-end rationality of the bureau but rather concerns that level of procedures through which particular forms of knowledge and expertise organize the materials with which they work and prepare the social surfaces to which those materials are to be applied in ways which make them amenable to particular kinds of governmental action.[16]

The history of the relations between culture and government is littered with technical considerations of this kind. These include, in the visual arts, the roles of different theories of the aesthetic, of different conceptions of art's public, of different ideologies of the visible and their role in relation to specific techniques of vision,[17] and of different conceptions of visual education. All of these play a crucial role, in any actual context, in influencing the ways in which art is exhibited, to whom it is exhibited, and why, and all of which – as Habermas's account of the refunctioning of culture associated with the formation of the classical bourgeois public sphere acknowledges – involve specific forms of technical expertise which do not fall in the same category as bureaucratic rationality. It is, moreover, through the role which these forms of technical expertise play that cultural resources are adapted to new purposes and, in the process, made infinitely pliable as they are bent to first one governmental project and then another – and all of this through the activities of intellectuals working in the cultural sphere who are neither critics, as McGuigan defines them, nor bureaucrats.

Notes

1   This chapter is a slightly modified version of an earlier essay published under the same title as no. 2 in the series of Papers in Social and Cultural Research published by the Pavis Centre for Social and Cultural Research at the Open University in 2000. A shortened version of this was subsequently published as "Intellectuals, culture, policy: the practical and the critical" in Miller (2001).

2   This is not to imply that these are the only two theoretical traditions that have contributed to debates in this area. There have been notable feminist contributions to our understanding of the role of gender in organizing distinctively feminized intellectual personas and assigning these distinctive functions within the cultural sphere: see, for example, Garrison (1976) and McCarthy (1991). Bourdieu's nuanced accounts of the role of different groups of intellectuals, cultural specialists, and intermediaries have also made a significant contribution: see Bourdieu (1988, 1993a, and 1996b). However, a somewhat different assessment is called for of his account of intellectuals as the bearer of the "historical universal." I have discussed this elsewhere: see Bennett (2005c).

3   See, however, for a thoughtful assessment of the limitations of this legacy, Collins and Murroni (1996).

4   Important critical theoretical and historical investigations of the concept of the public sphere conducted from a feminist perspective include Landes (1988), Riley (1988) and Ryan (1990). On the question of indigenous cultures and public spheres, see Michaels (1994). For Habermas's response to feminist engagements with his work, see Habermas (1992).

5   I should add, to avoid possible confusion, that my attention is limited to Habermas's initial account of the public sphere. While acknowledging that that Habermas has subsequently revised this in the light of the critical debates it has generated – see especially the chapter "Civil Society and the Public Sphere" in Habermas (1996: 328–87) – no account is taken of these revisions here. Although Habermas's revisions are significant ones, especially in relocating his original account of the public sphere as a historically specific form of what have proved to be more mutable public sphere/civil society relations, these revisions do not bear significantly on the accounts of intellectuals that I am concerned with here as these have drawn mainly on the earlier work.

6   McGuigan has since generously acknowledged some of the problems his formulations on this subject gave rise to and has clarified his position in ways that indicate both the limits of the place occupied by academic intellectuals and the need for them to be open to learn from other intellectuals in the cultural sector. See the postscript to McGuigan (2003).

7   There are, however, other traditions of analysis that might be drawn on for the same purpose. Bruno Latour, for example, concludes his *Science in Action* with an equally spirited defense of bureaucracy from the scorn and loathing of science: see Latour (1987: 254–7).

8   See, for an account which locates the emergence of the "good bureaucrat" in a longer historical perspective, Saunders (1997). Saunders's interest is with the development of the common law as a specific mode of practical reason and with the cultivation of an ethical obligation on the part of lawyers to uphold the procedures of the law rather than act out of their own religious or political convictions.

9   A more expanded version of the line of argument proposed by Hunter has also become available since the first version of this paper was published: see Du Gay (2000), especially the chapter on Bauman.

10 This is not to suggest that Said's criticisms of that complex are unsound. This question, together with Said's criticisms of the USA's Israel–Palestine policies and his broader criticisms of ongoing colonialisms, are not under discussion here.

11 The literature here is vast. The best representative sample of the varied range of work Habermas's concept of the public sphere has given rise to is the collection edited by Craig Calhoun (1992).

12 While it is true that Habermas's work has been drawn on in discussions of the role that the press and other media played, in a variety of Asian contexts, in the development of political movements directed against both indigenous and colonial forms of autocratic rule (see, for example, Milner, 1996), such usage has rarely implied an acceptance of the more specific historical and theoretical aspects of Habermas's writings on this subject. The historical limitations of applying Habermas's concept of the public sphere to Japan, where the emperor system imposed a different structure on the space of public meanings, have thus been fully argued by Tatsuro Hanada (see Hanada, 1995). In Allen Chun's perspective, the post-war public cultures of Taiwan, Hong Kong, and Singapore have been shaped mainly by the hegemonic imperatives of nation-state formation; only since the 1980s have democratic conceptions of the public sphere played a major role in questioning the closures of these officially administered, proto-national public cultures (see Chun, 1996). For Ping-hui Liao, the proto-nationalistic aspects of these territorial public cultures is now being eroded, or at least complicated, by the emergence of a "hyphenated and transcultural" Chinese public sphere

constituting a shared field of political action and social habitus formed by the new forms of cultural connectivity and exchange created by satellite communications networks (see Liao, 1995). Similar qualifications have attended the application of the concept of the public sphere to Australian debates. For Indigenous Australians, for example, the acquisition of equal entitlements in the field of public culture which accompanied the acquisition of citizenship has been accompanied by an ongoing history of the defense of kinship rights whose legitimacy is organized in terms which stand outside of, and in critique of, the universalist rhetorics of "public" and "citizen-ship" (see Rowse, 1993).

13 It is symptomatic of lapsarian discourse that what is for one theorist a degeneration of a previous norm is, for another, the normative ideal from which other lapses are to be assessed. The adult education class that is, for Habermas, a purely administered form of culture represents, for Raymond Williams, a democratic norm of face-to-face mutuality and curriculum democracy which later mass-mediated distance teaching systems surrender to the demands of a technological rationality. See Williams (1989).

14 I have argued this point at greater length in relation to the role played by liberal appropriations of Darwin's thought in organizing a morally interventionist role for government that would either complement or override the laws of nature: see Bennett (1997e). For more direct statements of the extent to which the liberal thought of this period explicitly pitted against itself the closure of the gap between state and society, see Huxley (1890 and 1894).

15 I have since dealt with these matters in greater detail. See Bennett (1995c).

16 See Rose and Miller (1992) for a fully elaborated account of the role which different forms of technical expertise play in translating specific forms of knowledge into programs of government.

17 See, on this question, Crary (1996).

Chapter Nine   The Historical Universal:
The Role of Cultural Value
in the Historical Sociology
of Pierre Bourdieu

In a revealing reflection on *The Love of Art*, Bourdieu contends that the ostensible object of this study (the social composition of the art museum public) had detracted attention from its real object: a sociology of artistic perception whose purpose was to demonstrate "the historicity of the categories of perception, naively held to be universal and eternal, that we apply to a work of art" by making apparent "the social conditions of possibility of this *historical transcendental* that we call 'taste' " (Bourdieu, 1993b: 266). That he had in mind not merely a sociological critique of cultic forms of aesthetic consumption is made clear when Bourdieu goes on to say that there was something more at stake for him in this study – something which he had deliberately hidden in case his work fell foul of the positivist climate which prevailed in sociology, especially American sociology, when *The Love of Art* (Bourdieu and Darbel, 1991) was first published in 1969. That something was "to found a science of aesthetic knowledge" conceived as "a particular and privileged case of practical knowledge" (Bourdieu, 1993b: 267) that depended on distinctive cognitive operations which, while different from those of theoretical or scientific knowledge, are not reducible to the kinds of "mystical communion or ineffable participation" (Bourdieu, 1993b: 267) that characterize charismatic forms of arts consumption. His aspiration, in other words, was to examine the social and historical conditions underlying the development of aesthetic forms of perception in a manner which, far from relativizing questions of aesthetic judgment, would make it possible to recognize the universal value that inhered in particular works as a result of their emergence from historical processes of a particular kind.

In what follows, my primary concern is with the forms of historical reasoning Bourdieu deploys in advancing an account of aesthetic value that is neither idealist nor essentialist but which nonetheless insists that literary and artistic works differ in value in accordance with the degree to which they have stored up the material history that has shaped them. This involves a consideration of Bourdieu's account of the autonomy of the artistic and literary fields and their role in providing the enabling conditions for the emergence and development of what he calls the "historical universal." In examining the forms of historical reasoning that are involved here, I draw on the role that competitive struggle plays in Darwinian narratives of natural history to highlight the distinctive form of temporality that characterizes Bourdieu's account of the history of the literary and artistic fields. I then consider how the specific narratives of time that characterize Bourdieu's work inform his account of the practice of historical anamnesis and its role in the formation of the collective intellectual as the bearer of the "historical universal." This prepares the ground for a review of the more evident difficulties associated with the role that concepts of historical transcendence and universality play in Bourdieu's historical sociology and the political program for the conduct of intellectuals he derives from these. I conclude by considering some of the ambiguities associated with Bourdieu's commitment to a politics of freedom derived from Enlightenment aesthetics. First, though, I look at the more general currency of references to the "historical universal" in Bourdieu's work to highlight the difficulties this concept creates for the widespread interpretation of Bourdieu as an icon of relativism.

The Historical Universal: Cultural Politics and Policies

Distinction opens with a move which "discrowns" the Kantian aesthetic in a Bakhtinian sense by bringing it down to the same level as the popular and sensuous pleasures of everyday life.[1]

> The science of taste and of cultural consumption begins with a transgression that is in no way aesthetic: it has to abolish the sacred frontier which makes legitimate culture a separate universe, in order to discover the intelligible relations which unite apparently incommensurable "choices", such as preferences in music and food, painting and sport, literature and hairstyle. This barbarous reintegration of aesthetic consumption into the world of ordinary consumption abolishes the opposition, which has been the basis of high aesthetics since Kant, between the "taste of sense" and the "taste of reflection", and between facile pleasure, pleasure reduced to a pleasure of the senses, and pure pleasure, pleasure purified of pleasure, which is predisposed to become a symbol of moral excellence and a measure of the capacity for sublimation which defines the truly human man. (Bourdieu, 1984: 6)

It is in the light of passages like this that Bourdieu's work has often been interpreted as relativist, widely celebrated (or condemned) for placing all tastes, popular and high, on a similar footing, equally rooted in specific class practices. There are a number of different variants of this position. In cultural studies, Bourdieu has often been invoked to contest the validity of aesthetic distinctions between high and popular forms – sometimes, in ways that Bourdieu would have endorsed, to insist on the need to take the latter seriously, and, at others, asserting or implying an equivalence of value of all cultural forms in ways he would clearly have contested. Fiske (1992) is an example of this second position. In literary and aesthetic theory, the most influential interpretation of Bourdieu's work in support of aesthetic relativism has been Smith (1988), albeit that Guillory (1993) provides a compelling critique of this position. Shusterman (1992) proposes a nuanced combination of Bourdieu's work and the aesthetic pragmatism of John Dewey that often unsettles Bourdieu's distinction between the fields of restricted and extended cultural production.

Bourdieu's essays on the organization of cultural production and the economy of symbolic goods also seem to point in a similar direction. In his account of the field of restricted cultural production, Bourdieu insists that "the disavowal of the 'economy' " associated with the commitment to art as an end in itself that characterizes the behavior of various agents in this field (the author, artist, critic, art dealer, publisher or theater manager) is itself a form of "economic rationality" which, once the symbolic capital it represents has been cashed in, will yield both symbolic and economic profit to its champions (Bourdieu, 1993a: 76). Here, as in *Distinction*, the ethos of disinterestedness is brought down to earth in being depicted as tangled up with specific kinds of interested economic calculation. In the cultural policy literature, similarly, Bourdieu's name is routinely invoked to provide a theoretical context and legitimation for policies which aim to promote a greater equality of access to, participation in, and support for all kinds of cultural activity irrespective of the value placed on them within official hierarchies of the arts. McGuigan thus takes Bourdieu as his example of a relativizing approach to the relations between cultural theory and cultural policy against which to pitch his own advocacy of aesthetically normative approaches to such questions (McGuigan, 1996: 30–50). Rowse (1985) had a significant influence on cultural policy debates in Australia, invoking Bourdieu in support of funding priorities focused on the popular arts. Relativist interpretations of Bourdieu have similarly informed a number of studies of museum visitor profiles – see, for example, Merriman (1991) – and are invoked in support of more generalized forms of cultural measurement (see Mercer, 2002). In the context of recent debates concerning the need for aesthetic evaluations that will establish distinctions of quality within television, Street (2000) similarly opposes a concern with such questions to what he characterizes as Bourdieu's neo-functionalism.

Yet Bourdieu has always maintained a careful distance from such interpretations of his work. Take the passage I reproduce below in which Bourdieu, drawing on the research he had undertaken for *The Love of Art* (originally commissioned by the Ministry for Cultural Affairs), took to task the belief that cultural animation projects and access and equity programs could significantly affect the patterns of social participation in the arts. For Bourdieu, such programs could amount to little more than bad faith given their inability to significantly impede the dynamics of social distinction arising out of the relations between cultural capital, the education system, and the institutions of art:

> Indeed, we can also question the real function of the policy that consists in encouraging and supporting marginal and largely inefficient bodies as long as everything possible has not been implemented that might force and authorize the academic institution to fulfil the function incumbent on it both *de facto* and *de jure*, which is to develop in all members of society, without distinction, an aptitude for those cultural practices considered by society as most noble. (Bourdieu, 2002: 67)

Bourdieu's immediate target in this study was the charismatic ideology of art underlying André Malraux's program as France's first Minister for Culture. To Malraux's belief that great art could be made immediately and intuitively accessible to all, Bourdieu counterposes the need for a "rational pedagogy of culture" as the only means of promoting more general forms of accessibility to works of high culture.[2] Yet Bourdieu does not challenge the emphasis that Malraux's policies placed on access to those cultural practices which society considers "most noble." Nor has he ever done so. He was, to the contrary, hostile to the cultural development programs developed during the cultural ministries of Jacques Duhamel in the 1970s and of Jacques Lang in the 1980s as condescendingly populist in assigning an equal value to all kinds of culture irrespective of the structural forces organizing them into relations of domination and subordination.

The basis for these objections consists in his view of the distinctive forms of value that have been stored up and accumulated within works of art as a consequence of the dynamics governing the development of the literary and artistic fields and their relationships to the economic and political fields. This defense of their role as repositories of what he called the "historical universal" was particular clear in his later work. Here, for example, is what he says in *Pascalian Meditations*:

> There is, appearances notwithstanding, no contradiction in fighting *at the same time against* the mystificatory hypocrisy of abstract universalism *and for* universal access to the conditions of access to the universal, the primordial objective of all genuine humanism which both universalistic preaching and nihilistic (pseudo-) subversion forget. (Bourdieu, 2000: 71)

To dispel any doubt as to what "nihilistic (pseudo-) subversion" might mean, he adds, a few pages later, that the "cult of 'popular culture' " usually amounts to little more than an "inversion of the class racism which reduces working-class practices to barbarism or vulgarity... which, under the guise of exalting the working class, helps to enclose it in what it is by converting privation into a choice or an elective accomplishment" (Bourdieu, 2000: 76). These formulations echo those of two earlier texts – Bourdieu's conversations with Hans Haacke (Bourdieu and Haacke, 1995), and his book on television (Bourdieu, 1998b) – in which Bourdieu champions the right of artists and intellectuals to defend the autonomy of the artistic and intellectual fields against the increasing "marketization" of cultural production associated with neo-liberal cultural and economic policies, and to do so even at the price of appearing elitist. For it is, Bourdieu argues, only the autonomy of these fields that can secure the conditions needed if works of universal value are still to be produced. But this defense is accompanied by the demand that those respon- sible for protecting and nurturing the universal must also accept responsibility for generalizing access to it: "In other words, we have to defend the conditions of production necessary for the progress of the universal, while working to generalise the conditions of access to that universality...We must work to universalise the conditions of access to the universal" (Bourdieu, 1998b: 66).

There is then, for Bourdieu, no equivalence of value stretching across the fields of restricted and general cultural production. Since only the former can serve as the incubator for the "historical universal," generalizing social access to this while at the same time providing the means of intellectual access that will allow the works produced in this field to be appropriated as instances of the historical universal, rather than as signs of social distinction, are the ultimate guiding principles for the direction of education and cultural policies – always, for Bourdieu, necessarily paired – that can be derived from Bourdieu's work. At the same time, however, there is nothing essentialist in this attribution of value to the field of restricted cultural production. To the contrary, it is clear that Bourdieu aimed, through the particular form of historicizing cultural products that he proposed, to produce an account of the historical formation of value that would steer a way between what he saw as the equally false options of relativism and the eternalization of a-historical essences:

> But historicising them [cultural products: TB] is not only (as some think) to relativise them, recalling that they have meaning only with reference to a determined state of the field of struggles; it also means giving them back their necessity by tearing them out of the indeterminacy which stems from a false eternalisation and relating them back to the social conditions of their genesis – a truly generative definition. (Bour- dieu, 1996b: 298)

Neither indifferently relativizing nor abstractly universalizing, Bourdieu's historical universalism arises out of a relationist perspective in which different forms of value accrue to different kinds of work, depending on the positions they occupy in relation to one another within the processes of production and consumption informing the organization and dynamics of different fields of cultural production. It is to this matter, therefore, that I now turn.

The Historical Structure of the Literary and Artistic Fields

In the Preface to *The Rules of Art*, Bourdieu asks whether scientific analysis is doomed to destroy aesthetic pleasure, and whether the sociologist must be "wed- ded to relativism, to the levelling of values, to the lowering of greatness" (Bourdieu, 1996b: xiv). These are purely rhetorical questions, setting the scene for Bourdieu's contention that only a sociological perspective – correctly conceived and applied – holds out the prospect of enriching and deepening aesthetic appreciation and understanding. It does so, he argues, by simultaneously being able to show how the work of art is both historic and trans-historic: historic in the sense that it is the product of a particular set of social and historical circumstances and relations of cultural production; trans-historic in the sense that it is the very mode of the work of art's conditioning by the social relations of its production that allows it to pull free from and transcend the time-bound and limiting effects of its historical period to achieve ongoing value as a source of valid knowledge and self-knowledge.

How does he do this? I want to place the accent here on the *how* since Bourdieu is by no means the first to advance claims of this kind. They are, to the contrary, a fairly well-worn trope in the sociology of art and literature and, even more so, in Marxist aesthetic theory. Here, however, the injunction – to paraphrase Fredric Jameson (1981) – that analysis should always historicize has usually turned out to mean placing the work of art within a narrative of History and to so read the relations between the two that canonical works emerge as offering privileged forms of historical self-understanding.[3] This is, however, very much history in the abstract which, while assigning works of art their place within larger narrative accounts of the direction and meaning of social development, rarely descends to consider the mundane details of particular forms of literary production and distribution except to denigrate these as, in one of Georg Lukács's favorite phrases, "vulgar sociology."[4] Bourdieu's procedure differs to the extent that these are precisely the kinds of issues he is concerned with, grounding his account of the social production of aesthetic value in the organization of the literary and artistic fields and its consequences for the material calculations and strategies of producers, consumers, and a whole range of intermediary agents – publishers, museum directors, gallery owners, etc. – involved in the practical functioning of those fields.

Yet there is still a narrative at work in Bourdieu's account, albeit a surprising one in as much as its governing metaphors – ones of evolution and struggle, of survival and accumulation – are clearly Darwinian. And conspicuously so: in *The Rules of Art* Bourdieu parades a whole series of evolutionary conceptions in his account of the organization of the literary and artistic fields and the struggle – a "struggle for life, for survival" (Bourdieu, 1996b: 157) – this gives rise to between different positions in those fields and the strategies of capital accumulation they permit. This partly reflects the fact that, especially through Flaubert, Darwinian conceptions informed the vocabulary through which artists and writers in the late nineteenth-century French literary and artistic fields – the only cases Bourdieu studies in detail – represented their struggles for autonomy. However, the matter runs more deeply than this in as much as Darwinian metaphors also provide the key to Bourdieu's understanding of the distinctive form of temporality governing the literary and artistic fields and regulating the relations between the different positions that are available within those fields.

In Darwin's account of the evolution of species, the relations between species as they exist at any one point in time is a historical summation of all that has gone before as variations which have proved successful in the struggle for life are viewed as a part of the accumulated inheritance of each species. Temporalization, in Darwinian narratives, is thus the result of struggle, just as struggle always leaves its mark in the present as a set of decipherable traces through which the history of the past struggles that have led to the present organization of life can be reconstructed.[5] This essentially archaeological historicity in which each stage of evolution both stores and registers a departure from those preceding it, recapitulating the past even as it breaks with it, played an important role in Darwin's concern to distance his work from two rival forms of historicity: the idealist biblical account of creation and Georges Cuvier's account of species development as a discontinuous history in which different creations are separated from one another by catastrophes (Rudwick, 1997). The continuous, cumulative sequences of lineal descent Darwin's account established thus demonstrated that "species are produced and exterminated by slowly acting and still existing causes, and not by miraculous acts of creation and by catastrophes" (Darwin, 1968: 457).

For Bourdieu, similarly, "the history of the field is the history of the struggle for a monopoly of the imposition of legitimate categories of perception and appreciation," just as "it is in the very *struggle* that the history of the field is made; it is through struggles that it is temporalised" (Bourdieu, 1996b: 157). In the space of the artistic field, Bourdieu therefore argues, "distances between styles or lifestyles are never better measured than in terms of time" (Bourdieu, 1996b: 159). This same principle applies to all agents and institutions in the field:

> galleries or publishing houses, like painters or writers, are distributed at any one time according to their artistic age, that is according to the antiquity of their mode of artistic production and according to the degree of canonisation and the influence of that generative schema which is at one and the same time a schema of perception and appreciation. (Bourdieu, 1996b: 158)

While empirically illuminating when applied to the forms of historicization that result from the struggles between agents in particular artistic fields at particular historical moments – and not just in the French context[6] – Bourdieu further contends that the history of art as such, at least in its western forms, is governed by similar principles. This partly reflects what others have identified as the metaphysical role that Bourdieu accords competition as a constitutive aspect of human social practice. Hubert Dreyfus and Paul Rabinow thus argue that the basic principle underlying Bourdieu's account of the organization of social life, providing the dynamism propelling each field and the relations between them, is "competition, not just for life and security as in Hobbes, but for advantage, and not just material advantage as in Marx, but more general symbolic advantage" (Dreyfus and Rabinow, 1993: 40). What the references to Hobbes and Marx miss, however, are the respects in which this account of the role of competition is also connected to the distinctive historical ontology that characterizes Bourdieu's account of the relations between habitus and field. Craig Calhoun (1993) has usefully highlighted this aspect of Bourdieu's work, noting the respects in which the structure of any field is always immanently historical, thus calling for, as Bourdieu puts it, "a structural history which finds in each state of the structure both the product of previous struggles to transform or conserve the structure, and, through the contradictions, tensions and power relations that constitute that structure, the source of its subsequent transformations" (Bourdieu, 1990: 42). The sources of social action, whether it be that of the artist, scientist, or civil servant, Bourdieu argues, are to be found in the legacies of past struggles that are stored up in the relations between both things, in the forms of institutions, and persons in the form of "the history incarnated in bodies, in the form of that system of enduring dispositions which I call habitus" (Bourdieu, 1990: 190). The socio-somatic aspects of habitus as a social storage mechanism operative within the person owes much to Merleau Ponty (Butler, 1999) and, of course, to Marcel Mauss and, via Mauss, to the range of socio-somatic mechanisms associated with Darwinian and post-Darwinian accounts of evolutionary inheritance (see Otis, 1994).

It is in the relations between field and habitus, then, that the different temporalities of events and structures can be integrated into one. They provide, as Bourdieu puts it, "the means of filling in the gap between the slow and imperceptible movements of the economic or demographic infrastructure and the surface agitation recorded by the day-to-day chronicles of political, literary or artistic history" (Bourdieu, 1990: 190). They also provide, in the case of the literary and artistic fields, for a mechanism of temporalization that is unidirectional, progressive, and cumulative owing to the extent to which the innovations of form, style, content, or genre resulting from past struggles are "recorded, codified and canonised by the whole corpus of professionals of conservation and celebration – historians of art and literature, exegetes, analysts" to become "part of the conditions of entry into the field of restricted production" (Bourdieu, 1996b: 242). Such innovations and their conservation, that is to say, become a part of the history of the field that has to be mastered by those cultural producers whose capital accumulation strategies bank on the symbolic profits that accrue to those who make a new move within the field, opening it up to new possibilities. Each innovation, however, displaces not only its immediate predecessor but, at the same time, the whole series of displaced predecessors that comprises the history of art:

> This model stands out with particular clarity today because, by virtue of an almost perfect unification of the artistic field and its history, each artistic act which leaves its mark by introducing a new position in the field "displaces" the entire series of previous artistic acts. By the fact that the whole series of pertinent "coups" is present in practice in the last one, an aesthetic act is irreducible to any other act situated in another position in the series and the series itself tends towards uniqueness and irreversibility. (Bourdieu, 1996b: 160).

It is true, of course, that the narrative trope of accumulation that is so strong in Bourdieu's work owes as much to Marx as to Darwin, especially in view of the influence that Darwin's account of the struggle for existence exerted on Marx's account of the relationships between competition and capital accumulation (see Beer, 1985: 57–8). There is, however, an important difference, long noted in the literature. For whereas Marx's account of capital accumulation is one of inter-rupted development in which value is lost or written off as a result of successive crises of profitability, Darwin always stressed the long, continuous, step-by-step progression of natural evolution in which nothing is lost without at the same time being preserved and carried forward into the next step. It is this trope, in particular, that Bourdieu draws on so extensively in *The Rules of Art*. "The history of the field," Bourdieu thus contends, "is thus truly irreversible; and the products of this relatively autonomous history present a kind of '*cumulativity*'" (Bourdieu, 1996b: 242) – a formulation which he later extends in contending that "'time' in the history of art is really irreversible, and that it presents a form of *cumulativity*" (Bourdieu, 1996b: 301). Avant-gardes, by expanding the reach of this "cumulativ-ity," simultaneously historicize prevailing aesthetic conventions by making them obsolete and, thereby, unable to generate symbolic profits in the field of restricted cultural production. This is a form of temporality which Bourdieu, drawing on the language of evolutionary thought, argues also generates its throwbacks and sur-vivals in those artists who continue to produce using codes and conventions which have been historically superseded. "Fossils of another age," Bourdieu writes of those painters who supplied the galleries of the Right Bank in *fin-de-siècle* Paris, "these painters who do in the present what was done by the avant-garde of the past (just like *forgers*, but on their own account) make an art that is not, if one may say so, of their age" (Bourdieu, 1996b: 150).

There are close parallels between this account and the Russian Formalists' account of the evolution of literary systems as the outcome of practices of estrangement and defamiliarization through which the literary devices developed in previous cycles of literary innovation are ruptured, shown to be arbitrarily conventional and limiting, and thereby rendered historically canonical, valued, and preserved as significant moments in the prehistory of the literary present, but as prehistory none the less (Bennett, 2003: 149–53). There are, however, equally significant differences between the two accounts. For the Russian Formalists, the temporalization of the literary field was viewed as *sui generis*, arising out of a dynamic that was entirely internal to the literary field. For Bourdieu, by contrast, it is not the purely internal logic of an abstracted and a-historical process of defa-miliarization that determines the periodization of the literary and artistic fields or provides the motor power for their accumulative momentum. This rather comes directly from the strategies and calculations guiding the actions of the different "players" – writers, painters, sculptors, art historians, curators, gallery owners, literary agents, and critics – within the processes through which art and literature are produced, reproduced, circulated, and consumed. On the one hand, then, Bourdieu concurs with the Russian Formalists that the repertoire of moves that are possible at any given moment depends on how different literary and artistic schools, genres, writerly and painterly conventions, and so on, are positioned in relation to one another within existing literary or artistic systems (for the Formal-ists) or fields (for Bourdieu). On the other hand, he contends that the actual directions and dynamics of change – the actual paths taken amid myriad possibil-ities – can only be understood by referring this plane of formal analysis to the interested exercise of both material power and symbolic force on the part of agents and institutions within the field.[7] "Having totally vital interests in the possibilities offered as instruments and stakes in the struggle," he writes, "these agents and institutions use all the powers at their disposal to activate those which seem the most in accord with their specific intentions and interests" (Bourdieu, 1996b: 201–2). This means that literariness is construed not as a given trans-historic essence, as in Formalist theory, but as a historical artifact – "a sort of *historical quintessence*, that is, the product of a long and slow work of historical alchemy which accompanies the process of autonomization of the fields of cultural pro-duction" (Bourdieu, 1996b: 139). The "sublimated essence of the universal," Bourdieu contends, can thus only be extracted from "the often merciless clash of passions and selfish interests," requiring a stoic renunciation of the "angelic belief in a pure interest in pure form" (Bourdieu, 1996b: xviii).

The development of the literary and artistic fields and their acquisition of an accumulating depth and complexity is thus the outcome of competitive struggles between agents in those fields. Bourdieu's account of their progressively developing autonomy is based on similar principles to his account of the history of reason as one which, in contrast to what he sees as the "transcendental illusionism" of Habermas's account (Bourdieu, 1998a: 89–90), must be based on a realpolitik of reason that can account for the production of a constituency with a material interest in the disinterested pursuit of truth.[8] I therefore look next at the implica-tions Bourdieu draws from this account of the historical structure of the literary, artistic, and intellectual fields for the ways in which the achievements that have been stored up and accumulated within them are to be retrieved and related to the present in an intellectual politics based on the principles of "historical universalism."

Historical Anamnesis and the Practice of Freedom

In *Pascalian Meditations*, Bourdieu records that he never "felt justified in existing as an intellectual" (Bourdieu, 2000: 7) and tried hard to exorcise from his work all those manifestations of scholastic reason which entail a denial of, and distancing from, the necessities of the social world. This has always been an aspect of Bourdieu's literary persona. Writing as both an insider to the fields of culture and knowledge, as one familiar with the rules of the game and, indeed, an adept player, and as an outsider, he draws on the distancing methods of sociology to show how the moves of such games derive their intelligibility – otherwise invisible or, in cultic conceptions of the arts, simply denied – from their relations to the vulgar material conditions of cultural production and the strategies of capital accumulation to which these give rise. Yet Bourdieu was equally concerned that something that has been painstakingly made should not be thrown away or dismissed out of hand. This helps to explain why aesthetic value is, for Bourdieu, no more something to be written off than, for Bruno Latour (1999a), the results of scientific work are to be discounted because they can be shown to be the result of the practice of scientists in particular and determinate relations of knowledge production. I make this comparison with Latour not because either Bourdieu or Latour does but because the accounts of the production of, respectively, aesthetic and scientific entities that the two offer are, in some respects, strikingly similar. Both, for example, make extended use of the concepts of purification and fabrication to stress the made-up nature of those entities, and both insist that their "made-upness" does not detract in the least from their reality and effectivity.[9] To the contrary, it is true for both that the reality and force of entities in the cultural and epistemological fields increase in proportion to the amount of effort that is invested in their initial fabrication and subsequent reproduction. This is why Bourdieu so insistently stresses the laborious work that was involved in the processes through which Flaubert and his generation fabricated the autonomy of the literary and artistic fields by distancing their activities from the twin poles of necessity (the economy) and power (politics and bureaucracy). And it is why he stresses the need for continuing work of this kind – by writers, artists, curators, and critics – if the autonomy of these fields is to be maintained and developed.

He also sees a need for a distinctive kind of intellectual practice to sustain and generalize such efforts. Though the perspective that "being is history" means that one must "demand of biological history (with the theory of evolution) and sociological history (with the analysis of the collective and individual sociogenesis of forms of thought) the truth of a reason which is historical through and through and yet irreducible to history," it takes a particular kind of historical self-reflection "to extract reason most effectively from historicity" (Bourdieu, 1996b: 310). Or again:

> To escape (however slightly) from history, understanding must know itself as historical and give itself the means to understand itself historically; and it must, in the same movement, understand historically the historical situation in which what it labours to understand was formed. (Bourdieu, 1996b: 310).

The project through which understanding is thus to reflect on, and bring to consciousness, the history of its own formation, and, thereby, distill the value that has been stored up within the artistic, literary ,and intellectual fields is that of historical anamnesis. A term which, via Freud, he borrows from Plato, anamnesis is, for Bourdieu, a process of recovery and recollection – a bringing to consciousness of forgotten or hidden processes. When applied to aesthetic works, anamnesis aims to retrieve such works from the kinds of essentialist and cultic misunderstandings that afflict those whose vantage point is restricted to a position within the field and, as a consequence, merely registers the lived experience of the aesthetic work while bracketing out the history of autonomization that has made that experience possible. "It is only by mobilising all the resources of the social sciences," Bourdieu argues, "that one can bring to fruition that historicist form of the transcendental project which consists of reappropriating, by historical anamnesis, the historical forms and categories of artistic experience" (Bourdieu, 1996b: 288).

The procedures of anamnesis thus return thought to itself historically by recalling the cumulative weight of those successive determinations which have formed it in accordance with a temporal logic that is irreversible. Recalling to thought the forgotten history that has shaped it, anamnesis offers the means for "a true reconquest of the self" (Bourdieu, 1996b: 312) that will, in its turn, enable a practice of freedom in the prospect it opens up, not of escaping, but of regulating the determinations that have shaped it. In this way, the promise of a "*historical transcendental*" (Bourdieu, 1996b: 288) that is opened up by the historical autonomization of the artistic, literary, and intellectual fields might, Bourdieu suggests, "be carried to its conclusion" (Bourdieu, 1996b: 312). The contemporary form that this project must take, Bourdieu suggests in his postscript to *The Rules of Art*,[10] is that of the organization of a "collective intellectual" in which intellectuals and artists will act corporately in their own interests in view of the congruence between these and the historical transcendental value of the autonomy of the artistic and intellectual fields. Their current task, Bourdieu argues, is to defend the value of this autonomy against the increasingly corrosive encroachments of the economy, bureaucracy, and technical reasoning. In such a context the practice of historical anamnesis becomes directly political in view of the importance of making "as explicit as possible the unconscious deposited in each intellectual by the very history of which intellectuals are the products" (Bourdieu, 1996b: 340).

We can see, in the light of these considerations, why questions concerning the mode of appropriation of works of art, literature, and restricted culture more generally are so important for Bourdieu. The critical ideal he has in mind is one that would simultaneously weaken the connections through which the cultural consumption of aesthetically coded works is tied to practices of social distinction while simultaneously expanding the influence of artists, writers, and intellectuals – and their ways of reading aesthetic texts as a means for a deepened and cumulating historical self-understanding – to overcome the division between restricted and extended culture by extending the principles governing the former into the latter. This requires, he argues in *On Television and Journalism*, the vigilant defense of the autonomy of restricted culture, securing its "ivory tower" modus operandi by supporting the production of cultural works that meet the specialist standards of judgment of agents within that field (artists, writers, etc.) against the requirements of "marketablity" or, indeed, of immediate accessibility (Bourdieu, 1998b: 59–64). And this in turn requires a dualistic orientation in relation to the state,[11] as Bourdieu urges that cultural producers should both argue for an enhanced role of cultural sponsorship for the state – as the only possible agent capable of acting in the general interest – while at the same time insisting on the right, indeed duty, of intellectuals and artists to be independent of the state as they "learn to use against the state the freedom that the state assures them" (Bourdieu and Haacke, 1995: 72).

The reality of the issues Bourdieu is concerned with here is undeniable. The need to secure continuing state involvement in the cultural field while simultaneously warding off its intrusive political and administrative effects has become a regular aspect of the position adopted by intellectuals in relation to neo-liberalism. It needs to be said, too, that Bourdieu's interest in these questions was not purely theoretical. He devoted considerable energy to translating the principle of the collective intellectual into active organizational forms that would empower intellectuals vis-à-vis the state more significantly than the devolved forms of "arm's length" administration that govern the relations between the state and different fields of arts, cultural, and intellectual production (arts councils and universities, for example) in many liberal democratic societies (Ahearne, 2004: 67–8). At the same time, however, there are many grounds on which Bourdieu's formulations can be criticized: his failure to realize how closely his characterization of state/ intellectual relations is dependent on post-Revolutionary French traditions, for example, and the somewhat bemusing mismatch between his championing of the collective intellectual and his extreme partisanship for his own particular brand of sociology.[12] It is, however, the principles of the historical ontology underlying his formulations that need to be engaged with if Bourdieu is to be criticized on grounds that take account of the complexity of his position in these regards.

"False Fossilization": the Contradictions of Bourdieu's Historical Reasoning

Bourdieu's conversation with Gunther Grass on the importance of intellectuals "speaking up" provides a convenient route into these questions since, here, time is not quite so irreversible as it appears in *The Rules of Art*:

> *Bourdieu:* It [neo-liberalism: TB] recasts the past in its own light and at the same time presents itself as progressive so that those who fight the return to the old ways are perceived themselves as yesterday's news. Both of us are constantly facing this; we are always being treated as eternally behind the times. In France, one is an "old iron."
>
> *Grass:* Dinosaurs . . .
>
> *Bourdieu:* Exactly. There it is, the great power of conservative revolutions, "progressive" restorations. (Bourdieu and Grass, 2000)

The problem here, recalling Bourdieu's remarks concerning the artists of the Right Bank who had become "fossils of another age," is one of "false fossilization" as unanticipated political tremors have placed time so out of joint with itself as to make those who are at the forefront of the literary and artistic fields seem historically superseded.

At one level, Bourdieu here simply registers the effects of a shift in the balance of power between different agents within the field of cultural production, and between this field and the economic and political fields. However, Bourdieu sees this as "a threat of a totally new sort" (Bourdieu and Grass, 2000) brought about by a change of a qualitative kind in which the division between the fields of restricted and extended cultural production is now scarcely tenable owing to the degree to which commercial, bureaucratic, and technocratic pressures have – quite suddenly it would seem – invaded the field of restricted production. What are we to make of an account which oscillates between stressing the unstoppable cumulative momentum of the literary and artistic fields, construing this as a property of those fields themselves, and the possibility that this momentum might be subject to sudden checks and reversals that can only be registered as historical aberrations or outside shocks? I want to briefly consider three aspects of the ways in which Bourdieu uses and interprets the forms of historical reasoning he proposes for the light they throw on this question.

The first concerns his failure to distinguish properly between, first, the processes of autonomization characterizing particular artistic and literary fields in particular moments of their history and, second. autonomization as a cumulative process that is held to be operable across different epochs and national societies in the form of a generalized account of the development of western art. While Bourdieu's own accounts of autonomization in *fin-de-siècle* France are concrete, focused, empirically based and theoretically probing, his longer histories are constructed by stitching together different moments in the development of western artistic practices as connecting parts of cumulative narratives which occlude significant aspects of their specific histories.[13] *Pascalian Meditations* (Bourdieu, 2000) thus offers an account of the autonomization of the artistic and literary fields as a process that starts, alongside the development of the philosophical and scientific fields, with the Greeks. Bourdieu then traces the subsequent autonomization and differentiation of these fields through the Renaissance, hitching his account on to Norbert Elias's (1994) account of the civilization process and the development of Kantian aesthetics, contending that the process of autonomization achieved its mature and developed form in the late nineteenth century. And there is then relatively little after this: for. Bourdieu, the *fin-de-siècle* laid down the rules of a game which persist, with no room for manoeuver except to repeat moves that have already been made (Bourdieu, 1996b: 342). There are, however, real difficulties for accounts cast in this mold when faced with the evidence of the more disjunctive histories of visual culture that Hans Belting (1994, 2001), for one, has made available, especially in distinguishing the forms of temporality of both medieval religious painting and contemporary art from that of the modern art system.

The second difficulty concerns Bourdieu's account of the role that different kinds of power play in the historical dynamics of the literary and artistic fields. Bourdieu sees these fields as being structured by the relations between forms of power that are autonomous to them and those that arise from outside. Construing these relations in the form of a zero-sum game in which one form of power can only increase its sway at the expense of the other, Bourdieu sees the literary and artistic fields as being riven by an unending struggle between two principles:

> the heteronomous principle, which favours those who dominate the field economically and politically (for example, "bourgeois art") and the autonomous principle (for example, "art for art's sake"), which leads its most radical defenders to make of temporal failure a sign of election and of success a sign of compromise with the times. (Bourdieu 1996b: 216–17)

The form taken by struggles within the literary and artistic fields, and between these fields and the field of power, is that of a constant competition over "the transformation or conservation of the relative value of different kinds of capital, which itself determines, at any moment, the forces liable to be engaged in these struggles" (Bourdieu, 1996b: 215). This means that the relations between different fields – the economic, the social, the political, and the cultural – are concerned solely with the strategies for, and rules governing, the conversion of different forms of capital (economic, social, and cultural) into one another. It is not difficult to see how this set of assumptions makes it possible to "think" the historicity of fields as either unilinear movements along the direction of increasing autonomy, or checks and reversals to this tendency, arising from the relative power of different capitals. Step outside Bourdieu's theoretical framework, however, and it becomes clear pretty quickly that the activities of agents within the literary, artistic, and cultural fields are no more reducible to capital accumulation or conversion strategies than relations of culture and power can be exhaustively described in terms of capital theory. The aesthetic hierarchies, forms of exclusion and the specific forms of subjection associated with the relations between culture, race, and colonialism, for example, simply cannot be recounted in these terms. This necessarily calls into question the validity of unidirectional accounts of the histories of cultural fields as if the play of power within them could be satisfactorily accounted for in terms of a single axis of autonomy versus dependence.

The third set of difficulties arises from Bourdieu's use of the term "historical transcendental" to identify two different mechanisms – first, the reproduction of relations of domination as if they were grounded in necessity, and second, the genesis of the "historical universal" as a force transcending the particular historical conditions of its making. This results in a confusion of the two different kinds of historical reasoning informing these two concepts. In its most frequent usage, the historical transcendental refers to the mechanisms through which particular dispositions or social relations developed in particular circumstances are perpetuated through time via definite methods of social reproduction in ways that generate the illusion of the universality, the necessity and inevitably of what they reproduce. *Masculine Domination* (Bourdieu, 2001) thus offers an account of the construction of masculine domination as a historical transcendental in this sense, invoking the procedures of historical anamnesis to account for the incessant labor of reproduction through which this effect is produced. In this case, Bourdieu invokes the practice of anamnesis for the analysis of *stabilities* through time produced by historical processes of reproduction. When it comes to analyzing the development of the literary and artistic fields and the formation of the collective intellectual, however, the very same practice is invoked to analyze *cumulative changes* through time. It is in the context of this latter concern that the historical transcendental slips over to become something else – the historical universal as a set of enduring values that accumulates and deepens through time.

This discrepancy introduces two different principles into the historical shaping of the habitus. Bourdieu's account of masculine domination as a historically transcendental force rests, in part, on an analysis of the forms that masculine domination takes in the peasant society of the Kabyle and in Bloomsbury, London, as revealed by a symptomatic reading of Virginia Woolf's *To The Lighthouse*. This is presented as an analysis of the processes through which masculine domination is reproduced by treating contemporary Kabyle society *as if* it were an archaic forerunner of 1930s Bloomsbury. Drawing on the widely discredited tropes of late nineteenth-century anthropology, Bourdieu interprets present-day Kabyle society as one in which, "abstracted from time," archaic social relations have "survived" into the present (Bourdieu, 2001: 6). From this he moves to construe the forms of masculine domination evident among the Kabyle, as well as in Bloomsbury, "as the instruments of an archaeological history of the unconscious which, having no doubt been originally constructed in a very ancient and very archaic state of our societies, inhabits each of us, whether man or woman" (Bourdieu, 2001: 54).

This is, by any standards, a remarkable piece of legerdemain. A procedure which presents as "historical" the similarities observed between a set of ethnographic field notes relating to an Algerian peasant society gathered in the 1950s and an English novel written in the 1920s by converting the former into the archaic prehistory of the latter is, of course, anti-historical in its methods since it simultaneously evacuates two societies of their particular histories.[14] My point here, though, is that the habitus of the collective intellectual is differently organized since this contains both this ancient layer of the self and the successive accretions that later histories have laid across it in a complex process of self-formation that ultimately achieves self-consciousness through the critical practice of anamnesis. To briefly explore the implications of this, I conclude by looking at Bourdieu's construction of the politics of freedom and some unresolved tensions this highlights concerning Bourdieu's relations to Kant and to the art museum.

Aesthetics and the Politics of Freedom

John Guillory, discussing Bourdieu's classic essay on the field of cultural production (Bourdieu, 1983), notes that it adds an issue that was not visible in *Distinction*: namely how artists who subject themselves to the demands of the autonomous world of art represent a relationship to the aesthetic disposition of disinterested-ness that is different from the cultic consumption of the dominant classes (Guillory, 1993: 331). This is a distinction that Bourdieu activates in his postscript to *The Rules of Art* when stating that he is addressing

> not all those who conceive of culture as a patrimony, a dead culture to be made into an obligatory cult of ritual piety, or as an instrument of domination and distinction, cultural bastion and Bastille, to be erected against the Barbarians within and with-out...but rather those who conceive of culture as an instrument of freedom pre-supposing freedom...a "collective intellectual" who might be capable of making a discourse of freedom heard, a discourse that recognises no other limit than the constraints and controls which each artist, each writer and each scholar, armed with all the acquisitions of his or her predecessors, enjoin upon themselves and all others. (Bourdieu, 1996b: 340)

Guillory also notes that, with Bourdieu, Kant's concern with the aesthetic as a distinctive mode of production disappears entirely owing to the emphasis Bour-dieu places on the aesthetic disposition as a mode of consumption (Guillory, 1993: 332). The omission is significant since what it forgets are the complex relations between the role of the aesthetic in Kant's politics of freedom and the earlier tradition of civic humanism in which the new discourse of aesthetics – particularly as fashioned by Shaftesbury – played a key role in articulating a new set of relations between freedom and governance in the context of the market society that emerged in the wake of the 1688 Revolution.[15]

While I cannot go into this aspect of the history of aesthetics in any detail (see, however, Chytry, 1989, Klein, 1994, and Poovey, 1998), I raise it here since it forms a part of the historical formation of the discursive space in which Bourdieu seeks to articulate a politics of freedom. It therefore bears directly on the practice of anamnesis he advocates in calling to mind past–present continuities that would otherwise remain unconscious. For in calling on the collective intellectual to take arms against neo-liberalism, Bourdieu asks not only that intellectuals should take issue with encroachments on their autonomy of both state and market, but that they should do so as self-conscious bearers of the universal that has been deposited in the unconscious of intellectuals (but not others) as a consequence of the histories of which they are the outcomes. In projecting this universality as some-thing still to be achieved, Bourdieu remains in the space opened up by Kant's notion of the *sensus communis* except that, rather than projecting, as Kant did, a consensus regarding judgments of taste, he makes the more Hegelian move of projecting a universalism of reason to be progressively constructed by intellectuals, who can alone represent the universal until the conditions in which it can be recognized by all have been created.

It is, in this light, worth recalling how Hegel's understanding of the relations between Spirit and History were linked to the art museum, particularly as Bour-dieu underlines the close connection that binds the history of aesthetic theory and the philosophy of art to the development of modern artistic institutions (Bourdieu, 1996b: 294). For as well as its role in shaping the "pure gaze" that Bourdieu discusses, the art museum has also functioned as an important aesthetic and epistemological technology of modernity through the particular form of historicity that it effects. Donald Preziosi (2003) thus argues that, over the period from the late eighteenth century to the present, art history and art museums have differentiated cultural works and practices by attributing to them different degrees of "semantic weight" or "carrying capacity." What he means by this is that it is only by virtue of the operations of this disciplinary and institutional nexus that different kinds of art are credited with the ability to store and preserve different degrees of information from their historical environments, and to make this available, in the future, for intellectual retrieval. This effect, he argues, arises from the capacity of art museums to detach particular works from their originating cultural contexts and to arrange them in sequential toil in relation to one another so that they might stand as the indexes of the universal histories they thus make visible. The role that Bourdieu envisages for the practice of historical anamnesis in relation to the historical universal is, in this respect, similar to the form of historicity produced by the art museum. Indeed, it is arguable that Bourdieu's conception of the historical universal reflects the operation of such institutions. As loci for the history that is stored up within them, they both make intelligible and provide the means through which a historically shaped universality might acquire a consciousness of itself as such by communing with the accumulated record of its own formation. The concluding paragraph of Hegel's *Phenomenology of Mind* makes the point. For when summarizing his sense of how Spirit comes into being through History as a process of conscious self-mediation, Hegel chooses the image of the art gallery as the imaginary scene for this act of historical self-shaping:

> This way of becoming presents a slow procession and succession of spiritual shapes (*Geistern*), a gallery of pictures, each of which is endowed with the entire wealth of Spirit, and moves so slowly just for the reason that the self has to permeate and assimilate all of this wealth of its substance. (Hegel, 1971: 807)

If we can see here how Bourdieu's understanding of cultural value affected his interpretation of the tasks of historical sociology in ways that were shaped by his own deeply modernist formation, we can also see the limitations of the political conclusions he drew from these for a period in which time is more flattened out than it used to be. But we can see also how these political formulations have their roots in the forms of historical reasoning underlying the concepts of field and habitus and the relations between them. These are clearly both matters that would warrant further investigation than has been possible here. It is hoped, however, that the lines of inquiry that have been suggested will prove fruitful for future work on these questions.

Notes

1   For Bakhtin, "discrowning" referred to the lowering of high or official forms of culture brought about through their parodic inversion or debasement in the practices of carnival: see Bakhtin (1968).

2   My assessments of Bourdieu's position in French cultural policy debates draw substantially on the accounts presented in Ahearne (2004) and Loosely (1995, 2004)

3   I draw here on an earlier discussion (Bennett, 1990a) of this aspect of Marxist theory.

4   Sometimes directed against what he characterized as bourgeois forms of empiricism, Lukács also used this phrase to criticize the mechanical materialism of the Soviet doctrine of socialist realism. The essays in Lukács (1970) give a good sense of both sets of issues.

5   The literature on this subject is vast. I draw here mainly on Canghuilem (1988), Steadman (1979), and Bennett (2004b).

6   See, for example, Grenfall and Hardy (2003) for a telling application of this aspect of Bourdieu's work to the organization of the contemporary British art field.

7   This also distinguishes Bourdieu's approach to the development of the literary and artistic fields from the systems theory approach of Niklas Luhmann (2000).

8   Bourdieu's insistence that the development of critical intellectual practice has to be understood as connected to the interests of particular strata stands in marked contrast to Adorno's attempt to establish a basis for critique in a position of redemption outside the clash of interests (Karakayali, 2004).

9   This is not to overlook the differences between them, however. Bourdieu's accounts of such processes remains cast within the framework of a realist epistemology in contrast to Latour's constructivism. Bourdieu, moreover, is clearly the main target Latour has in mind in his generalized criticisms of sociology's claim to be able to uncover the real motives of social action in underlying structural causes which remain hidden from, or only partially accessible to, social actors (see, e.g., Latour, 2004: 154–6).

10   Bourdieu presents this postscript as an explicitly normative departure from the scientific analysis put forward in the earlier chapters of *The Rules of Art*, albeit one he suggests is warranted by the conclusions reached in those chapters. My purpose is to suggest that the normative position Bourdieu takes here also imbues the categories of analysis he deploys in his scientific discussion.

11   Ahearne (2004: 47) usefully traces the transformations from Bourdieu's earlier suspicion of state interventions in the sphere of culture to his later, but still guarded, insistence on their necessity.

12   Bourdieu's endless attempts to privilege the sociologist over other intellectuals as a consequence of the forms of self-reflexivity that he sees as the necessary by-product of sociological reasoning are as tedious as they are unconvincing, and it is difficult to disagree with those who, like Latour (2004) and Dreyfus and Rabinow (1993), see this as a part of a power play aimed at epistemologically privileging sociology in relation to all other disciplines in the social sciences and humanities.

13   The specificity of the cumulative historicity Bourdieu attributes to western art fields is tellingly highlighted in Morishita's (2003) discussion of the different historicity governing the Japanese art field.

14   Bourdieu is clearly anxious on this point in the lengthy explanation he offers to justify this procedure. However, he fails to address Johannes Fabian's (1983) objection that

the primary distancing move of anthropology has always consisted in its denial of coevalness between the time of the observer and that of the observed.

15 Although Bourdieu acknowledges the relationship between Kant and Shaftesbury, he disconnects it from a concern with the politics of freedom and converts it into one concerning aesthetics as consumption (Bourdieu, 1996b: 295).

Selected Bibliography

I provide below details of the main publications relating to the major organizing foci of my work from the late 1970s through to the present. I have given the first place of publication in all cases. Where essays have subsequently been republished alongside other material in *Outside Literature*, *The Birth of the Museum* or *Culture: A Reformer's Science*, this is indicated by the bracket reference to *Outside*, *Birth* or *Culture* respectively at the end of the reference. The original location for the essays collected in this volume is also included here.

Aesthetics and literary theory

Bennett, T. (1979) *Formalism and Marxism*, London: Methuen.

Bennett, T. (1980) "Macherey and Marxist criticism," *Sociological Review* (February): 215–24.

Bennett, T. (1981) "Marxism and popular fiction," *Literature and History* 7(2), 138–65.

Bennett, T. (1982a) "Text and history," in P. Widdowson (ed.), *Re-reading English*, London: Methuen, pp.221–36.

Bennett, T. (1982b) "Texts, readers and reading formations," *Bulletin of the Mid-Western Modern Languages Association* (Winter): 3–17.

Bennett, T. (1982c) "Marxism and popular fiction: problems and prospects," *Southern Review* (Autumn): 218–33.

Bennett, T (1984a) "Texts in history: the determination of readings and their texts," *Australian Journal of Communication* 5 and 6.

Bennett, T. (1984b) "The text in question," *Southern Review* 17(2): 118–25.

Bennett, T. (1985) "Really useless 'knowledge': a political critique of aesthetics," *Thesis Eleven* 12: 28–52 (*Birth*).

Bennett, T. (1990a) *Outside Literature*, London and New York: Routledge.

Bennett, T. (1991a) "Literature/history: an uncoupling," *Journal of the Australasian Universities Language and Literature Association* 75 (May): 38–52.

Bennett. T. (1995a) "Figuring the audience," in J. Hay, L. Grossberg, and E. Wartella (eds.), *The Audience and its Landscape*, Boulder, CO: Westview Press, pp. 145–60.

Bennett, T. (2007a) "Habitus clivé: aesthetics and politics in the work of Pierre Bourdieu," *New Literary History,* 38(1): 201–28.

Popular culture and everyday life

Bennett, T. (1982d) "A thousand and one troubles: Blackpool Pleasure Beach," *Formations of Pleasure,* London: Routledge (*Birth*).
Bennett, T. (1984c) "James Bond: theorising a popular hero," *Southern Review* 16(2): 195–225.
Bennett, T. (1984d) "Marxist cultural theory: in search of 'the popular'," *Australian Journal of Cultural Studies* 1(2): 2–28.
Bennett, T. (1986a) "Hegemony, ideology, pleasure: Blackpool," in T. Bennett, C. Mercer and J. Woollacott (eds.), *Popular Culture and Social Relations,* pp. 6–21.
Bennett, T. (1986b) "The politics of the 'the popular' and popular culture," in T. Bennett, C. Mercer and J. Woollacott (eds.), *Popular Culture and Social Relations,* Milton Keynes and Philadelphia: Open University Press, pp.6–21.
Bennett, T. and J. Woollacott (1987) *Bond and Beyond: The Political Career of a Popular Hero,* London: Macmillan and New York: Methuen.
Bennett, T. (1996a) "Art and theory: the politics of the invisible," in J. Berland, W. Straw and D. Thomas (eds.), *Theory Rules: Theory and Art,* Toronto: University of Toronto Press, pp. 297–314 (*Birth*).
Bennett, T., M. Emmison, and J. Frow (1999) *Accounting for Tastes: Australian Everyday Cultures,* Cambridge: Cambridge University Press.
Bennett, T., M. Emmison, and J. Frow (2001) "Social class and cultural practice in contemporary Australia," in T. Bennett and D. Carter (eds.), *Culture in Australia: Policies, Publics, Programs,* pp. 193–216.
Bennett, T. (2002a) "The invention of the modern cultural fact: toward a critique of the critique of everyday life," in Silva and Bennett (eds.), *Contemporary Culture and Everyday Life,* Durham: The Sociologypress, pp. 21–36.
Bennett, T. (2003) *Formalism and Marxism* (2nd edn.), London: Routledge.
Bennett, T. (2006a) "Distinction on the box: cultural capital and the social space of broadcasting," *Cultural Trends,* 15(2 and 3): 193–212.

Culture and governance: cultural policy and cultural studies

Bennett, T. (1989a) "Museums and the public good: economic rationalism and cultural policy," *Culture and Policy* 1(1): 37–51.
Bennett, T. (1991b) "Putting policy into cultural studies," in L. Grossberg, C. Nelson and P. Treichtler (eds.), *Cultural Studies,* London and New York: Routledge, pp. 22–37.
Bennett, T. (1992a) "Coming out of English: from cultural studies to cultural policy studies," in K. K. Ruthven (ed.), *Beyond the Disciplines: The New Humanities,* Canberra: Australian Academy of the Humanities, pp.33–44.
Bennett, T. (1993) "Being 'in the true' of cultural studies," *Southern Review* 26(2): 217–38 (*Culture*).

Bennett, T. (1996b) "Out in the open: reflections on the history and practice of cultural studies," *Cultural Studies* 10(1): 133–53 (*Culture*).

Bennett, T. (1997a) "Culture and utility," in C. O'Farrell (ed.), *Foucault: The Legacy*, Brisbane: Queensland University of Technology, pp.398–404.

Bennett, T. (1997b) "Toward a pragmatics for cultural studies," in J. McGuigan (ed.), *Theory and Method in Cultural Studies*, London: Sage Publications, pp. 42–61 (*Culture*).

Bennett, T. (1997c) "Culture, government and the social," *Culture and Policy* 8(3): 169–76.

Bennett, T. (1998a) "Cultural studies: a reluctant discipline," *Cultural Studies* 12(4): 528–45 (*Culture*).

Bennett, T. (1998b) *Culture: A Reformer's Science*, Sydney: Allen and Unwin: London and New York: Sage.

Bennett, T. (2000) "Acting on the social: art, culture, and government," *American Behavioural Science* 43(9): 1412–28.

Bennett, T. (2001a) "Cultural policy," *International Encyclopedia of Social and Behavioural Sciences*: 3092–7.

Bennett, T. (2001b) "Culture and policy," in *Culture, Society and the Market*, Stockholm: Bank of Sweden Tercentenary Foundation and the Swedish National Council for Cultural Affairs, pp. 13–28.

Bennett, T. (2001c) *Differing Diversities: Cultural Policy and Cultural Diversity*, Strasbourg: Council of Europe.

Bennett, T. (2002b) "Culture and governmentality," in Jack Bratich, Jeremy Packer and Cameron McCarthy (eds.), *Foucault, Cultural Studies and Governmentality*, New York: SUNY Press, pp. 47–66.

Bennett, T. (2006b) "Culture and differences: the challenges of multiculturalism," in Simona Boda and Maria Rita Cifarelli (eds.), *When Culture Makes the Difference: Heritage, Arts and Media in Multicultural Society*, Rome: Meltemi Editore, pp. 21–37.

Bennett, T. (2007b) "Making culture, changing society: the perspective of culture studies," *Cultural Studies*.

Bennett, T. (2007c) "The work of culture," *Journal of Cultural Sociology*, 1(1): 31–48.

History and theory of museums and exhibition practices

Bennett, T. (1988a) "The Exhibitionary Complex," *New Formations* 4: 73–102 (*Birth*).

Bennett, T. (1988b) "History on the Rocks," in D. Barry and S. Muecke (eds.), *The Apprehension of Time*, Sydney: Local Consumption Press, pp. 4–15.

Bennett, T. (1988c) "Museums and 'the people,' " in R. Lumley (ed.), *The Museum Time-Machine: Putting Cultures on Display*, London and New York: Comedia/Methuen, pp. 63–85 (*Birth*).

Bennett, T. (1988d) *Out of Which Past? Critical Reflections on Australian Museum and Heritage Policy*, Occasional Papers in Cultural Policy Studies, no. 3, Institute for Cultural Policy Studies, Griffith University (*Birth.*)

Bennett, T. (1988e) "Museums and public culture: history, theory, policy," *Media Information Australia* 53 (August): 56–65.

Bennett, T. (1989b) "1988: history and the bicentenary," *Australian Canadian Studies* 7(1–2): 154–62.

Bennett, T. (1990b) "The political rationality of the museum," *Continuum* 3(1): 35–55 (*Birth*).

Bennett, T. (1991c) "The shaping of things to come: Expo '88," *Cultural Studies* 5(1): 30–51 (*Birth*).

Bennett, T. (1992b) "Useful culture," *Cultural Studies* 6(3): 395–408.

Bennett, T. (1992c) "Museums, government, culture," *Sites* 25: 9–23.

Bennett, T. (1995b) *The Birth of the Museum: History, Theory, Politics,* London and New York: Routledge.

Bennett, T. (1995c) "The multiplication of culture's utility," *Critical Inquiry* 21(4): 859–89 (*Culture*).

Bennett, T. (1996c) "The museum and the citizen," in T. Bennett (ed.), *Museums and Citizenship: A Resource Book,* special issue of *Memoirs of the Queensland Museum,* pp. 1–15.

Bennett, T. (1997d) "Speaking to the eyes: museums, legibility and the social order," in S. Macdonald (ed.), *Politics of Display: Science as Culture,* London: Routledge, pp. 25–35.

Bennett, T. (1997e) "Regulated restlessness: museums, liberal government and the historical sciences," *Economy and Society* 26(2) (*Culture*): 161–90.

Bennett, Tony (1997f) "Museums and their constituencies," *New Zealand Museums Journal* 26(2): 15–23.

Bennett, T. (1998c) "Pedagogic objects, clean eyes and popular instruction: on sensory regimes and museum didactics," *Configurations: A Journal of Literature, Science and Technology* 6(3): 345–71.

Bennett, T. (2001d) "Pasts beyond memories: the evolutionary museum, liberal government and the politics of prehistory," *Folk: Journal of the Danish Ethnographic Society* 43 (Autumn): 49–76.

Bennett, T. (2002c) "Archaeological autopsy: objectifying time and cultural governance," *Cultural Values* 6(1–2): 29–48.

Bennett, T. (2002d) "Stored virtue: memory, the body and the evolutionary museum," in S. Radstone and K. Hodgin (eds.), *Regimess of Memory,* London and New York: Routledge, pp. 40–54.

Bennett, T. (2004a) "Metropolis, colony, primitive: evolution and the politics of vision," in K. Kopp and K. Müller-Richter (eds.), *Metropolis and Primitive,* Berlin: Metzler Verlag.

Bennett, T. (2004b) *Pasts Beyond Memory: Evolution, Museums, Colonialism,* London and New York: Routledge.

Bennett, T. (2005a) "Civic seeing: museums and the organisation of vision," in S. MacDonald (ed.), *Companion to Museum Studies,* Oxford: Blackwell.

Bennett, T. (2005b) "Civic laboratories: museums, cultural objecthood, and the governance of the social," *Cultural Studies* 19(5): 521–47.

Bennett, T. (2006c) "Exhibition, difference and the logic of culture," in I. Karp, C.A. Kratz, L. Szwaja, and T.Ybarra-Frausto (eds.), *Museum Frictions: Public Culture/Global Transformations,* Durham and London: Duke University Press, pp. 46–69.

Bennett, T. (2007d) "The art museum as civic machinery," in B. Jaschke, C. Martinz-Turek and N. Sternfeld (eds.), *Sammlungen Austellen,* Vienna: Verlag Turia.

The politics of intellectuals

Bennett, T. (1987) "The prison-house of criticism," *New Formations* 2: 127–44 (*Outside*).

Bennett, T. (1988f) "Critical illusions," *Poetics* 17(1–2): 135–58 (*Outside*).

Bennett, T. (1999) "Intellectuals, culture, policy: the technical, the practical and the critical," *Pavis Papers in Social and Cultural Research*, no. 2, Milton Keynes: Pavis Centre for Social and Cultural Research, The Open University.

Bennett, T. (2005c) "The historical universal: the role of cultural value in the historical sociology of Pierre Bourdieu," *British Journal of Sociology* 56 (1): 141–64.

References

Details of my own publications that are referred to in the text are contained in the preceding Selected Bibliography and have not been repeated here.

Adams, T. R. (1939) *The Museum and Popular Culture*, New York: American Association for Adult Education.

Adorno, T. (1967) "Valéry Proust Museum," in *Prisms*, London: Neville Spearman.

Ahearne, J. (2004) *Between Cultural Theory and Policy: The Cultural Policy Thinking of Pierre Bourdieu, Michel de Certeau and Régis Debray*, Coventry: Centre for Cultural Policy Studies, University of Warwick.

Alexander, E. (1983) *Museum Masters. Their Museums and their Influence*, Nashville, Tennessee: The American Association for State and Local History.

Allor, Martin (1988) "Relocating the site of the audience," *Critical Studies in Mass Communication* 5.

Althusser, Louis and Etienne Balibar (1970) *Reading Capital*, London: New Left Books.

Anderson, Perry (1976) *Considerations on Western Marxism*, London: New Left Books.

Ang, Ien (1989) "Wanted: audiences. On the politics of empirical audience studies," in E. Seiter, G, Kreutzner, H. Borchers and E-M. Warth. (eds.), *Remote Control: Television, Audiences, and Cultural Power*, London: Routledge.

Attali, Jacques (1985) *Noise: The Political Economy of Music*, Manchester: Manchester University Press.

Bakhtin, Mikhail M. (1968) *Rabelais and His World*, Cambridge, MA: MIT Press.

Balfour, Henry (1890) "Special Report," *Foundations and Early History*, folio 38, Oxford: Pitt Rivers Archives, Pitt Rivers Museum.

Balfour, Henry (1904) "The relationship of museums to the study of anthropology," *The Museums Journal* 3.

Barry, Andrew (2001) *Political Machines: Governing a Technological Society*, London and New York: The Athlone Press.

Barry, Andrew, Thomas Osborne, and Nikolas.Rose (eds.) (1996) *Foucault and Political Reason: Liberalism, Neo-liberalism and Rationalities of Government*, London: UCL Press.

Barthes, Roland (1987) *Criticism and Truth*, Minneapolis: University of Minnesota Press.

Baudrillard, Jean (1982) "The Beaubourg effect: implosion and deterrence," *October* 20: 3–13.

Baxendall, Lee and Stefan Morawski, (1974) *Karl Marx, Frederick Engels: On Literature and Art*, New York: International General.

Beer, Gillian (1985) *Darwin's Plots: Evolutionary Narrative in Darwin, George Eliot and Nineteenth-Century Fiction*, London: Ark Paperbacks.

Belting, Hans (1994) *Likeness and Presence: A History of the Image before the Era of Art*, Chicago: University of Chicago Press.

Belting, Hans (2001) *The Invisible Masterpiece*, London: Reaktion Books.

Bohrer, Frederick N. (1994) "The times and spaces of history: representation, Assyria and the British Museum," in Daniel J. Sherman and Irit Rogoff (eds.), *Museum Culture: Histories Discourses Spectacles*, Minneapolis: University of Minnesota Press.

Bonnell, Victoria E. and Lynn Hunt (1999) (eds.) *Beyond the Cultural Turn: New Directions in the Study of Society and Culture*, Berkeley and Los Angeles: University of California Press.

Bottomore, Tom (ed.) (1963) *Karl Marx: Early Writings*, London: C.A.Watts.

Bouquet, Mary (2000) "Figures of relations: reconnecting kinship studies and museum collections," in Janet Carsten (ed.), *Cultures of Relatedness: New Approaches to the Study of Kinship*, Cambridge: Cambridge University Press.

Bourdieu, Pierre (1979) "Public opinion does not exist," in A. Mattelart and S. Siegelaub, (eds.), *Communication and Class Struggle: Capitalism and Imperialism*, New York: International General.

Bourdieu, Pierre (1983) "The field of cultural production, or: The economic world reversed," *Poetics*, 12.

Bourdieu, Pierre (1984) *Distinction: A Social Critique of the Judgement of Taste*, London: Routledge and Kegan Paul.

Bourdieu, Pierre (1988) *Homo Academicus*, Cambridge: Polity.

Bourdieu, Pierre (1990) *In Other Words: Essays Towards a Reflexive Sociology*, Cambridge: Polity.

Bourdieu, Pierre (1993a) *The Field of Cultural Production: Essays on Art and Literature*, Cambridge: Polity.

Bourdieu, Pierre (1993b) "Concluding remarks: For a sociogenetic understanding of intellectual works," in C. Calhoun, E. LiPuma, and M. Postone (eds.), *Bourdieu: Critical Perspectives*, Cambridge: Polity.

Bourdieu, Pierre (1996a) *The State Nobility: Elite Schools in the Field of Power*, Cambridge: Polity.

Bourdieu, Pierre (1996b) *The Rules of Art: Genesis and Structure of the Literary Field*, Cambridge: Polity.

Bourdieu, Pierre (1998a) *Practical Reason*, Cambridge: Polity.

Bourdieu, Pierre (1998b) *On Television and Journalism*, London: Pluto Press.

Bourdieu, Pierre (2000) *Pascalian Meditations*, Cambridge: Polity.

Bourdieu, Pierre (2001) *Masculine Domination*, Cambridge: Polity.

Bourdieu, Pierre (2002) "Inequality at school as the key to cultural inequality," in J. Ahearne (ed.), *French Cultural Policy Debates: A Reader*, London and New York: Routledge.

Bourdieu, Pierre and A. Darbel (1991) *The Love of Art: European Art Museums and their Public*, Cambridge: Polity.

Bourdieu, Pierre and Gunther Grass (2000) "Speaking up," web translation of January 2000 television interview.

References

Bourdieu, Pierre and Hans Haacke (1995) *Free Exchange*, Cambridge: Polity.

Brewer, John (1995) " 'The most polite age and the most vicious.' Attitudes towards culture as a commodity, 1660–1800," in Ann Bermingham and John Brewer (eds.), *The Consumption of Culture, 1600–1800: Image, Object, Text*, London: Routledge.

Brewer, John (1997) *The Pleasures of the Imagination: English Culture in the Eighteenth Century*, London: Harper Collins Publishers.

Bromley, Roger (1978) "Natural boundaries: the social function of popular fiction," *Red Letters*, no. 7.

Brown, Lee Rust (1997) *The Emerson Museum: Practical Romanticism and the Pursuit of the Whole*, Cambridge, MA: Harvard University Press.

Burchell, Graham, Colin Gordon and Peter Miller (eds.) (1991) *The Foucault Effect: Studies in Governmentality*, Hemel Hempstead: Harvester Wheatsheaf.

Burkhardt, Richard W. (1997) 'La Ménagerie et la vie du Muséum', in C. Blanckaert, C. Cohen, P. Corsi and J-L. Fischer (eds.), *Le Muséum au primier siècle de son histoire*, Paris: Éditions de Muséum National D'Histoire Naturelle, pp. 481–508.

Butler, Judith (1999) "Performativity's social magic," in R. Shusterman (ed.), *Bourdieu: A Critical Reader*, Oxford: Blackwell.

Calhoun, Craig (ed.) (1992) *Habermas and the Public Sphere*, Cambridge, MA: MIT Press.

Calhoun, Craig (1993) "Habitus, field, and capital: The question of historical specificity," in C. Calhoun, E. LiPuma and M. Postone (eds.), *Bourdieu: Critical Perspectives*, Cambridge: Polity.

Candy, Philip and John Laurent, (eds.) (1994) *Pioneering Culture: Mechanics' Institutes and Schools of Art in Australia*, Adelaide: Auslib Press.

Canghuilhem, Georges (1988) *Ideology and Rationality in the History of the Life Sciences*, Cambridge, MA: MIT Press.

Caygill, Howard (1989) *Art of Judgement*, Oxford: Basil Blackwell.

Caygill, Marjorie and John Cherry (eds.) (1997) *A. W. Franks: Nineteenth Century Collecting and the British Museum*, London: The British Museum.

Chartier, Roger (1988) *Cultural History: Between Practices and Representations*, Cambridge: Polity.

Chartier, Roger (1997) *On the Edge of the Cliff: History, Language, and Practices*, Baltimore: Johns Hopkins University Press.

Chun, Allen (1996) "Discourses of identity in the changing spaces of public culture in Taiwan, Hong Kong and Singapore," *Theory, Culture and Society* 14(1).

Chytry, J. (1989) *The Aesthetic State: A Quest in Modern German Thought*, Berkeley and Los Angeles: University of California Press.

Clifford, James (1997) *Routes: Travel and Translation in the Late Twentieth Century*, Cambridge, MA: Harvard University Press.

Cole, Sir H. (1884) *Fifty Years of Public Work of Sir Henry Cole, K.C.B., Accounted for in his Deeds, Speeches and Writings*, (2 vols.) London: George Bell and Sons.

Collins, Richard and Christina Murroni (1996) *New Media, New Policies: Media and Communications Strategies for the Future*, Cambridge: Polity.

Coombes, Annie E. (1994) *Reinventing Africa: Museums, Material Culture and Popular Imagination in Late Victorian and Edwardian England*, New Haven and London: Yale University Press.

Crary, Jonathan (1996) *Techniques of the Observer: On Vision and Modernity in the Nineteenth Century*, Cambridge, MA: MIT Press.

Crary, Jonathan (2001) *Suspensions of Perception: Attention, Spectacle, and Modern Culture*, Cambridge, MA: MIT Press.

Crimp, Douglas (1993) *On the Museum's Ruins*, Cambridge, MA: MIT Press.

Dana, John Cotton (1917a) *The New Museum*, Woodstock, Vermont: The Elm Tree Press.

Dana, John Cotton (1917b) *The Gloom of the Museum*, Woodstock, Vermont: The Elm Tree Press.

Dana, John Cotton (1920) *A Plan for a New Museum: The Kind of Museum it will Profit a City to Maintain*, Woodstock, Vermont: The Elm Tree Press.

Darwin, Charles (1968) *The Origin of Species by Means of Natural Selection or The Preservation of Favoured Races in the Struggle for Life*, Harmondsworth: Penguin Books.

Daston, Lorraine and Katharine Park (1998) *Wonders and the Order of Nature, 1150–1750*, New York: Zone Books.

Davison, Graeme (1993) *The Unforgiving Minute: How Australians Learned to Tell the Time*, Melbourne: Oxford University Press.

Dean, Mitchell (1991) *The Constitution of Poverty: Toward a Genealogy of Liberal Governance*, London: Routledge.

Dean, Mitchell (1999) *Governmentality: Power and Rule in Modern Society*, London: Sage Publications.

Demetz, Peter (1967) *Marx, Engels and the Poet: Origins of Marxist Literary Criticism*, Chicago: University of Chicago Press.

Desmond, Adrian (1982) *Archetypes and Ancestors: Palaeontology in Victorian London*, Chicago and London: University of Chicago Press.

Dias, Nélia (1994) "Looking at objects: memory, knowledge in nineteenth-century ethnographic displays," in G. Robertson, M. Mash, L. Tickner, J. Bird, B. Curtis and T. Putnam (eds.), *Travellers' Tales: Narratives of Home and Displacement*, London and New York: Routledge, pp. 164–76.

Dias, Nélia (1998) "The visibility of difference: nineteenth-century French anthropological collections," in Sharon Macdonald (ed.), *The Politics of Display: Museums, Science, Culture*, London and New York: Routledge, pp. 36–52.

Dias, Nélia (2003) "Cultural difference, diversity of cultures and cultural diversity: the case of the Musée du quai Branly," paper presented at the *Museums and Difference* conference, Centre for Twenty-first Century Studies, University of Milwaukee.

Donzelot, Jacques (1980) *The Policing of Families: Welfare versus the State*, London: Hutchinson.

Dreyfus, Howard and Paul Rabinow (1993) "Can there be a science of existential structure and social meaning?" in C. Calhoun, E. LiPuma, and M. Postone (eds.), *Bourdieu: Critical Perspectives*, Cambridge: Polity.

Du Gay, Paul (2000) *In Praise of Bureaucracy: Weber – Organisation – Ethics*, London: Sage Publications.

Duncan, Carol (1995) *Civilising Rituals: Inside Public Art Museums*, London and New York: Routledge.

Eagleton, Terry (1976) *Criticism and Ideology* London: New Left Books.

Eagleton, Terry (1983) *Literary Theory: An Introduction*, Oxford: Blackwell.

Eamon, William (1994) *Science and the Secrets of Nature: Books of Secrets in Medieval and Early Modern Culture*, Princeton, New Jersey: Princeton University Press.

Eco, Umberto (1981) *The Role of the Reader: Explorations in the Semiotics of Texts*, London: Hutchinson.

References

Edwards, Elizabeth (2001) *Raw Histories: Photographs, Anthropology and Museums*, Oxford and New York: Berg.

Elias, Norbert (1987) *Time: An Essay*, Oxford: Blackwell.

Elias, Norbert (1994) *The Civilising Process*, Oxford: Blackwell.

Escarpit, Robert (1961) "Creative treason as a key in literature," *Yearbook of Comparative and General Literature*, no. 10.

Fabian, Johannes (1983) *Time and the Other, How Anthropology Makes Its Object*, New York: Colombia University Press.

Findlen, Paula (1994) *Possessing Nature: Museums, Collecting, and Scientific Culture in Early Modern Italy*, Berkeley, Los Angeles and London: University of California Press.

Finney, Colin (1993) *Paradise Revealed: Natural History in Nineteenth-Century Australia*, Melbourne: Museum of Victoria.

Fisher, Phillip (1991) *Making and Effacing Art: Modern American Art in a Culture of Museums*, New York: Oxford University Press.

Fiske, John (1988) "Critical response: Meaningful moments," *Critical Studies in Mass Communication*, no. 5.

Fiske, John (1992) "Cultural studies and the culture of everyday life," in Larry Grossberg, Crary Nelson and Paula Treichler (eds.), *Cultural Studies*, New York and London: Routledge.

Fiske, John and Jon Watts (1985) "Video games: Inverted pleasures," *Australian Journal of Cultural Studies* 3(1).

Foucault, Michel (1970) *The Order of Things: An Archaeology of the Human Sciences*, London: Tavistock Publications.

Foucault, Michel (1972) *The Archaeology of Knowledge*, London: Tavistock Publications.

Foucault, Michel (1980 [1976]) "Two lectures," in Colin Gordon (ed.) *Power/Knowledge: Selected Interviews and Other Writings, 1972–1977*, New York: Pantheon Books.

Foucault, Michel (1977) *Discipline and Punish: The Birth of the Prison*, London: Allen Lane.

Foucault, Michel (1980) *Power/Knowledge: Selected Interviews and Other Writings, 1972–1977* (ed. C. Gordon), New York: Pantheon Books.

Foucault, Michel (1988) "Technologies of the self," in L. H. Martin, H. Gutman, and P. H. Hutton (eds.) *Technologies of the Self: A Seminar with Michel Foucault*, London: Tavistock.

Foucault, Michel (1991 [1978]) "Governmentality," in Graham Burchell, Colin Gordon and Peter Miller (eds.) *The Foucault Effect: Studies in Governmentality*, Hemel Hempstead: Harvester Wheatsheaf.

Foucault, Michel (1997) *Ethics: The Essential Works*, Vol. 1., Paul Rabinow. (ed.) London: Allen Lane.

Frow, John (1986), *Marxism and Literary History*, Cambridge, MA: Harvard University Press.

Fuller, Nancy J. (1992) "The museum as a vehicle for community empowerment: the Ak-Chin Indian community ecomuseum project," in I. Karp, C. M. Kreamer, and S. D. Lavine (eds.), *Museums and Communities: The Politics of Public Culture*, Washington and London: Smithsonian Institution Press, pp. 327–66.

Gallup, George and Saul Rae (1968) *The Pulse of Democracy*, New York: Greenwood.

Garrison, Dee (1976) "The tender technicians: The feminisation of public librarianship, 1876–1905," in Mary S. Hartman and Lois Banner (eds.), *Clio's Consciousness Raised: New Perspectives on the History of Women*, New York: Octagon Books.

Gascoigne, John (1994) *Joseph Banks and the English Enlightenment: Useful Knowledge and Polite Culture*, Cambridge: Cambridge University Press.

Gibson, Lisanne (1997) "Art, citizenship and government: 'Art for the people' in New Deal America and the 1940s in England and Australia," *Culture and Policy* 8(3).

Giddens, Anthony (1998) *The Third Way: The Renewal of Social Democracy*, Cambridge: Polity.

Ginzburg, Carlo (1980a) *The Cheese and the Worms: the Cosmos of a Sixteenth-Century Miller*, London: Routledge and Kegan Paul.

Ginzburg, Carlo (1980b) "Clues and scientific method," *History Workshop Journal* 9 (Spring): 12.

Golinski, Jan (1998) *Making Natural Knowledge: Constructivism and the History of Science*, Cambridge: Cambridge University Press.

Grayson, Donald (1983) *The Establishment of Human Antiquity*, New York: Academic Press.

Grenfall, Michael and Carole Hardy (2003) "Bourdieu and the Young British Artists," *Space and Culture* 6(1): 19–34.

Griffiths, Alison (2002) *Wondrous Differences: Cinema, Anthropology, and Turn-of-the-Century Visual Culture*, New York: Columbia University Press.

Grossberg, Lawrence (1988) "Wandering audiences, nomadic critics," *Cultural Studie.* 2(3).

Grossberg, Lawrence (1989) "The context of audiences and the politics of difference," *Australian Journal of Communication* 16.

Guillory, J. (1993) *Cultural Capital: The Problem of Literary Canon Formation*, Chicago and London: University of Chicago Press.

Guyer, Paul (2005) *Values of Beauty: Historical Essays in Aesthetics*, Cambridge: Cambridge University Press.

Habermas, Jürgen (1974) *Theory and Practice*, London: Heinemann.

Habermas, Jürgen (1989) *The Structural Transformation of the Public Sphere – An Inquiry into a Category of Bourgeois Society*, Cambridge: Polity.

Habermas, Jürgen (1992) "Further reflections on the public sphere," in Craig Calhoun (ed.), *Habermas and the Public Sphere*, Cambridge, MA: MIT Press.

Habermas, Jürgen (1996) *Between Facts and Norms: Contributions to a Discourse Theory of Law and Democracy*, Cambridge: Polity.

Hall, Martin (2006) "The reappearance of the authentic," in I. Karp, C. A. Kratz, L. Szwaja, and T. Ybarra-Frausto (eds.), *Museum Frictions: Public Culture/Global Transformations*, Durham and London: Duke University Press, pp. 70–101.

Hall, Stuart (1980a) "Cultural studies: two paradigms," *Media, Culture and Society* 2(1).

Hall, Stuart (1980b) "Encoding/decoding," in S. Hall, D. Hobson, A. Lowe and P. Willis (eds.), *Culture, Media, Language*, London: Hutchinson.

Hall, Stuart (1981) "Notes on deconstructing the popular," in R. Samuel (ed.), *People's History and Socialist Theory*, London: Routledge and Kegan Paul.

Hall, Stuart (1986a) "On postmodernism and articulation" (interview edited by Lawrence Grossberg), *Journal of Communication Inquiry* 10(2).

Hall, Stuart (1986b) "The problem of ideology: Marxism without guarantees," *Journal of Communication Inquiry* 10(2): 28–44.

Hall, Stuart (1986c) "Popular culture and the state," in T. Bennett, C. Mercer and J. Woollacott (eds.), *Popular Culture and Social Relations*, Milton Keynes and Philadelphia: Open University Press.

References

Hall, Stuart (1996) "Who needs identity?" in Stuart Hall and Paul du Gay (eds.), *Questions of Cultural Identity*, London: Sage Publications.

Hall, Stuart (1997) "The centrality of culture: notes on the cultural revolutions of our time," in Kenneth Thompson (ed.), *Media and Cultural Regulation*, London: Sage Publications.

Hall, Stuart and Tony Jefferson (eds.) (1976) *Resistance through Rituals: Youth Subcultures in Post-War Britain*, London: Hutchinson.

Hall, Stuart and Paddy Whannel (1964) *The Popular Arts*, London: Hutchinson Educational.

Hall, Stuart, Chas Critcher, Tony Jefferson, John Clarke and Brian Roberts (eds.) (1978) *Policing the Crisis: Mugging, the State and Law and Order*, Basingstoke: Macmillan.

Hanada, Tatsuro (1995) "Can there be a public sphere in Japan?" *ISICS Research Papers* 50.

Harris, Neil (1975) "All the world a melting pot? Japan at American fairs, 1876–1904," in Iriye Akira (ed.), *Mutual Images: Essays in American–Japanese Relations*, Cambridge, MA: Harvard University Press.

Harris, J. (1995) *Federal Art and National Culture: The Politics of Identity in New Deal America*, Cambridge: Cambridge University Press.

Hawkins, Gay (1993) *From Nimbin to Mardi Gras: Constructing Community Arts*, Sydney: Allen and Unwin.

Heath, Stephen (1978) "Difference," *Screen* 19(3), Autumn: 105–6.

Heath, Stephen (1987) "Literary theory, etc.," *Comparative Criticism*, vol. 9, Cambridge: Cambridge University Press,

Hegel, George Wilhelm Friedrich (1971) *The Phenomenology of Mind*, London: George Allen and Unwin.

Helsinger, Elizabeth (1994) "Ruskin and the politics of viewing: constructing national subjects," *Harvard University Art Museums Bulletin* 3(1).

Hetherington, Kevin (1999) "From Blindness to blindness: museums, heterogeneity and the subject," in John Law and John Hassard (eds.), *Actor Network Theory and After*, Oxford: Blackwell Publishers/The Sociological Review.

Hetherington, Kevin (2002) "The unsightly: touching the Parthenon Frieze," *Theory, Culture & Society* 19(5/6): 187–205.

Hilpern, K. (1998) "Arts and soul," *The Guardian Society*, 26 August: 8–9.

Hirst, Paul (1976) "Althusser and the theory of ideology," *Economy and Society* 5(2).

Hoggart, Richard (1969) *The Uses of Literacy: Aspects of Working-Class Life, with special reference to Publications and Entertainment*, Harmondsworth: Penguin.

Hooper-Greenhill, E. (1989) "The museum in the disciplinary society," in S. M. Pearce (ed.), *Museum Studies in Material Culture*, Leicester and London: Leicester University Press.

Hunter, Ian (1988a) *Culture and Government: The Emergence of Literary Education*, London: Macmillan.

Hunter, Ian (1988b) "Setting limits to culture," *New Formations* 4: 103–24.

Hunter, Ian (1994) *Rethinking the School: Subjectivity, Bureaucracy, Criticism*, Sydney: Allen and Unwin.

Huxley, Thomas H. (1868) "A liberal education; and where to find it," *Macmillan's Magazine*, March.

Huxley, Thomas (1882) "On the method of Zadig: retrospective prophecy as a function of science," in *Science and Culture and Other Essays*, London: Macmillan.

Huxley, Thomas (1890) "Government: anarchy or regimentation," *The Nineteenth Century*, May.

Huxley, Thomas (1894) "Evolution and ethics," in James Paradis and George C. Williams (1989), *Evolution and Ethics: T. H. Huxley's* Evolution and Ethics *with New Essays on its Victorian and Sociobiological Context*, Princeton, New Jersey: Princeton University Press.

Huxley, Thomas (1896) "Suggestions for a proposed natural history museum in Manchester," *Report of the Museums Association*.

Iser, W. (1978) *The Act of Reading: A Theory of Aesthetic Response*, London: Routledge and Kegan Paul.

Jameson, Fredric (1981) *The Political Unconscious: Narrative as a Socially Symbolic Act*, London: Methuen.

Jameson, Fredric (1998) *The Cultural Turn: Selected Writings on the Postmodern, 1983–1998*, London: Verso.

Jenkins, David (1994) "Object lessons and ethnographic displays: museum exhibitions and the making of American anthropology," *Comparative Studies in Society and History* 36(1): 242–70.

Jenkins, Ian (1992) *Archaeologists and Aesthetes in the Sculpture Galleries of the British Museum 1800–1939*, London: British Museum Press.

Johnson, Leslie (1988) *The Unseen Voice: A Cultural History of Early Australian Radio*, London: Routledge.

Johnson, R., G. McLennan, B. Schwartz and D. Sutton (eds.) (1982) *Making Histories: Studies in History-Writing and Politics*, London: Hutchinson.

Jones, P. (1994) "The myth of 'Raymond Hoggart': on 'founding fathers' and cultural policy," *Cultural Studies* 8(3): 394–416.

Karakayali, N. (2004) "Reading Bourdieu with Adorno: The limits of critical theory and reflexive sociology," *Sociology* 38(2): 351–68.

Kasson, J. S. (1990) *Marble Queens and Captives; Women in Nineteenth-Century American Sculpture*, New Haven and London: Yale University Press.

Klein, Lawrence E. (1994) *Shaftesbury and the Culture of Politeness: Moral Discourse and Cultural Politics in Early Eighteenth-Century England*, Cambridge: Cambridge University Press.

Knell, Simon (1996) "The roller-coaster of museum geology," in Susan Pearce (ed.), *Exploring Science in Museums*, London: Athlone.

Kohlstedt, Sally Gregory (1983) "Australian museums of natural history: public practices and scientific initiatives in the 19th century," *Historical Records of Australian Science*, 5.

Kuper, Adam (1999) *Culture: The Anthropologists' Account*, Cambridge, MA: Harvard University Press.

Laclau, Ernesto and Mouffe, Chantal (1985) *Hegemony and Socialist Strategy*, London: Verso.

Lampert, R. J. (1986) "The development of the Aboriginal Gallery at the Australian Museum," *Bulletin of the Conference of Museum Anthropologists*, no. 18.

Landes, Joan B. (1988) *Women and the Public Sphere in the Age of the French Revolution*, Ithaca and London: Cornell University Press.

Latour, Bruno (1987) *Science in Action*, Cambridge, MA: Harvard University Press.

Latour, Bruno (1999a) *Pandora's Hope: Essays on the Reality of Science Studies*, Cambridge, MA: Harvard University Press.

References

Latour, Bruno (1999b) "Ein ding ist ein thing: a (philosophical) platform for a left (European) party", *Soundings*, no. 12.

Latour, Bruno (2004) "Why has critique run out of steam: From matters of fact to matters of concern," in B. Brown (ed.), *Things*, Chicago and London: University of Chicago Press.

Law, John (1999) "After ANT: complexity, naming and topology," in John Law and John Hassard (eds.), *Actor Network Theory and After*, Oxford: Blackwell Publishers and The Sociological Review.

Levell, Nicky (1997) *The Collectors Gallery: A Textual and Visual Summary*, Horniman Museum.

Levin, M. R. (1982) "The wedding of art and science in late eighteenth-century France: a means of building social solidarity," *Eighteenth Century Life* 7(3).

Liao, Ping-hui (1995) "Taiwan and the hyphenated public sphere" (unpublished paper).

Lifshitz, Mikhail (1974) *The Philosophy of Art of Karl Marx*, London: Pluto Press.

Lilpern, K. (1998) "Arts and soul," *The Guardian Society*, 26 August, pp. 8–9.

Lloyd, Genevieve (1984) *The Man of Reason: "Male" and "Female" in Western Philosophy*, London: Methuen.

Loosely, D. L. (1995) *The Politics of Fun: Cultural Policy and Debate in Contemporary France*. Oxford and Washington DC: Berg.

Loosely, D. L. (2004) "The development of a social exclusion agenda in French cultural policy," *Cultural Trends*, 13(2): 1–13.

Low, T. L. (1942) *The Museum as a Social Instrument*, New York: Metropolitan Museum of Art/The American Association of Museums.

Lubbock, John (1865) *Pre-Historic Times as illustrated by Ancient Remains and the Manners and Customs of Modern Savages*, London: Williams and Norgate.

Luhmann, N. (2000) *Art as a Social System*, Stanford, CA: Stanford University Press.

Lukács, Georg (1970) *Writer and Critic, and Other Essays*, London: Merlin Press.

Lull, James (1988) "The Audience as Nuisance," *Critical Studies in Mass Communication*, no. 5.

Lynd, Robert S. and Helen M. Lynd (1929) *Middletown*, London: Constable.

MacDonald, Sharon and Roger Silverstone (1990) "Rewriting the museum's fictions: Taxonomies, stories and readers," *Cultural Studies* 4(2).

Macherey, Pierre (1978) *A Theory of Literary Production*, London: Routledge and Kegan Paul.

Marchand, Suzanne (2000) "The quarrels of the ancients and moderns in the German museums," in Susan A. Crane (ed.), *Museums and Memory*, Stanford: Stanford University Press.

Marx, Karl (1973) *Grundrisse: Foundation of the Critique of Political Economy*, Harmondsworth: Penguin.

McCarthy, Kathleen D. (1991) *Women's Culture: American Philanthropy and Art, 1830–1930*, Chicago and London: University of Chicago Press.

McClellan, Andrew (1994) *Inventing the Louvre: Art, Politics, and the Origins of the Modern Museum in Eighteenth-century Paris*, Cambridge: Cambridge University Press.

McClellan, Andrew (2003). "A brief history of the art museum public," in A. McClellan (ed.), *Art and its Publics: Museum Studies at the Millennium*, Oxford: Blackwell, pp. 1–49.

McGregor, Russell (1998) *Imagined Destinies: Aboriginal Australians and the Doomed Race Theory, 1880–1939*, Melbourne: Melbourne University Press.

McGuigan, Jim (1996) *Culture and the Public Sphere*, London and New York: Routledge.

McGuigan, Jim (2003) "Cultural policy studies," in Justin Lewis and Toby Miller (eds.), *Critical Cultural Policy Studies: A Reader*, Oxford: Blackwell.

Medvedev, Pavlev and Mikhail Bakhtin (1978) *The Formal Method in Literary Scholarship: A Critical Introduction to Sociological Poetics*, Baltimore: Johns Hopkins University Press.

Mercer, Colin (2002) *Towards Cultural Citizenship: Tools for Cultural Policy and Development*, Stockholm: The Bank of Sweden Tercentenary Foundation and Gidlunds Förlag.

Merriman, Nick (1991) *Beyond the Looking Glass: The Past, Heritage and the Public in Britain*, Leicester: University of Leicester Press.

Michael, Michael (2000) *Reconnecting Culture, Technology and Nature: From Society to Heterogeneity*, London and New York: Routledge.

Michaels, Eric (1994) *Bad Aboriginal Art: Tradition, Media and Technological Horizons*, Minneapolis: University of Minnesota Press.

Miller, David Philip and Peter Hanns Reill (eds.) (1996) *Visions of Empire: Voyages, Botany, and Representations of Nature*, Cambridge: Cambridge University Press.

Miller, Toby (ed.) (2001) *A Companion to Cultural Studies*, Oxford: Blackwell.

Milner, Anthony (1996) *The Invention of Politics in Colonial Malaya: Contesting Nationalism and the Expansion of the Public Sphere*, Cambridge: Cambridge University Press.

Milner, A. and J. Browitt (2002) *Contemporary Cultural Theory: An Introduction*, London: Routledge.

Minson, Jeffrey (1993) *Questions of Conduct: Sexual Harassment, Citizenship, Government*, London: Macmillan.

Mitchell, Timothy (1988) *Colonising Egypt*, Cambridge: Cambridge University Press.

Modleski, Tania (1982) *Loving with a Vengeance: Mass-produced Fantasies for Women*, New York and London: Methuen.

Moores, Shaun (1990) "Texts, readers and contexts of reading: developments in the study of media audiences," *Media, Culture, Society*, vol. 12.

Morishita, Masaaki (2003) *Empty Museums: Transculturation and the Development of Public Museums in Japan*, PhD thesis, The Open University.

Morley, David (1980a) "Texts, readers, subjects," in S. Hall, D. Hobson, A. Lowe and P. Willis (eds.), *Culture, Media, Language*, London: Hutchinson.

Morley, David (1980b) *The "Nationwide" Audience: Structure and Decoding*, London: BFI Monograph 11.

Morley, David (1989) "Changing paradigms in audience studies," in E. Seiter, G, Kreutzner, H. Borchers and E-M. Warth. (eds.), *Remote Control: Television, Audiences, and Cultural Power*, London: Routledge.

Morley, David and Roger Silverstone (1990) "Domestic communication – technologies and meaning," *Media, Culture, Society* 12.

Mulhern, Francis (1979) *The Moment of "Scrutiny"*, London: New Left Books.

Mulhern, Francis (2000) *Metaculture*, London: Routledge.

Neveu, E. (2005) "Bourdieu, the Frankfurt School, and cultural studies: on some misunderstandings," in R. Benson and E. Neveu (eds.), *Bourdieu and the Journalistic Field*, Cambridge: Polity.

Nightingale, Virginia (1989) "What's 'ethnographic' about ethnographic audience research?" *Australian Journal of Communication* 16.

Norris, Christopher (1985) *Contest of Faculties: Philosophy and Theory after Deconstruction*, London: Methuen.

References

O'Regan, Tom (1992) "(Mistaking) policy: notes on the cultural policy debate," *Cultural Studies* 6(3): 409–24.

O'Shea, Alan and Bill Schwarz (1987) "Reconsidering popular culture," *Screen* 28(3): 104–9.

Oldroyd, David R. (1990) *The Highlands Controversy: Constructing Geological Knowledge through Fieldwork in Nineteenth Century Britain,* Chicago: University of Chicago Press.

Otis, Laura (1994) *Organic Memory: History and the Body in the Late Nineteenth and Early Twentieth Centuries,* Lincoln and London: University of Nebraska Press.

Outram, Dorinda (1996) "New spaces in natural history," in N. Jardine, J. A. Secord and E. C. Spary (eds.), *Cultures of Natural History,* Cambridge: Cambridge University Press.

Ozouf, M. (1988) *Festivals and the French Revolution,* Cambridge, MA: Harvard University Press.

Parry, Ann (1985) "Reading formations in the Victorian press: The reception of Kipling, 1888–1991," *Literature and History* 11(2):254–63.

Pêcheux, M. (1982) *Language, Semantics and Ideology: Stating the Obvious,* London: Macmillan.

Physick, J. (1982) *The Victoria and Albert Museum: The History of its Building,* London: Victoria and Albert Museum.

Pickstone, John V. (1994) "Museological science?" *History of Science* 32 (part 2, no 96): 111–38.

Poovey, Mary (1998) *A History of the Modern Fact: Problems of Knowledge in the Sciences of Wealth and Society,* Chicago and London: University of Chicago Press.

Poulot, Dominique (1994) "Le musée et ses visiteurs," in C. George (ed.), *La jeunesse des musées: Les musées de France au XIXe siècle.* Paris: Musée d'Orsay, pp. 332–50.

Prakash, Gyan (1992) "Science 'gone native' in colonial India," *Representations,* no. 40.

Prawer, S. S. (1978), *Karl Marx and World Literature,* Oxford: Oxford University Press;

Preziosi, Donald (2003) *Brain of the Earth's Body: Art Museums, and the Phantasms of Modernity,* Minneapolis/London: University of Minnesota Press.

Prior, Nick (2003) "Having one's Tate and eating it: transformations of the museum in a hypermodern era," in A. McClellan (ed.), *Art and its Publics: Museum Studies at the Millennium* Oxford: Blackwell.

Prosler, Martin (1996) "Museums and globalization," in Sharon MacDonald and Gordon Fyfe (eds.), *Theorizing Museums,* Oxford: Blackwell Publishers/The Sociological Review.

Radway, Janice (1984) *Reading the Romance: Women, Patriarchy and Popular Literature,* Chapel Hill: University of North Carolina Press.

Radway, Janice (1988) "Reception study: Ethnology and the problems of dispersed audiences and nomadic subjects," *Cultural Studies* 2(3).

Report of the Select Committee of the House of Commons on the Paris Exhibition (1867), Parliamentary Papers 10.

Riley, Denise (1988) *Am I That Name? Feminism and the Category of "Women" in History,* London: Macmillan.

Rose, Margaret (1984) *Marx's Lost Aesthetic: Karl Marx and the Visual Arts,* London: Cambridge University Press.

Rose, Nikolas (1996) "The death of the social? Re-figuring the territory of government," *Economy and Society* 25(3).

Rose, Nikolas (1998) *Inventing Ourselves: Psychology, Power and Personhood,* Cambridge: Cambridge University Press.

Rose, Nikolas (1999) *Powers of Freedom: Reframing Political Thought,* Cambridge: Cambridge University Press.

Rose, Nikolas and Peter Miller (1992) "Political power beyond the State: Problematics of government," *British Journal of Sociology* 43(2).

Rowse, Tim (1985) *Arguing the Arts: The Funding of the Arts in Australia,* Ringwood, Vic.: Penguin Books.

Rowse, Tim (1993) "Diversity in indigenous citizenship," in Ghassan Hage and Lesley Johnson (eds.), *Republicanism, Citizenship, Community,* vol. 2 of *Communal/Plural,* Research Centre in Intercommunal Studies, University of Western Sydney.

Rudler, F. W. (1897) "On the arrangement of ethnographical collections," *Museums Journal.*

Rudwick, Martin J. S. (1997) *Georges Cuvier, Fossil Bones, and Geological Catastrophes,* Chicago: University of Chicago Press.

Rupke, N. A. (1983) *The Great Chain of History: William Buckland and the English School of Geology,* Oxford: Clarendon Press.

Ryan, Mary P. (1990) *Women in Public: Between Banners and Ballots, 1825–1880,* Baltimore and London: The Johns Hopkins University Press.

Said, Edward W. (1984) *The World, the Text, and the Critic,* London: Faber.

Said, Edward W. (1994) *Representations of the Intellectual,* London: Vintage.

Saisselin, R. G. (1970) "The transformation of art into culture: from Pascal to Diderot," *Studies in Voltaire and the Eighteenth Century* LXX.

Saunders, David (1997) *Anti-Lawyers: Religion and the Critics of Law and State,* London and New York: Routledge.

Schnapp, Alain (1996) *The Discovery of the Past: The Origins of Archaeology,* London: British Museum Press.

Shapin, Steven (1994) *A Social History of the Truth: Civility and Science in Seventeenth-Century England,* Chicago and London: University of Chicago Press.

Shapin, Steven and Simon Schaffer (1985) *Leviathan and the Air-Pump: Hobbes, Boyle, and the Experimental Life,* Princeton, NJ: Princeton University Press.

Sheehan, J. J. (2000) *Museums in the German Art World: From the End of the Old Regime to the Rise of Modernism,* Oxford: Oxford University Press.

Shusterman, Richard (1992) *Pragmatist Aesthetics: Living Beauty, Rethinking Art,* Oxford: Blackwell.

Slatoff, W. J. (1970) *With Respect to Readers: Dimensions of Literary Response,* Ithaca and London: Cornell University Press.

Smith, B. H. (1988) *Contingencies of Value: Alternative Perspectives for Critical Theory,* Cambridge: Harvard University Press.

Spray, E. (1997) "Le spectacle de la nature: contrôle du public et vision républicaine dans le Muséum Jacobin," in C. Blanckaert, P. Claudine Cohen, P. Corsi and J-L. Fischer (eds.), *Le Muséum au premier siècle de son histoire,* Paris: Éditions de Muséum National D'Histoire Naturelle, pp. 457–80.

Stafford, Barbara (1994) *Artful Science: Enlightenment Entertainment and the Eclipse of Visual Education,* Cambridge, MA: MIT Press.

Steadman, Philip (1979) *The Evolution of Designs: Biological Analogy in Architecture and the Applied Arts,* Cambridge: Cambridge University Press.

Steele, T. (1997) *The Emergence of Cultural Studies, 1945–65: Cultural Politics, Adult Education and the English Question,* London: Lawrence and Wishart.

References

Stewart, Susan (1995) "Death and life, in that order, in the works of Charles Wilson Peale," in L. Cooke and P. Wollen (eds.) *Visual Display: Culture Beyond Appearances*, Seattle: Bay Press, pp. 30–53.

Stocking Jr., George W. (1999) "The space of cultural representation, circa 1887 and 1969: reflections on museum arrangement and anthropological theory in the Boasian and evolutionary traditions," in Peter Galison and Emily Thompson (eds.), *The Architecture of Science*, Cambridge, MA: MIT Press.

Stoler, Laura Ann (1995) *Race and the Education of Desire: Foucault's History of Sexuality and the Colonial Order of Things*, Durham and London: Duke University Press.

Street, J. (2000) "Aesthetics, policy and the politics of popular culture," *European Journal of Cultural Studies* 3(1): 27–43.

Therborn, Göran (1976) *Science, Class and Society: On the Formation of Sociology and Historical Materialism*, London: New Left Books.

Thompson, Edward P. (1967) "Time, work-discipline and industrial capitalism," *Past and Present*, no. 38.

Thompson, Edward P. (1977) "Caudwell," in J. Saville and R. Miliband (eds.), *Socialist Register 1977*, London: Merlin, pp. 228–76.

Thompson, M. W. (1977) *General Pitt-Rivers: Evolution and Archaeology in the Nineteenth Century*, Bradford-on-Avon: Moonraker Press.

Trigger, Bruce (1989) *A History of Archaeological Thought*, Cambridge: Cambridge University Press.

Turnbull, Paul (1991) " 'Ramsay's regime': the Australian Museum and the procurement of Aboriginal bodies, c. 1874–1900," *Aboriginal History* 15(2).

Turner, Graeme (2003) *British Cultural Studies: An Introduction*, London: Routledge.

van Keuren, David Keith (1982) *Human Sciences in Victorian Britain: Anthropology in Institutional and Disciplinary Formation, 1863–1908*, PhD thesis, University of Pennsylvania.

van Riper, A. Bowdoin (1993) *Men among the Mammoths: Victorian Science and the Discovery of Human Prehistory*, London and Chicago: University of Chicago Press.

Vazquez, Adolfo Sanchez (1978 [1973]) *Art and Society: Essays in Marxist Aesthetics*, London: Merlin Press.

Vidich, A. J. and J. Benseman (1960) *Small Town in Mass Society*, New York: Anchor Books.

Virilio, Paul (1994) *The Vision Machine*, London: British Film Institute.

Volosinov, V. N. (1973) *Marxism and the Philosophy of Language*, New York: Seminar Press.

Walkerdine, Valerie (1986) "Video replay: families, films and fantasy," in V. Burgin., J. Donald and K. Caplan (eds.), *Formations of Fantasy*, London: Methuen.

Wallach, Alan (1998) *Exhibiting Contradiction: Essays on the Art Museum in the United States*, Amherst: University of Massachusetts Press.

Williams, Raymond (1958) *Culture and Society*, London: Chatto and Windus.

Williams, Raymond (1961) *The Long Revolution*, London: Chatto and Windus.

Williams, Raymond (1971) "Literature and sociology: in memory of Lucien Goldmann," *New Left Review* 67.

Williams, Raymond (1974) *Television: Technology and Cultural Form*, London: Fontana.

Williams, Raymond (1976) *Keywords: A Vocabulary of Culture and Society*, London: Fontana/Croom Helm.

Williams, Raymond (1977) *Marxism and Literature*, Oxford: Oxford University Press.

Williams, Raymond (1989) *The Politics of Modernism: Against the New Conformists*, London: Verso.

Willis, P. (1978) *Learning to Labour: How Working-Class Kids Get Working-Class Jobs*, Farnborough: Saxon House.

Wu, Chin-tao (2002) *Privatising Culture: Corporate Art Intervention since the 1980s*, London: Verso.

Yanni, Carla (1999) *Nature's Museums: Victorian Science and the Architecture of Display*, London: The Athlone Press.

Yoshimi, Shunya (1993) "Industrial expositions in modern Japan: a gauge of the changing city," paper presented at the annual meeting of the Association for Asian Studies.

Young, Robert M. (1985) *Darwin's Metaphor: Nature's Place in Victorian Culture*, Cambridge: Cambridge University Press.

Index

Index